WHAT PEOPLE

"Pick up *Breaking Bad Faith* if you're tired of the stench emitting from the Christian crapola that has come to define Western Christianity and the cult of Christian celebrity in particular. See what happens when you turn out the white noise emanating from the Christian Industrial Complex and tune in to where the spirit is actually speaking these days."

— Becky Garrison, author of *Roger Williams's Little Book of Virtues*
and board member with The Wittenburg Door

"Thanks for writing this book ... so important and needed!"

— Brian McLaren, author of *Faith After Doubt*
and *Do I Stay Christian?*

"Michael Camp sees what's wrong. The God so many tout isn't a deity we should imitate or worship. But Camp also points a way forward to what's right. Exchanging unhelpful views of God for helpful ones is crucial to not only our personal lives but to civilization as we know it. I recommend Michael Camp's diagnosis and medicine!"

— Thomas Jay Oord, author of *Open and Relational Theology*
and dozens of other books

"In *Breaking Bad Faith*, Michael Camp methodically walks us through the web of our inherited beliefs and untangles the mess of toxic theology covering up the revelations of Jesus. Until we can objectively examine our unconscious beliefs, they will continue to wreak havoc on our personal lives and the culture we live in. Camp does a fantastic job of explaining how these unexamined beliefs perpetuate current-day violence and leave us feeling helpless to stop it. He sets us on a path to peace that actually feels attainable. Breaking Bad Faith is a book our fractured society desperately needs right now."

— Heather Hamilton, bestselling author of *Returning to Eden: A Field Guide for the Spiritual Journey*

"Just when I thought I had read all the "deconstruction" books worth reading, Michael Camp came along and said, "Hold my beer." Michael's offering, *Breaking Bad Faith* takes deconstruction and reconstruction of one's faith to a whole new level. Of course, the reference to the beer is intentional when you consider that Michael's podcast is called, *The Spiritual Brewpub*. This book is not a sugar coated, syrupy repetition of typical deconstruction complaints. Michael unpacks conventional Christian theological myths using reason, critical thinking, experience, and grounding his observations solidly in historic precedent and fact. This is a book that carries *gravitas* and is a *tour-de-force* of damaging Christian theology based on retribution and violence that affects individuals, the church, and society today in extremely negative ways. But Michael goes beyond simply deconstructing the negative elements of this destructive theology, but also provides a beautiful picture of the authentic, radical love-ethic of Jesus and provides a path toward peace and restoration. Michael gives us hope and an alternative to the corrosive elements of Christianity we see playing out today. Anyone that is looking for an alternative to conservative Christian theology, and a guide to find your way through the labyrinth of myths Christians have devised over the centuries will appreciate this book."

— Dan Henderson, author of *Confessions of a Recovering Evangelical*

"*Breaking Bad Faith* is a fun, easy-to-read exposé of the corruption of American Evangelicalism's gospel and ethic. Although I would also have preferred an equal opportunity dissection of progressive Christianity, nevertheless, Michael Camp highlights the growing awareness that sacrificial warrior Christendom is not the liberating Gospel of Jesus. Hopefully, *Breaking Bad Faith* will encourage those with questions to continue boldly asking them."

— Michael Hardin, independent theologian, author of *The Jesus Driven Life*, *Mimetic Theory and Biblical Interpretation*, and *Knowing God? Consumer Christianity and the Gospel of Jesus*

"Divorcing our image of God from the myth of redemptive violence couldn't be more important than it is today, where so many of us are unwittingly bearing the image of that violent God in the way we interact with one another online and in real life. Michael's book helps us understand the appeal of this violent depiction of God, the base tendencies that draw us to it, but more importantly, how to break away from the desire for the retribution that this God represents."

— Kevin Miller, Director of *J.E.S.U.S.A.* and *Hellbound?*

"We are in an age where millions of Christians are leaving behind the harsh infernalist faith they inherited for theologies in which salvation is universal in scope. In this book, Michael Camp, in good faith, articulates just such a vision."

— David Artman, author of *Grace Saves All: The Necessity of Christian Universalism*

"I appreciate Camp's work in *Breaking Bad Faith* because he fearlessly rakes through our theology to discover the good and expose the bad so that we can move on intentionally and consciously, rather than by simply accepting without question the dogmas we have inherited or adopted. While respecting the faith, he is not afraid to help us discard the parts that are hurting us, others, and the world, and to reinterpret or recreate better theologies that translate into better policies and practices for everyone."

— David Hayward, aka 'NakedPastor,' author of *Flip It Like This*

"Michael Camp gives us all a generous gift by not only helping us understand the nature of dangerous religion, but also gives us tools for freeing our minds of a contrived and menacing image of God. Jesus said we must love our neighbor as ourselves. There is nothing more cruel we can do to ourselves than construct in our minds an angry and sadistic deity who terrifies us in our dreams. If we can't be kind to ourselves when it comes to our deepest beliefs, then we can't be kind to others. Thank you Michael, for helping us free ourselves, so we can free others and help repair the world!"

— Rev. Rob Schenck, author of *Costly Grace: An Evangelical Minister's Rediscovery of Faith, Hope and Love*

BREAKING BAD FAITH

EXPOSING MYTH AND VIOLENCE IN POPULAR
THEOLOGY TO RECOVER THE PATH OF PEACE

MICHAEL CAMP

Copyright © 2023 by Michael Camp; First Edition

Cover Design by Rafael Polendo (polendo.net)
Interior Layout by Matthew J. Distefano

Scriptures taken from the Holy Bible, New International Version®, NIV®. Copyright © 1973, 1978, 1984, 2011 by Biblica, Inc.™ Used by permission of Zondervan. All rights reserved worldwide. www.zondervan.com The "NIV" and "New International Version" are trademarks registered in the United States Patent and Trademark Office by Biblica, Inc.™

Scripture taken from the NEW AMERICAN STANDARD BIBLE(r), Copyright (c) 1960, 1962, 1963, 1968, 1971, 1972, 1973, 1975, 1977 by The Lockman Foundation. Used by permission.

The quote by Michael Hardin in chapter 12 used by permission.

ISBN 978-1-957007-69-4
Printed in the United States of America

Published by Quoir
Chico, California
www.quoir.com

CONTENTS

DEDICATION — VIII

ACKNOWLEDGMENTS — IX

INTRODUCTION — XI

1. UNCOVERING VIOLENT SACRIFICIAL RELIGION — 1

2. HOW RELIGIOUS MYTHS AND FRAUDS WORK — 9

3. THE MAJOR MYTHS VERSUS REALITY — 25

4. THE TWO-FACED GOD OF POPULAR THEOLOGY — 51

5. THE ERRONEOUS WAY PEOPLE VIEW THE BIBLE — 81

6. THE PROBLEM WITH A TRANSACTIONAL GOD — 97

7. VIOLENCE IN POPULAR THEOLOGY AND AMERICAN CULTURE — 107

8. THE MYTH OF REDEMPTIVE VIOLENCE — 135

9. THE ROOTS OF PEACE — 151

10. RECLAIMING THE PATH OF PEACE — 165

11. MODERN PEACE MOVEMENTS AS OUR GUIDE — 183

12. BREAKING BAD FAITH FOR THE SAKE OF PEACE — 193

END NOTES — 217

BIBLIOGRAPHY — 233

For my children,
Joel, Jordan, Nathan, and Bethany

ACKNOWLEDGMENTS

So many people deserve acknowledgment for helping me directly and indirectly to finally complete this book and get it off the ground.

To my wife, Lori, thank you for your constant love and support. To my "discussion group" friends, thank you for inspiring me to keep seeking and writing. To the many reviewers and commentators on my first two books who encouraged me that I was on the right track on this journey. Your kind words and descriptions of how your life was impacted inspired me to write another book.

To the many authors of articles and books in the Bibliography. Your work laid the foundation for this book with your historical research, biblical scholarship, and theological or social insights.

To those who participated in my Religious Deconstruction Workshop, thank you for walking with me and sharing your thoughts. Your feedback helped me with tips to break bad faith.

Many thanks goes to the Quoir Publishing team for creating a beautifully formatted and designed book. Thanks, Keith Giles, for believing in this book, Matthew Distefano for your hard work and expertise, and Rafael Polendo for the cover design. Plus, all your marketing advice was invaluable.

To my editor, Anna Rhea, thank you so much for making this book so much better with your polishing skills and patience with my ongoing changes.

I'm blown away by each person who endorsed the book. I'm humbled by what you wrote and it's an honor to have your support. Thank you!

To my book launch team, I'm so grateful that you were willing to take the time and effort to help propel this book. Each of you made a huge difference. Thanks to those who gave me early feedback that really encouraged me.

Finally, thanks to anyone who is brave enough to address harmful and unhistorical theologies in their spiritual journey. This book is for you.

INTRODUCTION
Exposing Bad Faith

Bad faith is all around us. It is present when people embrace a non-historically informed religious belief system. It arises when there are beliefs and practices that are legalistic, spiritually abusive, and manipulative. You can find it when people divide the world into "us vs. them," and look down on unbelievers as hopelessly lost unless they convert to the religious (or political) faith of "us."

Bad faith is present when people insist the Bible is inerrant (without error) and infallible (incapable of being wrong) in everything it teaches and is the supreme authority in all matters of faith and conduct and who think all who don't believe this are backslidden or heretics. It appears when people read the Bible without concerns for an accurate translation of the original language or literary, historical, and cultural context. It's present when people believe one must be a committed member of a "Bible-believing" church to be right with God and that God uses modern "church" as an authoritative covering to keep people on the right path. Moreover, it's present when people think women can't be pastors or leaders in the church.

Bad faith is present when people believe that all of humanity is born in total depravity due to "original sin," and without some form of "born again Christian" experience, every person is a hopeless sinner destined to an afterlife of eternal punishment upon death.

You can find it when people think those who identify as LGBTQ can't be true Christians and are lost unless they repent, practice abstinence, or become heterosexual. It is present when men use Bible verses to justify domestic violence or when churches teach divorce (and remarriage) is a sin even in cases of physical and emotional abuse. Or when people think corporal punishment of children is God's will and commanded in the Bible and think parents who don't spank their children are being disobedient. Or when people believe "church discipline" merits shunning people who don't toe the doctrinal line or consider others heretics because they believe in things like universalism or gender equality.

Bad faith is present when people believe in a retributive god who advocates for largely punitive "tough-on-crime" policies to bring order to society and who commands capital punishment for high crimes. It is lurking when people believe this retributive god endorses and even encourages that believers pack a concealed weapon to be ready to prevent crime and take down a bad guy with a gun; or when people believe God supports violent retaliation in general and is okay with most if not all of America's wars. It arises when people believe this retributive god supposedly sent Jesus to earth to suffer a torturous, violent punishment as a substitute for what humanity deserves to appease God's wrath over sin. Or when they believe Jesus will return to earth in final judgment to reward believers and punish unbelievers in an apocalyptic tribulation before the world ends. Or when people believe that the majority of the human race will be separated from God for eternity because they haven't accepted Christ as their personal Lord and Savior or aren't sufficiently dedicated to some sectarian "biblical" theology or haven't sufficiently obeyed.

This brand of faith teaches that God is transactional, duplicitous, and demands sacrifice—time, talents, careers, prayers, fasting, tithes, money, church commitment, life dedication, obedience, rejection of one's own sense of reason, imprisonment or execution of criminals, and the torture and murder of an innocent victim (Jesus of Nazareth around 30 CE) before this god will bless and forgive humanity and bring true justice to the world. As you shall discover in these pages, this god ultimately advocates and promotes retribution and violence and requires his worshippers to do the same. This brand of "faith" needs to be exposed and broken as it harms both its adherents and its victims. Exposing this "bad faith" with historical, logical, and biblical facts is the first goal of this book.

Incidentally, this doesn't mean anyone who has any of the aforementioned beliefs—what I call *bad faith*—are all bad people. No, as we will see, many of us are just victims of misinformation and someone else's misconstrued study of history. Others of us should know better. But many of us are programmed to believe certain ways or are just mimicking what we hear in our faith communities without thinking too hard about it. This book will force you to think. *Not thinking through what you believe is a huge problem.*

The second goal of this book is to reveal what matters most about what people call "Christianity." What matters most boils down to the radical non-violent love ethic of Christ, i.e., the path of peace. The big problem with just diving into this topic is that most people's view of "Christianity" is so fraudulent and distorted, it clouds any core message. One cannot possibly address things like Jesus' egalitarianism, his command to love our enemies, his modeling the forgiving victim, and his call for peacemaking until (s)he is clear-eyed on the history of what we call Christianity. Without exposing a collection of various Christian frauds and myths that our society buys into, one can never really see what matters most, let alone have a guide to breaking bad faith.

We need to shed this false lens from which most people view Jesus and his early followers. You see, "Christianity," the way most people think of it, has almost nothing—or at best, very little—to do with the historical Jesus epic that began in the first century. "Christianity," and particularly Western Christianity and its variety of popular modern streams of evangelicalism and fundamentalism, is full of mythical, fraudulent, and violent theologies that cloud one's mind so much that it's almost impossible to see the beauty of the magnanimous message that Jesus still brings the world. French theologian, Jacques Ellul, called this "the subversion of Christianity," arguing that there was not just deviation from the core message but "radical and essential contradiction, or real subversion."[2] Russian author of *War and Peace* and theologian, Leo Tolstoy, said both believers and unbelievers typically are wearing this false lens, being "fully persuaded that they have understood Christ's teachings a long time, and that they understand it so fully, indubitably, and conclusively, that it can have no other significance, than the one they attribute to it. And the reason for this conviction is that the false interpretation and consequent misapprehension of the Gospel is an error of such long standing."[3]

In short, we must expose long standing "bad faith" in our theology before we can ever see good faith. Then we'll be ready to break the bad faith habit. Many people have called this process "deconstructing" one's theology before you reconstruct it. That is, cutting out the falsehoods and zeroing in on historical facts and truth. This bad faith that needs deconstructing is everywhere, but particularly in popular Christianity, that is, its conservative, fundamentalist, and evangelical streams—in both Protestantism and

Catholicism. But it can also just as easily seep into progressive and liberal Christianity.

I'm most familiar with conservative Christianity in the West. I spent twenty-five plus years of my life active in the American evangelical movement as a young convert during the 1970s Jesus Movement, a lay church leader in independent and charismatic churches, and an ordained, evangelical missionary to Muslims working for both Christian aid agencies and evangelical "church-planting" organizations.

Through a very long process, I deconstructed from this form of Christianity and survived to write about it. In my first book, *Confessions of a Bible Thumper*, I tell the story of my initial conversion, the many mistakes I made along the way, and my subsequent long deconstruction. One of the things I discovered in this experience was how much history matters. My evangelical faith may have had a number of good things going for it, but it was not based on a good study of history. I discovered other traditions in history that more accurately reflect the original Jesus story—for example, some of the Eastern streams of early Christianity like the Nestorian and the early Jacobite movements, branches of Eastern Orthodoxy, many of the church fathers (whose views were very different from Augustine's) like Clement, Origen, Didymus, Nestorius, Gregory of Nyssa, Gregory of Nazianzus, and Theodore of Mopsuestia, church mothers like Macrina the Elder and Macrina the Younger, and medieval mystics like Julian of Norwich and Meister Eckhart. Then there were the Protestant streams that became minorities in the West, such as the Celtic tradition, the Anabaptists, Quakers, and Moravians, and finally some of the most astute historians and theologians of the 19th through 21st centuries, such as Tolstoy, Ellul, E. Stanley Jones, Dietrich Bonhoeffer, Karl Barth, Martin Luther King, Jr., Robin Meyers, Harvey Cox, Marcus Borg, Diane Butler-Bass, Karen Armstrong, Desmond Tutu, John Dominic Crossan, Rene Girard, Phyliss Tickle, David Bentley Hart, Michael Hardin, and Hal Taussig.

This new understanding of history and these alternative theologies that I found, although not identical in their conclusions, were much closer to the original content of Jesus' teachings. They helped me identify bad faith and break it. They led me to not only deconstruct a number of my beliefs but also reconstruct a more historically accurate faith.

In my second book, *Craft Brewed Jesus*, I described how I reconstructed my faith and explored a new Christ-like spirituality—new to evangelicalism, but not new to the record of history. And, actually one that fits more in line with my own and many others' experiences of what we trust God—the divine source of the universe—is really like. Or, if you will, it fits more in line with what a truly loving God would be like if one really exists: consistently compassionate to all and restorative in nature rather than retributive. One that still holds people accountable for sin and wrongdoing, but whose goal is restoration rather than punishment that somehow balances the scales of justice. This spirituality is inclusive and supportive of good, healthy, human experiences. It appreciates a variety of life's joys, such as diverse community, cross-cultural understanding, unbridled music, the arts, and responsible sexuality. Another example is celebrating today's now-ubiquitous craft beer and brewery movement, much like the Celtic Christians did in the early Middle Ages, and Christian monks did or as the early gatherings around Jesus appreciated wine, food, and celebration.

This book you hold in your hands seeks to expose and deconstruct the bad faith in modern, American theology and then reveal what matters most as a foundation for reconstructing faith, or, at the very least, a new philosophy of life. I've tried my best to base it on a good study of history. It seeks to go back far enough in history as well as interpret later history (4th century through today) in light of early history (first through 3rd centuries). The conclusions it comes to will be called heretical by many. But you must decide for yourself. Is what this book claims based on a consistent view of what Jesus taught? Does earliest "Christian" history (and later history in light of it) verify its conclusions? Does it fit with the best biblical and ancient linguistic scholarship? When it does make claims of good faith from the prophets and parts of the New Testament, does it practice sound exegesis and hermeneutics?[4] Does it touch a chord in your heart, that most of us seem to know deep down, that equitable love for all humankind is what matters most?

I trust that once I help you expose issues like violent sacrificial religion, the two-faced transactional God our society believes in, how religious myths work, the erroneous way people view the Bible, violence in popular theology, our misunderstanding of "biblical" justice and judgment, and the many "Christian" myths historical studies reveal, only then will you be able to clearly see the subversive path of peace Jesus lays out for the world that can truly save us. These myths include the myths of redemptive violence, Christianity as a religion, the inerrancy of the Bible, institutional church, Christian nationalism, original depravity, hell, women as subordinates, the end times, and even the myth of morality. Once these myths are shed, the core of Jesus' egalitarian, inclusive, and peacemaking message for the world comes into sharp focus.

This core message is to be viewed lightly, not as finding the holy grail of Christian theology that everyone should embrace to form a rediscovered, definitive, Christian way, let alone create a new church movement or denomination and impose it on others. No, this message acknowledges that there are still mysteries of life and spirituality that we must all accept. It accepts that being absolutely certain about one's theology is actually bad, and that, whatever the core message is that one discovers, it transcends all religions, non-religion, and philosophies of life. It is truly inclusive, not exclusive.

The place to begin our journey is not in an ivory theological tower that many church members, elders, pastors, Christian college students, seminarians, professors, and theologians tend to climb and hang out in, but on an arid mission field near the ends of the earth with real-life Muslim adherents to which Christians are told they must go and preach the gospel.

ONE

UNCOVERING VIOLENT SACRIFICIAL RELIGION

THE OGADEN DESERT'S DRY, oppressive heat bore down from above penetrating my skin. Red sand kicked up from below as I walked down a dusty road. I was deep inside Bo'O refugee camp just 30 miles from the Ethiopian border. Children occasionally ran out from behind huts made of stick, mud, and grass—called *akals*—then greeted me with flashing smiles. I made my way to one of myriad, tiny tea shops throughout the camp to meet my Somali colleagues—fellow workers in an aid project. Then the thought came.

I was thunderstruck when it hit me. How can that be true? It tore at my heart. *There must be another explanation*, I told myself. I had just realized my Muslim friends, according to my own conservative Christian theology, were supposedly destined for eternal damnation. A strange thought for your average person. But not for me. I was a young, naïve, evangelical missionary in the Horn of Africa. As the rationale continued in my mind, I connected the dots. The generations before them, in their ancestral line, had supposedly already been doomed. I "knew" this in theory since becoming an evangelical Christian four years earlier—Muslims would supposedly not be "saved" unless they converted to Christianity. But now, on the ground in the real world, the implications of it hit home.

It was 1983. I was an evangelical working for a Christian aid agency in Somalia. Somalia and neighboring eastern Ethiopia are arid, ancient lands—home to exotic Cushitic tribes—Somalis and Oromos—whose traditions included pastoralism, nomadism, and Islam. On my first night in country in the capital city of Mogadishu, months before my epiphany, I awoke to the ubiquitous early morning call to prayer. The mesmerizing Arabic words confirmed that I had landed within a vastly different culture—a 99 percent Muslim society for the last twelve centuries. This was worlds away from my New England roots, secular American popular culture, and culturally Christian American mindset.

When the realization landed on that dusty track in Bo'O camp, I was all too cognizant of how much I had bonded with my Somali and Oromo friends, neighbors, and co-workers—interpreters, trainers, project managers—most of whom were refugees from Ethiopia as a result of the Somalia-Ethiopian border war that had begun in 1979. Many of them lived in the refugee encampments where I worked called Bo'O and Qorioley, and others lived in the city of Mogadishu.

Abdulahi, Gobi, Zarah, Shuru, Omar, Mohammed, Halimo, Abdul Fatah, Hiis and others had become dear to me. They were courageous and dedicated people with a keen sense of humor and love for their families. For the previous four months, I had labored with them as an aid worker and even lived within their communities—those mud/stick/grass huts or other rustic cinder block homes. Upon arriving as an aid worker, my initial job was managing a supplemental feeding program for the vulnerable in Bo'O camp. By the time I arrived, the program was small as the urgent need to feed desperate refugees with no means of self-reliance had waned. Later I helped spearhead a wood-conserving cookstove project in Qorioley and Bo'O that had promised to dramatically curtail the urgent problem of deforestation impacting all the camps. Thousands of people who relied entirely on open wood fires to cook food had denuded surrounding arid "forests," forcing women to walk up to ten hours to gather firewood from afar. My agency also spearheaded projects I had indirect involvement in, such as helping refugees become self-sufficient by developing farms, irrigation, beekeeping, and businesses that served the local community.

My Somali and Oromo co-workers and I had worked together on these initiatives that helped their fellow refugees—estimated up to 1.2 million—who had trekked across the Ethiopian border into Somalia. We often hung out together drinking spicy, sweet shah in one of those familiar tea shops of the refugee camps and towns—the equivalent of a Starbucks on every block in Seattle. We laughed and joked together many times. I grew to love their beaming smiles, dry sense of humor, women's colorful garments, traditional head coverings, men's traditional tube skirts, children playing happily in the streets with home-made toys, and babies strapped to their mothers' backs. Then there was the subculture of the Horn of Africa: nomads trekking across barren landscapes and crossing rural roads with herds of camels. My love for these people included their dedication to their own faith, but mostly, our increasingly deep friendships across disparate cultures. It was a human bond, not solely African or Western or Christian or Muslim.

To be sure, this wasn't a perfect society. Women were discriminated against and oftentimes abused. Misogyny reigned in this ancient culture. Female circumcision was a common practice (even though it is not derived from Islam). Sexual mores were oppressive. Progressive ideas like equal rights and democracy were in their infancy. Nevertheless, for the most part, the average Muslim person or family was friendly, hospitable, and decent. I saw them as no better or worse than people in American society, which has its own blemishes of racism, sexism, and ethnocentrism. "Islamism," the radicalization of Islam into a violent, authoritarian, and terrorist religion, was not present in East Africa at that time. Moreover, Islam in East Africa is a much more open society than it is in the Middle East. For example, despite sexist attitudes, women are allowed to work, travel alone, get an education (if given the opportunity), and are not confined to wearing a full hijab, only modest dress and head covering.

But my thought in that moment was not congruent to all this. I had just realized a serious problem with my evangelical worldview. Not just mine, but the worldview of the whole evangelical movement in America. According to that philosophy, all Muslims, unless they "accept Christ as their Lord and Savior," are destined for an eternal demise. Calvinists believe it is because people are inherently depraved and deserve hell as a default destination and God has pre-ordained both the saved and the damned. Arminianists believe it is because people choose to reject God when they don't accept Christ, or supposedly, when they never ask God to show them the true faith. If they had, the theology goes, God would have sent them Christian missionaries to convert them. Moreover, since the ancestors of my Muslim friends had not converted to Christ, they were presumably, at this very moment, in this place called hell. As our theology stipulated, Jesus was the only way to God, so if one did not trust Jesus for salvation, God's wrath was still on them, and they would face the judgment of God upon death. Once passing the doorway between life into death, the rationalization continues, it is too late to repent and accept Christ. One is doomed. Eternal. Conscious. Torment. This is the doctrine of hell.

The answer to the problem, according to evangelical theology, was to try to convert my Muslim friends to Christ (it was too late for their ancestors; we Protestants do not have a purgatory). My Christian colleagues and I tried. You try to convert them by "witnessing" about your faith, praying for them, reading the Bible together, and sharing the gospel message. After all, it was our mandate. We evangelical missionaries—not only in Africa but in Asia, Europe, and Latin America—were on the mission field to help fulfill The Great Commission: to take the gospel message throughout the world to all ethnic groups and help pave the way for the return of Christ.

In Somalia, many of the evangelical aid workers who served in several Christian humanitarian organizations held Bible studies and invited our Somali and Oromo friends to attend. Some of them were favorable to the love ethic of Jesus compared to the legalistic codes of conduct that they were taught in Islam—mandatory, five-times-a-day prayer, women subjected to strict dress codes, only using an Arabic Quran, a mandatory 30-day annual fast, and, in some circles the abhorrent tradition of female circumcision (again, not a Muslim practice). This African brand of folk Islam, although less strict than other societies in the Middle East, was burdensome enough to make Christianity appealing to some, particularly young people. Through a collection of evangelical organizations working in the camps, a handful of Muslims apparently converted to Christianity. A very small handful.

But what about those who do not accept Christ? What if the Quran schools, to which almost every Somali and Oromo Muslim child was obligated to attend, were successful in their programming? For example, implanting the notion that Islam was the only one true religion, that Jesus could never be the Son of God because God could never have a son, that Mohammed was the last prophet that supersedes all others, that the Christian gospels have been tampered with and cannot be trusted, and that the path of Islam was the only way to heaven? What if what I suspected was true: most Muslims I met were sincere believers in one true God who they called the all-powerful, all-merciful, all-compassionate Allah? They honestly believed Christians were polytheists (attributing divinity to the man Jesus denies there is only one God) who tried their best to live good lives.

Moreover, what if the conservative Muslim's view of hell was sufficiently ingrained in them, similar to how our own evangelical view of hell is ingrained in us, that the overwhelming majority of Muslims around me would never accept Christ—perhaps out of fear—and would supposedly die in their sins to face the wrath of God? What if most of my new-found friends wind up in hell for eternity? And join their great-grandfathers and great-grandmothers and ancestors down through the centuries? Again: Eternal. Conscious. Torment. Separated forever from the only source of life—the Creator God—for not believing the right way about Jesus and the Bible or for not living righteous enough due to their human sin.

What if? The questions only made me incredulous to my own theology and what I thought I had read in the Bible. I had uncovered violent sacrificial religion in my own faith.

Later in my journey, after I had studied the history of the doctrine of hell and had uncovered misinterpretations and mistranslations of Jesus' words, I realized that thinking someone is going to hell is a violent thought. If hell is eternal conscious torment or even an ongoing separation from God's goodness, it is violent. Tormenting someone, whether physically or mentally, is violence against them. In this life in democratic societies, consigning one to *hell* would be considered the crime of torture, forced imprisonment, or abandonment of people whose only supposed "crime" was they rejected, or simply didn't believe, the right religious doctrines. Or they weren't quite good enough to make it. This is what totalitarian governments or communist countries did and still do to dissidents. The doctrine of hell was tyrannical.

Evangelicals have a clever way of getting around these logical conclusions. They came up with the notion that people choose hell. By their rejection of the evangelical view of Jesus and his atonement (that Jesus took the punishment that people deserved to appease God's anger and opened a way for God to forgive them), people supposedly choose to be separated from God. They apparently can't stand to be with the true God and would rather be in hell. Even C.S. Lewis gave this view an air of respectability. In his book, *The Great Divorce*, he gave a fictional account in which a busload of people is transported from hell to heaven. Once there, the inhabitants of hell realize they didn't like the holy haven, decide not to stay, and return to their eternal demise. Because of their life choices, they are deemed irredeemable, Lewis's reasoning went. I read the book while in Somalia in search of a defense of the doctrine.

However, in this life, people don't choose to be tormented, and they rarely reject kindness. If they choose to reject a kind offer, they are usually afraid or have misunderstood the act. Moreover, Muslims don't reject God or *Allah*, which is simply the Arabic word for *God*, by rejecting Christianity. Jews don't reject God by not believing Jesus is the Messiah nor do secularists reject love for humanity by not believing in the Divine.

What this rationalizing really means is that evangelicals who are adamant about the doctrine of hell believe in a God who only gives two choices: either comply to a particular set of doctrines about Jesus or go to hell. God says something like, "Comply and I'll forgive you and be kind to you. Don't comply and I'll separate you from myself forever, placing you in torment because you have rejected me." Or something about how he can't look on sin as a holy God and the only way to remove sin is through belief in Christ, or it leads to destruction—an eternal destruction.

This is not unconditional love. Unconditional love does not limit people to only two choices. There are always other choices for people and for God. People can ask for help, repent, change their mind, be restored, and come home. God can leave the light on, reveal his loving nature, and correct or discipline people in love. God can see into a person's heart and know they are doing the best they can as a human being made in his image given their social environment, their ingrained religious beliefs, and the knowledge they have attained. God can see when a person is brainwashed by religious or social programming that keeps them from making right choices or blinds them from truth. God can reach people outside of religion and instill in them a desire to love their neighbor and humanity. God knows when people do evil and when they don't realize their own sin. God can simply forgive and show kindness that leads to repentance and redemption. God does not have to be under the authority of some self-imposed "justice" that says He cannot be in the presence of sin or can't forgive sin and forgo retribution without a religious transaction.

> "Father, forgive them, for they know not what they do."
> — Jesus, while being crucified (Luke 23:34)

But violent sacrificial religion must have scapegoats—people who are to blame, who are so bad that they have messed up the world, who have rejected

God and always will, who deserve to be sacrificed. And in this case, they deserve to go to hell.

After wrestling with these thoughts in Africa, I did ultimately find another explanation. I adopted an "inclusive" theology, in that it was possible that some people would be saved outside of Christendom because God is loving and just. He would not enforce a punishment that didn't fit the crime. For my Muslim friends and their ancestors, God would judge or had judged them according to how they lived their lives, in light of what they thought was true. Many would hopefully be saved, I surmised. Others would go to hell. Despite my rationalizations, I still believed in hell for those who didn't measure up. I still had a wrath-fueled theology. But I kept my inclusivist views to myself.

This inclusivism was the view of Billy Graham in the latter half of his ministry, although most people didn't realize it. He only expressed it in interviews and some sermons and not in his published work.[1] But it was, and still is, a very slim minority view within evangelicalism. When I went back to the mission field again in 1990, I was honest with my ordaining church about the fact that my inclusivist view of the afterlife didn't fit their statement of faith. They said they could only ordain me with a condition—that I would never teach inclusivism on the mission field. I agreed but later came to regret it.

Despite my acquiescence, I never felt right with the doctrine of hell. It would be another 15 years before the ancient path of peace that is ingrained in Jesus' teachings would become clear to me. Today the original peacemaking way has been lost in the fog of popular theology that pushes violent sacrificial religion as the norm for the way we interact with God and retribution as the norm for how God engages with us and, therefore, how we engage with others. For example, in our country's criminal justice system and wars. It's been lost because popular theologians refuse to take a second look at the many mistranslations of the words *hell* and *eternal punishment* in the New Testament. Also, they refuse to examine the history of what the church fathers called the doctrine of *apokatastasis*, or universal reconciliation.[2]

It's past time to clear the fog and expose the fraud of these twin heresies of violent sacrificial religion and retribution. They are part of a series of myths that have hoodwinked American evangelicalism and much of Western Christianity for centuries. Let's see how these myths and frauds played out.

Two
HOW RELIGIOUS MYTHS AND FRAUDS WORK

No one likes to get scammed—to be a victim of a fraud or realize they have believed a myth. It feels terrible. Like you were betrayed. You trusted someone. and they took advantage of you. You believed something, and then you realized it's not based on the facts. That's why most people have a hard time admitting they have been scammed. Often, they would rather double down on their belief in a myth so as not to be shamed by their victimhood.

RELIGIOUS AND POLITICAL FRAUDS OF OUR DAY

Frauds and myths take many forms in our day. Disseminators use cable news, social media, podcasts, websites, documentary films, and email to spread unsubstantiated information, conspiracy theories, or "fake news." I will highlight several examples from the last several years from religion and politics.

"Alabama State Police have arrested three poll workers in Birmingham for allowing 3,000 invalid votes for Doug Jones in Alabama's December 12, 2017, special election," a website named Reagan Was Right reported. Even though the site described its content as "satire," people spread this announcement as if it was true.[1]

QAnon Conspiracy Theories

Around 2018, I met a woman who was a QAnon follower. She sincerely believed John F. Kennedy, Jr. was still alive, having survived the plane crash in which most people thought he died. He was living undercover fighting various injustices, including the "deep state,"[2] and would soon reveal himself to the world as the running mate of Donald Trump for his 2020 re-election campaign. When I divulged my distaste for the politics of Donald Trump, she began a long description of the way the world really is—including how the deep state is controlling the U.S. government, why I am ignorant, and concluded with this story of Trump and JFK, Jr., fighting the "conspiracy." Later, I learned some versions of this notion of the deep state include the belief that Democrats are running a pedophile ring (Hillary Clinton ran one out of a pizza parlor that became known as Pizzagate), and the FBI (or Antifa) set up the January 6, 2021 insurrection to make it look like it was perpetrated by Trump supporters.[3] These and several other frauds were promoted by QAnon and related websites.

At the time of this encounter, I was flabbergasted that anyone in their right mind, let alone the likeable, smart, and articulate, person I met a moment earlier, could believe such things. The woman also gave me a book that she said explained how the JFK, Jr., and Donald Trump connection fit into the larger narrative of us being in the end times. It was one of those typical, biblical, last days, "prophetic" books with which I was all too familiar. I don't know if this woman gave up on QAnon conspiracy theories when the JFK, Jr., prediction never came true. But I do know many other QAnon conspiracy theories are still popular today.

The Mike Warnke Fraud

One of the most famous religious frauds in modern times was the story of Mike Warnke, the popular Christian comedian from the 1970s to 1990s who claimed he was a former drug-addicted, satanic high priest leading a witches' coven of 1,500 satanists in southern California in the mid-1960s. He wrote a book called The Satan Seller that described his involvement in the occult and dramatic conversion to Jesus, i.e., conversion to evangelical Christianity. I read this book around 1973 as a naïve, impressionable fifteen-year-old. The book included stories of Warnke in 1965-66 presiding over satanic rituals—magical spells, drinking blood and urine, summoning demons, worshiping Satan, and traveling to satanic conferences in places like Salem, Massachusetts. He claimed he and his fellow satanists also participated in sexual orgies that sometimes included kidnapping and rape.

In 1992, spurred by blatant inconsistencies found in his book and other writings, two reporters for the evangelical Christian magazine, Cornerstone, completed their several-months investigation of Warnke.[4] They interviewed over 100 of Warnke's personal friends and acquaintances. Their conclusion? The interviewees confirmed repeatedly that Warnke was a classic fraud. His friends laughed at some of his most outrageous claims (i.e., he was a wild drug addict who led a coven of 1,500 witches and warlocks during and after his one semester at a California community college) and voiced frustration over his minor ones (i.e., having long hair down to his shoulders and six-inch fingernails in college). It wasn't that nothing was true in his story but that he would take the smallest grains of truth and blow them up out of proportion until the real facts were unrecognizable.

The real story? In college, Warnke was an odd, flamboyant character. He drank, dabbled in Ouija boards and tarot cards, and joked about having a "coven" of 5 to 6 people that wasn't even active. There was no drug addiction (the marijuana craze didn't arrive on his campus until at least 1967), nor did he use speed or heroin let alone overdose on them. Photos of Warnke in college showed he was quite conservative looking. His friends testified to all this to the reporters as did his then-girlfriend during the nine months he was supposedly a sex crazed, drug-taking, satanic priest. She confessed they never even had sex because she was a devout Catholic. She said there's no way he could have done most of the things he claimed during the time she dated him. Moreover, his supposed dramatic conversion to Christ in boot camp before going to Vietnam—he enlisted in the Navy claiming he had to flee the coven that had turned violently against him—was even suspect. Another friend said he had already started participating in a college ministry called Campus Crusade for Christ before he joined the Navy.[5]

When Warnke wrote his book and started performing as a Christian comedian, he tapped into the popular theology of the 1970s that included fear of Satan, demons, the drug-induced youth culture, "end times," and the proposition that only Jesus (the evangelical variety, of course) can solve one's personal problems. Warnke became a successful evangelist, both cajoling with humor and scaring audiences into "the kingdom." But his whole case for persuading people to come to or follow Christ was based on a set of outrageous lies and deceptions.

After the exposé came out, Warnke only admitted to exaggerations and embellishments and never confessed to outright lying. This is part and parcel of the mindset that refuses to take lies, deception, and frauds seriously because in this case, people are supposedly coming to Jesus. When religious frauds are exposed, the common defense becomes just a rationalization that the ends justify the means.

The Norma McCorvey "Jane Roe" Story

There are the other frauds in today's politics that often touch on religion or are promoted by people with religious fervor. The most extraordinary one is the Norma McCorvey story. McCorvey is the "Jane Roe" in the 1973 Roe v. Wade case that legalized abortion nationwide and was overturned by the U.S. Supreme Court in June 2022. A complex individual, she was praised by the pro-choice movement for challenging criminal abortion law but was never allowed to be their spokesperson because she was considered too unpredictable. Then in 1995, she stunned the nation when she switched sides, became a "born again" Christian and a crusader against abortion. In fact, the truth was much more complicated. And it wasn't altogether revealed until the 2020 documentary, *AKA Jane Roe*.

At the time in 1995, I remember hearing that McCorvey became a believer and was now in the pro-life camp. I was still an avid pro-life activist, albeit not as active, having participated in two Operation Rescue (OR) "rescues" in 1989 in Los Angeles. OR was an evangelical Christian, anti-abortion movement that started in 1986. Today they go by the name Operation Save America. These "rescues" were obstructionist sit-ins by hundreds of people that blocked the doors at abortion clinics and usually culminated in mass arrests. Along with 700 others, I spent three days in the L.A. County jail after one such event in the spring of 1989. *Wow, Jane Roe is now a Christian!* I thought when I heard the news in the mid-90s. *This is such a boon for the pro-life movement.*

What I didn't hear until more than two decades later is what really happened behind the scenes. McCorvey, used as a poster girl for the pro-life movement, wasn't exactly the poster child for the evangelical movement. She smoked and drank heavily and was a lesbian in a long-term relationship. In normal circumstances, she would have been kicked out of most evangelical churches for not living a "holy" life. Finally, in the documentary, she confessed her about-face was all an act. When she spoke out against abortion, she was a paid actor although it wasn't a formal contract. She had many doubts about the pro-life message she was promoting, and she expressed pro-choice sentiments in the documentary. She wanted to have a voice that the pro-choice movement hadn't given her, so she tried the pro-life camp.

"We used her," said Robert Schenk, an evangelical pastor. "When you do what we did to Norma, you lose your soul." Schenk, who appears in *AKA Jane Roe*, was one of the evangelical leaders who paid Norma to make public appearances for Operation Rescue and the pro-life movement and later changed his mind about that and the way he looked at abortion. The pro-life, anti-abortion movement treated her like a trophy, he confessed.[6] At times, after Norma had been drinking, she would complain to Schenk and others for using her for fundraising purposes but not giving her an adequate percentage. Schenk admitted she was right.[7]

Norma McCorvey had a tragic, complicated life. She was terribly abused as a child and later sexually assaulted in a violent marriage. She had always been attracted to the same sex and was in a serious relationship with a woman while working for Operation Rescue. They cajoled her to end the relationship for "biblical" reasons claiming it was a "grievous sin." Schenk later admitted, "My callous part in their break-up will always be one of the worst sins I've committed against two human beings."[8] The narrative of the converted born-again Jane Roe of Roe v Wade who was now a pro-life, conservative Christian and her damning testimony against the pro-choice movement was a sham. Later, we'll examine the anti-abortion movement and why its claim that abortion is murder is another bogus contention.

It ain't what you don't know that gets you into trouble. It's what you know for sure that just ain't so.
— Mark Twain

The Big Lie of 2020 and "Stolen" Elections

Of course, we must examine the biggest political fraud of our time that hoodwinked many. Donald Trump successfully scammed millions of people to believe the 2020 election was rigged and fraudulent and that he had actually won.[9] And, one of the biggest blocks of supporters who believed this were white evangelical Christians. As late as November 2021, 60% of white evangelicals still believed the 2020 election was stolen from Trump.[10] "This is the only faith group surveyed to have a majority of respondents affirm the disproven claim asserted by former president Donald Trump and his allies..."[11] despite there being no court-sworn evidence presented to judges in 60-plus lawsuits—all but one of which were lost, including two that went to the Supreme Court.[12] And even though every audit that was later performed in battle-ground states didn't uncover major fraud, a majority of white evangelical Christians still bought into various unfounded theories. These included that thousands of dead people voted for Biden in major battleground states, ballots for Trump were routinely thrown out, and the company Dominion had voting machines across the country that had up to a 93% error rate. To his critics, this became known as "The Big Lie."[13] And it was.[14]

The avid Trump supporter and evangelical Christian, Mike Lindell, known as "the My Pillow Guy," spread Trump's "big lie" about the election to the nth degree. It's difficult to tell if he was a true believer—that is, if he was genuinely hoodwinked—or if he knowingly lied through his teeth. I suspect he was a victim of the scam rather than the latter. Interestingly enough, Lindell has his own story of redemption from opioid addiction through coming to Christ.

In late 2021, Lindell helped sponsor and spoke at a two-week-long bus tour that spread various lies about the election results. He promoted conspiracy theories—one being that the January 6th mob was actually associated with Antifa, and they were responsible for the attack. On January 25, Twitter permanently banned Lindell for spreading The Big Lie.[15]

Lindell produced three documentaries, *Absolute Proof, Absolute Interference*, and *Absolutely 9-0. Absolute Proof* was removed from YouTube and Vimeo for violating its election misinformation rules. In the documentaries,

Lindell falsely claimed he had proof of the election being stolen, that voting machine companies Smartmatic and Dominion, "conspired with foreign powers to rig voting machines to steal the election from Trump,"[16] that the Supreme Court would vote 9-0 to reinstate Trump once his evidence was fully revealed, and that it would happen on August 13, 2021. That day was the day after his "Cyber Symposium" ended, an event that he said would deliver irrefutable evidence of election fraud. The live streaming of the event was downright embarrassing. Lindell never presented any proof, only unintelligible data with no reasonable interpretation, and several rants about how he had been hacked.

Lindell's own cybersecurity expert denied he had proof of election fraud. He said it amounted to a "pile of nothing."[17] His documentary, *Absolute Proof*, won the Golden Raspberry Awards Worst Picture for 2020. Dominion sued Lindell for defamation. After an appeal, "a federal court judge ruled that Dominion's defamation lawsuit against Lindell and MyPillow can proceed, noting that Dominion has 'adequately alleged' that Lindell's accusations against the company were either knowingly false or made with 'reckless disregard for the truth.'"[18]

Later still, Trump's own Attorney General, William Barr, plus all of his serious advisors who investigated this, warned Trump there was no evidence of fraud anywhere near sufficient to overturn the results of the election. During testimony to the January 6th Committee in Congress, Barr said he had told Trump in three separate discussions, "I made it clear that I did not agree with the idea of saying the election was stolen and putting out this stuff, which I told the President was bullshit."

Barr also said as much about the 2000 Mules documentary from right-wing political commentator and evangelical Christian Dinesh D'Souza, who pleaded guilty in Manhattan Federal Court to Campaign Finance Fraud in 2014[19] (but later pardoned by Trump). "In my opinion then and my opinion now is that the election was not stolen by fraud, and I haven't seen anything since the election that changes my mind on that including the 2000 Mules movie," Barr said to the January 6th committee. He then immediately burst out laughing.[20]

The documentary, researched by a nonprofit named True to Vote, claimed that 2000 individuals ("mules") were paid to illegally collect ballots and drop them into ballot collection boxes in several swing states in the 2020 election. The "evidence" for this is based on only one supposed eyewitness whistleblower, a flawed study on cellphone geolocation data, and pure speculation. An AP fact check called "FACT FOCUS: Gaping holes in the claim of 2K ballot 'mules'"[21] thoroughly debunked the premise of the film. Republican Arizona Attorney General, Mark Brnovich, asked the FBI and the IRS to investigate True to Vote because of evidence they raised money from demonstrably false claims in the movie and elsewhere. In his letter to federal authorities, Brnovich wrote, "True to Vote lied about having provided evidence of Arizona election fraud to state investigators." Their spokespeople made public claims about voter fraud that supposedly helped Joe Biden get elected, and despite saying they would later provide evidence, they failed to provide proof in several meetings with state officials.[22] Moreover, a thorough examination by Reuters Fact Check revealed a host of problems with the claims for geolocation data and surveillance video.[23] Not to mention the fact that the flawed "mules" theory that people stuffed ballot boxes—if it even was true—had not one shred of evidence that the ballots being stuffed were actually cast for Joe Biden and not Donald Trump. It was pure speculation.

Later in 2022, there were reports surfacing that "anomalies" in voter rolls was proof that dead people and incompetent voters have voted in favor of Democrats in the past and would do so in the upcoming election. One such report in Skagit County, Washington, was shown to be categorically false by investigators of KING 5 News Seattle. Each specific claim was debunked.[24]

In all these cases, whether it's religious claims, general political misinformation, QAnon conspiracy theories, cries that the 2020 election was stolen from Donald Trump, or claims that voter rolls are being fraudulently used to gain votes by Democrats, people get scammed because they want to believe content that bolsters their religious, political, or ideological bend. When they spread the information to others, honestly believing it is true, they indirectly take part in the fraud without realizing it. What makes it a true scam is when contrary information through reputable fact-checking is ignored and/or demonized. This is in contrast to when false reporting is an honest mistake where a media source later corrects the misinformation after the real facts arise.

When Scams Lead to Violence

The ultimate fraud in the Trump era culminated on January 6, 2021, and was so pervasive it influenced many Trump supporters to commit acts of violence. Donald Trump and other speakers at his Washington "Save America" rally continued their blatant lies about the election being stolen. They had been perpetuating false claims for weeks that the vote count was fraudulent. At the rally, in an 11,000-word speech, in which he cited a list of unsubstantiated instances of voting fraud, Trump instilled both fear and misplaced zeal into the hearts of his hearers by saying things like:

> They should find those votes. They should absolutely find that just over 11,000 votes, that's all we need. They defrauded us out of a win in Georgia, and we're not going to forget it...The only way this can be explained is if tens of thousands of illegitimate votes were added to the tally, that's the only way you could explain it...We won't have a country if it happens...When you catch somebody in a fraud, you're allowed to go by very different rules. So I hope Mike [Pence] has the courage to do what he has to do. And I hope he doesn't listen to the RINOs and the stupid people that he's listening to. This is the most corrupt election in the history, maybe of the world...We must stop the steal and then we must ensure that such outrageous election fraud never happens again, can never be allowed to happen again...And we fight. We fight like Hell and if you don't fight like Hell, you're not going to have a country anymore.[25]

Rudy Giuliani riled up the crowd by admonishing them. Given the voter fraud he claimed was going on he said, "Let's have trial by combat."[26] Representative Mo Brooks, referencing the same, said things like, "Today is a time of choosing. And tomorrow is a time for fighting...Today is important in another way. Today is the day American patriots start taking down names and kicking ass...Our ancestors sacrificed their blood, their sweat, their tears, their fortunes, and sometimes their lives...I have a question for you. Are you willing to do the same?"[27]

Despite the claim that these speakers never meant to instill violence and said to march peacefully on the capital, the result was violence. Eight hundred Trump supporters—many or most of them conservative Christians—driven by fear of losing their country and believing to have the endorsement of Trump, marched on the capital building and forcefully attacked capital police and property using various implements as weapons, including stun guns, pepper spray, baseball bats, flag poles wielded as clubs, and their own fists. Once it started, Trump and his co-provocateurs didn't immediately announce this was not what they had intended to happen. They let it go on for three hours before Trump was finally pressured to make a statement to try to calm the rioters. It's also indicative of why so many people recognized Trumpism as a cult. It has all the signs of religious extremism, which ultimately leads to violent thoughts and, ultimately, violent deeds.

THE PREMISE OF RELIGIOUS MYTHS
IN WESTERN CHRISTIANITY

It is the contention of this book that major streams of Western Christianity have perpetuated frauds and myths on the masses for decades, even centuries, in very similar ways that the aforementioned frauds have been fostered on society today. To the unsuspecting, it seems so true. Trump was adamant and persuasive in preaching the Big Lie. Mike Warnke and Norma McCorvey were embraced by the evangelical establishment, so people surmised it must be true. When there is a belief in a particular narrative, whether it's that all liberals, Democrats, and the mainstream media are liars and promote evil, or that all unbelievers are depraved due to original sin, any claims that bolster that narrative are automatically accepted as truth. But when you look behind the curtain, they are shown for what they really are: frauds.

These frauds usually perpetuate what I call *violent sacrificial religion* and a retributive approach to law and life that I will explain in more detail in coming chapters. Admittedly, most people who did participate in disseminating these myths did not or do not realize what they are doing. Others are just promoting speculative or misinformed conclusions. This has resulted in most of modern Christendom teaching unhistorical claims. Not so much to gain fortune, although that is part of it—to pay the church bills and fill the coffers—but mostly to control people. It has used all three of these approaches to influence the masses: (1) carelessly passing on certain doctrines or speculations as truth, (2) stirring people's emotions, and (3) utilizing fear of ruin, judgment, and/or the afterlife.

As stated, most of the time, Christian apologists are not directly involved in scamming people. They are victims of myth spreading themselves, similar to my experience as a young missionary among Muslims, the woman who honestly believed JFK, Jr., was alive, the fans of Mike Warnke who sincerely believed his story to be true, or the evangelical Christians who accepted the conversion story of Norma McCorvey. Or when Trump supporters honestly thought that Biden and the Democrats stole the election. People are told something is true by a friend, online news source, social media, video presentation, documentary, church sermon, seminary class, book by an author they trust, a QAnon site, or even in a Bible (e.g., Greek words mistranslated in English or a narrative that is obviously inconsistent with Jesus' teachings). Over a period of time, they come to believe the content and pass it on to others unbeknownst of its fraudulent roots. Afterall, it bolsters their own worldview, whether that's a conservative Christian worldview or the view that Democrats and liberals are far Left extremists who would stoop to fraud and theft to win an election. So, although Western Christianity has scammed Western culture and perpetuated many myths, it has primarily been done so through unsuspecting adherents.

Sometimes, it's fear of God's punishment or fear of hell that will drive people to accept and spread a faith-myth. Fear prevents them from questioning a proposition. Although I questioned hell, I rarely did so publicly out of fear. Other times, people are influenced when their emotions are tapped. A message tugs at their heart strings, so they conclude its substance or underlying claims must be true. Finally, it's common for there to be a vibrant community surrounding a particular faith-fraud or conspiracy theory. It's the fear of losing that community or letting that community down that may drive someone to never question the narrative that is being purported.

I got scammed when I first made the decision to consider Christ at the age of 15 at a Billy Graham crusade. Meant to create a sense of urgency to "accept" Christ, one of the frauds was being led to believe we were in the "end times" and the "rapture" would soon occur. If I didn't accept Christ and Jesus returned, or if I died before accepting Christ, it would be too late. I would either face "the seven years of tribulation" or go to hell. And again, later when I decided to follow Jesus at the age of 22 after having a nervous breakdown in college, I accepted the fraud that I would never find peace unless I became an *evangelical Christian*.

I did have a genuine, life-altering spiritual experience. Yet, when entering evangelical sub-culture, I was subjected to a religious system full of faith-based myths. Despite being suspicious of some of them, as I later was with the doctrine of hell, I largely accepted what I was taught. Who was I to question what I understood to be long-standing Christian doctrines? Years later, I realized that part of my faith was real and part of it was based on fake claims. Another purpose of this book is to help you learn the difference. As Mark Yaconelli says, religious crap detectors are "really a healthy instrument in religion—discerning the bullshit from the gold."[28]

For sincere Christians, a Christian theology scam appears outrageous. "That's ridiculous! How can Western Christianity be a fraud and full of myths?" they protest. Evangelicals may concede that most of Catholicism is a fraud but vehemently object to their faith being one. The answer has to do with fact-checking the claims of Western Christianity through a good study of its origins. People are unaware of Christian myths because they are ignorant of history.

Diana Butler Bass calls this "spiritual amnesia," a kind of religious Alzheimer's. Believers are ignorant or forget or ignore their faith's history like an individual loses their memory. Without knowing the historical foundations of their faith or having knowledge of how many sacred doctrines cannot be traced back to the beginning, Western Christians are buying into fraudulent claims.

For religious skeptics, it may appear like an obvious claim. "Now that is definitely true! Christianity itself is a myth," they might say. Whether people have a scandalous or favorable reaction, many probably don't see the nuance behind the statement, Western Christianity is largely a fraud.

While agnostics, atheists, and some Christians may sense where these fake claims are coming from, few are familiar with the specific reasons for them. Nor are they generally aware why I would affirm that, although it has its problems, much of Eastern Christianity (certainly not all), does not rise to the level of promoting frauds. At the very least, much of its theology squares with a study of the first century Jesus Movement.

WHAT IT MEANS AND DOESN'T MEAN TO SAY WESTERN CHRISTIANITY IS LARGELY BASED ON MYTHS

I want to address these common reactions by first stating what I do *not* mean by the statement, *Western Christianity is largely based on myths*. Only by understanding what I don't mean, can one understand what I do.

I am not saying that Jesus' teachings are a fraud.

No, countless people throughout history have found solace, wisdom, and genius in Jesus' teachings, particularly his radical love and equality ethic. In modern history, some of those include heroic figures, such as Mahatma Gandhi, Dorothy Day, Martin Luther King, Jr., Mother Teresa, Desmond Tutu, and psychiatrist M. Scott Peck, who wrote *The Road Less Traveled*. The abolitionist movement of the 19th century was largely spurred by Protestant Christians. The Civil Rights Movement of the 1960s was as well. Many of our modern humanitarian aid agencies and hospitals are either Christian-based or can trace their roots back to ideas that have the mark of Christ's teachings.

Whether people call themselves a believer or not, it is common for those who encounter Jesus' teachings to be inspired and even more so if they become aware of some of the mistranslations and misconceptions that modern English New Testaments and churches convey. His teachings have a way of both encouraging people spiritually and inspiring them to live a life of love and service to others.

Nor am I saying that a person's personal faith as a Christian living in the West is a fraud.

No, millions of people have a vibrant faith in Jesus Christ, calling themselves followers of the first century Jewish Rabbi, who they either believe to be "the Messiah" and "Son of God" and "Savior" of humankind, or at least a human prophet used mightily by God. There are both conservative and liberal-minded Christians whose faith in Christ is real.

Nor am I saying that Christianity is based on a myth—that Jesus was actually not an historical figure, as mythicists like Robert Price and Richard Carrier argue.

Price and Carrier make a case that the figure of Jesus was fabricated over decades, from a synthesis of Egyptian, Jewish, and Greek mythologies. This theory says the Jesus story of the New Testament was adopted from popular dying-rising savior stories of Ancient Greece and the Near East. But mythicist theory is overall a minority viewpoint among historical scholars and even Bart Ehrman, known for being a staunch critic of conservative Christianity, forcefully refutes it in his book, *Did Jesus Exist?* He concludes, "Whatever else you may think about Jesus, he certainly did exist."[29] Jonathan Geoffrey Dean does the same in an early chapter of his new book, *Salt & Light: The Complete Jesus.*

No, the myths and fake claims I speak of are centered on Western Christianity *as a religious system*, and its generally accepted *worldview* and *doctrines*, whether they be Roman Catholic, Evangelical, Fundamentalist, Charismatic, and much of mainline Christianity.

Even though I can think of several notable and worthy exceptions (i.e., Celtic Christians, some Eastern Orthodox streams, Anabaptists, Quakers, Moravians, many progressive Christians, and modern Christian Universalists), many, if not most, Western Christians have bought into a worldview and belief system that is ironically contrary to the original meanings of the message of Jesus and Paul as articulated in the first century. Some of them are the exact opposite.

In other words, the DNA of ancient Christianity (i.e., Jesus' teaching and peace movement) has suffered grave mutations that the Western Reformation never completely corrected, and in some cases, made worse.

But how can we know this? Through careful historical, biblical, and linguistic study. And how can the Jesus of history be authentic, and this religion called Christianity in much of the West be substantially a fraud? By an historical sleight of hand. I laid out some of the major areas where this has occurred in my second book, *Craft Brewed Jesus.*

The conservative-minded believer of course reacts to this. Don't we have the Bible, in particular the New Testament, as our history? The Bible is clear, they will say, on a Christian worldview and doctrines!

No, the Bible may seem clear to some, but when you look under the hood, it's not clear. One's understanding of Jesus' and Paul's teachings when reading the modern English New Testament is typically clouded by mistranslations of Koine Greek[30] terms and phrases and misinterpretations based on a lack of knowledge of historical and cultural context. Moreover, other historical sources, such as the early church fathers, the Church of the East, the Jewish historian Flavius Josephus, and many more, steer one to conclusions contrary to many traditional views in Western Christianity, so much of which was influenced by only one church "father," Augustine. Finally, the way modern Christians typically view the Bible is contrary to the way Jesus, the Jews of his time, and the earliest followers of Jesus viewed the Bible. We will address this phenomenon in chapters 3 and 5.

As for agnostic- or atheist-minded people, they will undoubtedly agree with most of these contrary conclusions. However, they may or may not miss the larger point *Breaking Bad Faith* will make—that despite the presence of faith-based myths within Western Christianity, there is an authentic, historical voice derived from the teachings of this first century Jewish Rabbi, Jesus or Yeshua of Nazareth, that has a transformational message for our modern world.

This is not a message that would lead people to some reformed, rediscovered religion called *Christianity*. Rather it's one that would lead people to a profound *metaphysical and humanistic philosophy of life free of religion*. This philosophy of life (Leo Tolstoy called it a *theory of life*) includes what I'm calling the "path of peace," a message of good news on how to achieve peace and overcome violence within humanity. It's a way of leaving behind the human "mimetic" tendency to both mimic human retribution and "scapegoat" others, whether in our personal lives, communities, or on a global scale. Describing this peacemaking way of life will be the focus of the second half of the book.

So, what *are* these major fake claims and myths within Western Christianity that in some way promote or encourage violent sacrificial religion and a retributive approach to law and life? They have to do with how Western Christianity views the Bible, church, salvation, the cross, women, God's character, the afterlife, the end times, sexuality, and war. Before we look at the foundations that underpin them all, we need to understand 12 major faith frauds or myths.

THREE
THE MAJOR MYTHS VERSUS REALITY

THE FOLLOWING ARE NOT all of the frauds or myths that can be associated with Western and other forms of Christianity and have some association with violent sacrificial religion, but they are the major harmful ones that are easily refuted by a good study of history. Authors Erin Vearncombe, Brandon Scott, and Hal Taussig, in their historical narrative, *After Jesus Before Christianity*, tell us the reason there are so many myths is because our society tends to read Christian history backwards. We read everything through the lens of the present. We try to construct the building of Christianity from the top, like building a skyscraper by starting with the observation deck. We don't start with the foundation. By doing so "European and American societies [projected] their own power and belief systems back onto the earliest centuries"[1] reducing Christianity's story into a simple black-and-white perspective of orthodoxy vs. heresy as decided by the Catholic Church, the Protestant reformers, other Christian institutional streams, and today's modern popular theologians of evangelicalism and fundamentalism. When we start with the foundation, however, we start doing a good study of history and see things in a whole new light. We discover "in the first two centuries [after Jesus], what we think of as 'Christianity' did not exist."[2] When we start with the foundation—the true origins—we can uncover these myths and frauds that we still cling to in the present.

1 – THE FRAUD OF RELIGION

Jesus and/or the Apostle Paul did not start a new religion. Yet, Western Christianity, including evangelicalism, is a religion. Jesus and Paul were not Christians. Jesus was a Jewish Rabbi. Paul was a Jewish Pharisee who later converted to a non-violent, universalist brand of Judaism. Jesus and Paul advocated rethinking Judaism and the Torah per a re-reading of the Torah, reforms found in the Prophets, and Jesus' own revelations.

True Judaism, per Jesus and Paul, was to be a way of life based on love—love extended to all including enemies—that breaks down the barriers of Jew and Gentile and no longer uses violent animal or other sacrifices to "atone" for sins or appease a wrathful God. Jesus taught a way within Judaism, not a new religion. It wasn't until decades and centuries later that his way began to part from Judaism and became a separate religion. Up until then, the Nazarenes, as the earliest Jesus followers were often called, was one of up to 24 Jewish sects among four main divisions of first-century Judaism.[3] Moreover, individual groups of them were not all called "Christians." That was one of many names that others called them, or they called themselves. Those who followed the teachings of Jesus, the *Nazarenes*, or even *Galileans*, were not considered members of a new religion called Christianity but rather a sect within Judaism who welcomed outsiders and were also known as "followers of the Way."

Jesus told his Jewish hearers, "Go and learn what this means, 'I desire mercy, not sacrifice'" (Matthew 9:13 quoting Hosea 6:6). Jesus was critiquing the Jewish violent sacrificial system and the exclusivist and elitist religion that much of Judaism had become, just as the Prophets and Psalmist before him had often done.[4] He was not founding a new religion. Jesus did not found the Christian religion and his earliest followers, and Paul did not become what we moderns consider "Christians."

They challenged people, as stated above, not to convert to a new faith, but to a new humanistic way or theory of life—*free of the harmful elements of religion*. It was a *way of life* that trusted that a God of love was real, but trusting this God did not require, and in fact, was against almost all religious practices. In one way, for Jews, it was a challenge to become a universalist Jew, one who welcomed all, including Gentiles, as children of God. It retained the universalist elements in some of the Jewish scriptures but rejected the sacrificial system and violent retribution found in other parts of the scriptures. It wasn't a call for Jews to join a new faith called *Christianity* but to reform their own faith to become inclusive, reject exclusivism, and make loving one's neighbor, particularly the poor and marginalized, more important than strict adherence to the Law.

The fact that some evangelicals claim their message is not to join a "religion" but to enter into a "relationship" with Christ, is itself a type of fraud. Evangelicalism is still a religion.

One reason people today may not recognize early Christianity as a Jewish sect and not a new religion is because we are ignorant of what first century religion was like. All religions of the Roman Empire, including Judaism, the worship of Greco/Roman gods, mystery cults, and emperor worship, had four major components: a temple, a sacrificial system, a priesthood, and ritualistic practices and codes of conduct. Jesus and Paul did away with each of these. They both rejected the Jewish temple as irrelevant, uncovered the absurdity of a sacrificial system, taught that all were equal, that a priesthood was not necessary (because technically all were priests), and warned how religious codes (from vows to festivals to diet to Sabbath rules to penalties for disobeying the Law) all divert from true spirituality. This was why the Romans first called the followers of Jesus atheists. The early Jesus movement did not believe in "the gods," nor did the people sacrifice to any god, build or go to a temple, or have religious rituals.

But wait, didn't Jesus and his early followers meet and teach at the Jewish Temple? Yes, but it was not mandatory to meet there or follow Temple practices. Jesus predicted the Temple would be destroyed and taught that true worship happens in one's heart. He said the time had now come, in his day, that true worshippers need not worship in any temple (John 4:20–24).

As for the original communion, it was a "Love Feast," a communal meal held in people's homes with no precise religious code. Centuries later it became a ritual in the church.[5] As for baptism, it did not originate with Christianity, was practiced several different ways, and was never deemed required for salvation or for one to have a change of heart.[6] In fact, all of the four components of pagan religion in antiquity were not in the earliest Jesus movement but eventually crept into the Catholic Church and, for the most part, were retained by Protestants. Even sacrifice. As we will see, a violent sacrificial system became part of Christian theology.

Religion is problematic. Its dividing line between those inside and those outside eventually leads to violence. The ancient Jewish faith has a history of violence from the Canaanite conquest to the Zealot-driven Great Revolt against the Romans from 66 to 70 CE. Greco/Roman religion led to the violent persecution of some early Jesus followers by the Romans. After the fourth century, the new Romanized "Christian" religion led to heretics being violently persecuted by "Christians." Then there was the Crusades where two major religions, Christianity and Islam, fought each other. Today, extremists under the guise of Islam (Al Qaeda, ISIS, Al Shabab) or the guise of Christianity or Christian Nationalism (Ku Klux Klan, Army of God, Aryan Nations, the Jericho March of 2020, the January 6th Capitol Insurrection) resort to violence and sometimes terrorism. Even mainstream Christianity regularly endorses militarism and other retributive solutions to the problems of society.

Moreover, our popular Christian theology may not advocate direct violence against unbelievers or heretics, but it does so indirectly—it warns the world about a coming violent judgment and eternal damnation. It largely supports capital punishment. At times, it attributes acts of violence, such as 9/11, or a pandemic like COVID-19, to the bad behavior of scapegoats and/or the judgment of God.[7] And most importantly, in America, most of Christendom (with some notable exceptions), divides the world into "us" and "them," the saved and the lost, with the lost being depraved or rebellious sinners whose default destination is eternal damnation as designed by a wrathful God who must have his system of retributive justice satisfied.

The refreshing reality, however, is that the earliest, first-century Jesus Movement was a peacemaking and universalist sect within Judaism that welcomed all with no religious requirements accept to follow an inclusive love ethic.

2 – THE MYTH OF CHURCH

Jesus did not found an institutional church. His "church," or ekklesia in the Greek, was simply a gathering of people who followed the new way of life of love he taught. It was contrary to the religions of the day, whether Jewish, Roman, the state-sponsored Emperor Cult, or one of the many "mystery religions." As stipulated above, all religions of antiquity had a set of rituals, sacrifices, priests, and temples. Earliest Jesus gatherings were free of hierarchy, professional clergy, sacred people, sacred places, sacred buildings, and sacred objects. It was an "anti-religion" movement. Again, the Romans called the first followers of Jesus atheists because they didn't believe in the gods and didn't have a system of religion. That system didn't arise until a few centuries later.

E.P. Sanders tell us that "all scholars agree that Jesus did not foresee an institutional Church with a professional priesthood that would have authority to absolve sins" and by implication, have authority to "cover" church members with spiritual protection.[8]

Moreover, the notion that a wider Christian church could be connected to a state government was also absent from the thinking of the early gatherings of followers. Jesus taught the "kingdom" or reign of God did not come through careful observation so people can say, "it's over there" or "it's here." The reign of God was within the hearts of people and reflected among a loving community, Jesus taught (Luke 17:20-21). It's not a hierarchal system of laws and authority, therefore, can't be tied to an institution or government. The Christian nationalist movement today that tries to deny the separation of church and state and declare America a "Christian" nation is born out of a misunderstanding of what Jesus taught about how the reign of God works. Not to mention the fact that it has no basis in American history. You can clearly see that in the seminal book, *The Search for Christian America*, by Mark Noll and the later book, *The Myth of a Christian Nation*, by Gregory Boyd.

Our modern church institutions and denominations, whether rooted in Roman Catholicism or Protestantism, are not a reflection of the spiritual community espoused by Jesus and Paul. When Jesus said, "I will build my church," he wasn't talking about religious organizations, institutions, or denominations. He was talking about building *a following of people* who would change their way of thinking—this is the meaning of 'repentance'—and embrace his love ethic. It's also noteworthy that the word "church," *ekklesia*, is only referenced two times in the Gospel accounts, all in Matthew, where Jesus refers to building a following who walk his path and having a "gathering" of people confront an errant brother if he refused to listen to an individual or two or three others. It was not in reference to a religious institution or organization.

Our modern churches are ethically neutral. That is, they can be used for good, but more often than not, they become spiritually abusive due to a hierarchal system of "church" leaders (popes, cardinals, bishops, priests, pastors, elders, apostles, prophets, church home group leaders, etc.) and a legalistic set of non-negotiable doctrines, statements of faith, behaviors, and church rules.

Our modern practice of going to church is purely optional for a person following Jesus' way of love. The only real admonition for followers is to gather together in some way, shape, or form. In the first century, they did it informally in homes and courtyards with no pastors, bishops, or titled officers. Leadership was present but informal. In some gatherings (not all) it consisted of a plurality of "elders." There was no priestly or pastoral professional class nor hierarchy. The term "pastor" simply meant one who had a gift to care for others. It didn't denote the top leader(s) in an institutional church.

If one is honest, today's church systems by their structure are extremely problematic. Just look at the myriad denominations, fissures, and scandals within institutional churches, both Catholic and Protestant. And some of these issues, like spiritual abuse by church leaders, can easily become violent. When churches focus their main goal to be the protection of their own institution, not the marginalized, they succumb to violent and corrupt practices. The sexual abuse scandals by Catholic priests[9] and the Protestant evangelical sexual abuse coverup[10] are just two examples. They are violence against children. Another example is the church teaching of women submitting to their abusive husbands and strict teachings of divorce that tell wives to stay in physically abusive marriages. Moreover, there's the mounting formal accusation against mega churches and their leaders all over the country that are continually being caught in corrupt or spiritually abusive behavior.[11]

The refreshing reality, however, is that the earliest, first-century Jesus Movement did not go to church, have professional clergy, set up a hierarchy, or run things like a business. They were local groups of *followers of the way*, with designations of their groups that included "Jesus clubs, movements for the Savior, communities of the Anointed, and schools of the Lord."[12] They met in homes, courtyards, and informal gatherings around one common practice: have a meal together and remember Jesus and the love ethic he taught and demonstrated by his life, death, and non-retaliatory resurrection. Then go out and practice that ethic and encourage others to do the same. There are a variety of ways to emulate this practice without a church institution. Modern churches are optional for anyone who wants to follow the way of Jesus.

3 – BIBLE FRAUD

Jesus and Paul did not believe in an inerrant, universally applicable, and altogether authoritative Bible. Most modern theologies of the Bible are based on historical myths. The Bible is not an infallible rulebook by which we are to live (even if you stipulate infallibility of the original manuscripts, which we don't have).

I see the Bible as a wonderful book that contains divinely inspired messages, but to truly appreciate it, one needs to acknowledge its inherent problems. Just like any historian would view historical accounts with a critical eye until mistakes and inconsistencies sink to the bottom and probable truths and meaningful messages rise to the surface, we need to do the same with the Bible.

This is pure heretical thought to the conservative-minded Christian. But before you throw me off a cliff, bear this in mind: Jesus viewed the Bible this way. As we will learn later, he read it selectively, favored the word of the Prophets over sacrificial laws, made exceptions to Torah stipulations, and contradicted the character of the God of much of the Old Testament. In fact, so did the prophets with some exceptions. Jesus didn't see the Bible as a wholly divine book written by humans but as a human book with some of God's fingerprints on it.

Jesus, and most of the writings of the prophets, differentiated between two voices in the scriptures. A voice of love and forgiveness versus a voice of retribution and wrath. A voice of mercy versus a voice of murder. A voice of divine revelation versus a voice of human religion. We will see this dichotomy clearly later in the book when we look at concrete examples.

Moreover, the Jewish people of the first century did not have a settled "canon" (definitive list) of scriptures until the second century. There was always a debate on what was scripture and what wasn't (and which voices within scripture should be obeyed), and Jesus entered into this debate. This is why the Sadducees only considered the Torah scripture and not the Prophets and the Writings. And why the Greek Jews and earliest followers of Jesus used the Septuagint as their scriptures, which included the Apocrypha—14 books not in any Protestant Bible today! And why the Essenes had a set of writings they deemed authoritative to add to all these, some of them discovered among the Dead Sea Scrolls, and even one of them, I Enoch, quoted by the New Testament book of Jude.

As for the New Testament, it was not a settled "canon" until the fourth century, and even then, there were ongoing disputes about which books should be included and which should be left out. As I describe in *Craft Brewed Jesus*,[13] the process of establishing the New Testament reveals the dilemma with declaring the books we have today as infallible and thoroughly authoritative. Whereas some books were easily accepted (i.e., the four gospels were widely accepted, but not mandatory for all), others were highly disputed by many orthodox Christian leaders.

When one studies this history of how both the Old and New Testaments were debated, compiled, and canonized, it becomes clear that our modern concepts of an across-the-board, authoritative, and infallible Bible are pure myth.[14] This myth perpetuates what Michael Hardin calls a flat reading of the Bible—treating everything as an equally, internally, consistent message from God. As Christian Smith documents, it also makes the Bible impossible to read coherently.[15] This type of inerrant reading of the Bible messes with your mind. It does not allow us to think for ourselves as to what is worthy of the divine and what is not. It empowers certain religious leaders to use the Bible as a weapon to control others by citing passages that reinforce some warped theology while ignoring other passages that contradict that theology.

We will explore this later in the book, for if you get this wrong, you go down a slippery slope of incongruent theology that has been the foundation of Western Christianity—a theology that tries to have it all ways. It attempts to harmonize obvious biblical mistakes, theological inconsistencies, violent God narratives, and historical falsehoods with some of the most spiritually inspiring stories and teachings the world has ever known. In other words, it tries to mix the two voices within scripture. When this is done, we're left with people worshipping the Bible instead of God. And outsiders who wrongly reject the Bible altogether simply because they rightly reject this all-or-nothing mentality.

 We're also left with people using the Bible to justify violence and abuse. In America, it peaked with the theological justification of slavery and later Jim Crow laws. Unfortunately, today it continues in practices such as capital punishment, physically abusive discipline of children, the refusal to allow women in physically abusive marriages to divorce, and retributive methods of dealing with criminals and "the other." This includes solitary confinement, mandatory or harsh prison sentences, and scapegoating certain populations such as African Americans, immigrants, the LGBTQ community, liberals, and people of other religions.

Bear in mind, the problem of scapegoating can work in every way. It is equally true that liberals can use their own sacred theology and political correctness (which can become like a sacred text) to scapegoat conservatives or anyone who doesn't use the *right* words, do the *right* thing, or practice the *right* politics.

The refreshing reality is that the earliest, first-century Jesus Movement did not have a New Testament nor a definitive list of scriptures that were mandatory to follow. They did not view the Jewish scriptures or the later gospel accounts, letters, and other documents that eventually became the New Testament as an all-encompassing, mandatory rulebook. Rather, they focused on the love ethic and teachings of Jesus they gleaned from the oral tradition, the emerging gospels, and other new scriptures—some that made it into the New Testament eventually and others that did not. This will become clearer when we dive further into this issue in Chapter 5.

4 – THE MYTH OF THE
TWO-FACED GOD

After hearing the two voices in the Bible, one can recognize that the God of most of Western Christianity, particularly evangelicalism and fundamental-ism, is two-faced—a merciful God of love *and* a retributive God of wrath. A non-violent God of peace *and* a violent God of war. A God that has divided the fate of humanity to be consigned to either heaven *or* hell—blessed bliss for true believers or eternal conscious torment for everyone else. Yet both history and logic tell us this is superstitious hogwash.

If there is a God of love, he or she is only a God of love. If not, we are all in deep excrement, not just the unbelievers. David Platt, an evangelical preacher who clearly believes in a two-faced God, once said, "Yes, God is a Father who loves us, a loving Father who saves us, but he is also a wrathful Judge who may damn us."[16]

Imagine having an earthly father like this—one who claimed to love you but who also held the right to damn you to hell. We would rightfully judge him as two-faced and not trustworthy. Yet this opinion is the majority in Western Christendom. They believe in a God who both loves and damns people. This too messes with one's mind. And it reveals a violent streak in God.

Another popular preacher, Francis Chan, reminded his flock God once completely inundated the whole planet killing masses of people, *and* Jesus warned us that some who call him "Lord, Lord" would not enter heaven (Matthew 7:21). That meant some in his audience would wind up in hell.[17] Here is a violent God who drowned almost the entire human race—the elderly, men, women, children, infants, and the unborn—and will also destroy false believers. This God is not even pro-life. Scandalized pastor, Mark Driscoll, former head of Mars Hill Church in Seattle, once told his congregation that God hates some of them at that very moment—based on Old Testament verses that talk about God loving and hating whom he chooses.[18] So, now we have a God who arbitrarily both loves and hates. This is not a trustworthy divinity. "You are in grave danger," Driscoll preached. "You are filling your cup of wrath. If you die apart from Jesus, he will pour out full strength the full cup of that wrath on you forever."[19]

This paradox uncovers the two major problems with this two-faced, or Janus-faced, God.[20] First, with a two-faced God, we never know for sure which God will show up. Which is it? Is God angry at us and our sin? Angry enough to destroy us or consign us to hell because his justice demands punishment? Does God hate us because he simply chooses to hate *some* people? Or is he equally loving and merciful to all, patiently waiting for humanity to change, mature, and discover divine peace? Is Driscoll correct based on his take on the Bible or should we believe Jesus when he says, God is kind to the ungrateful and wicked (Luke 6:35)? Or the Psalmist when he says God will not harbor his anger forever (Psalm 103:9)? Is God wholly good or is he a mixed bag?

Second, Jesus' life and teaching affirms the God of love and, as we shall learn, completely contradicts the idea of a retributive God who destroys people and ultimately sends them to hell. Historical records and Greek biblical texts confirm this.

Conservative Christians have an answer to this, but it's found wanting. They claim that God can be both. God is angry at sin but loves humankind so much he sent Jesus to die for us so that anyone who freely chooses Christ will be saved from sin and death and hell. Since God doesn't force himself on people, if people freely choose to reject or ignore Christ, their default destination is eternal damnation. As if God is so angry at sin, he has to send people to hell. Later, we'll see how this is rationalized from the Bible, how it doesn't fit the history of early Christianity, and how non-sensical it is. The logical conclusion is we end up serving a God who needs a therapist.

The refreshing reality, however, is that the earliest, first-century Jesus Movement did not feel obligated to try to harmonize a two-faced God they found in the Jewish scriptures. They largely looked at the character of God through the lens of Jesus and the love ethic he taught. What was God like in their minds? He was like Jesus and how he acted and lived on earth.

This line of reasoning leads us to the next three scams: the doctrines of *hell*, *original sin*, and *substitutionary atonement*.

5 – THE MYTH OF HELL

Years after my experience on the mission field, I learned an important fact. Jesus did not teach the existence of hell. Tracing history, we know that the doctrine of hell is a fallacy derived from ancient pagan, Egyptian, and Near East religious beliefs and bolstered by political justifications. It didn't enter Jewish thought (it is not taught in the Old Testament) until the Jewish captivity in Babylon and, more specifically, until cited in certain intertestamental scriptures, such as I Enoch.[21]

Jesus taught a time of rehabilitation or remedial discipline was coming for the wicked, not eternal punishment.[22] When he referred to gehenna—the garbage dump outside Jerusalem that is mistranslated *hell*—he matched contemporary views of it being a metaphor for temporary judgment either in the here and now or the afterlife.[23] Several books starting in the early 2000s, including Rob Bell's logically sound *Love Wins* and the scholarly, historical study *The Christian Doctrine of Apokatastasis* by Ilaria Ramelli, make virtually impenetrable emotional, logical, biblical, and historical cases against eternal damnation. As does the 2012 documentary *Hellbound?*,[24] which examines the history of the doctrine and its roots outside early Christian thought. These examples are just the tip of the iceberg.[25]

The earliest church teachings from the Jewish prophets and Jesus regarding God's temporary anger and forgiving nature and his restorative plans for humanity are clearly recorded throughout scripture and history.[26] For this to become clear, one only needs to uncover them and step out of the mistaken translations and superstitious interpretations found in Western theology.

Moreover, history confirms this. Universalists were a majority in the ancient faith movement of Jesus for the first five centuries.[27] There have always been universalists among Christians throughout history, particularly among Eastern Christians (i.e., the Nestorians and Jacobites), but also among minority Western streams. Some examples of these are Julian of Norwich, the Moravians, the Anabaptists, the Quakers, and such notable figures as George Washington, Benjamin Franklin, Benjamin Rush (signer of Declaration of Independence), Charles Dickens, Harriet Beecher Stowe, Abraham Lincoln, Victor Hugo, Clara Barton, Hannah Whitall Smith, George MacDonald (mentor of C.S. Lewis), Jacques Ellul, Karl Barth, and a myriad of others.

History also confirms the translations found in most of our English Bibles that translate Greek words like *hades* and *gehenna* as hell are in serious error. The many books and resources cited in the footnotes get to the heart of these misguided mistranslations.

Another example is the Greek phrase *aionios kolasis*, most often translated as *eternal punishment* (Matthew 25:46). *Aionios* does not mean eternal. It is the adjective form of the word *age*, as in "a period of time."[28] In the Septuagint—the Greek translation of the Torah, Writings, Prophets, and Apocrypha—it is used for short periods of time. For example, Jonah was in the belly of the whale for aionios. This is cited in modern translations as "three days" (Jonah 1:17). The Jewish historian Josephus uses the word to describe the imprisonment of a man named Jonathan—*aionios* imprisonment. The prison sentence only lasted three years.[29]

The word *kolasis* was originally used to describe the pruning of a plant to get it to grow in a more desirable way. It is a corrective term that means "correction or rehabilitation." It is a certain type of discipline that restores and corrects. There is another word in Greek for punishment that means "retributive punishment": *timoria*. But Jesus does not use that word or the Aramaic equivalent, and people from that time commonly knew the difference. Even Aristotle made this point: "Now there is a difference between *timoria* and *kolasis*. *Kolasis* is inflicted in the interest of the sufferer; *timoria* in the interest of him in inflicts it, that he may obtain satisfaction."[30]

In other words, *kolasis* benefits the sufferer to make them better. This is why "rehabilitation" is an accurate translation of this word, and "punishment," which is meant to satisfy a retributive purpose (which hell could only be described as) is not. The time period is open-ended with short or long periods possible, but with eternity being impossible. This is also why Greek lexicographer, Ann Nyland, translates the phrase *eternal punishment* in Matthew 25 as "rehabilitation for a set period of time."[31]

Of course, this does not mean that God does not judge evil people or not hold them accountable or that we humans have no need to repent. It means history teaches us that early Christians believed God is a restorative God, not a retributive God. A God who uses the circumstances of one's life choices and arguably remedial experiences in the afterlife to correct and rehabilitate people, not to condemn or damn them forever. A God who always leaves the door open for change and forgiveness and doesn't trap people in eternal dungeons.

The refreshing reality is that the concept of hell is a pagan idea that was never taught in the Old Testament. It crept into Jewish thought in the intertestamental period and was never taught by Jesus nor his earliest followers.

6 – THE FRAUD OF ORIGINAL SIN

The source of the Western doctrine of original sin comes from Augustine, not the Jewish and New Testament scriptures. Robert Arnold claims, "This doctrine of 'original sin' is a hideous one and found its way into the Western theological construct through the flawed Latin text of St. Paul's Epistle to the Romans having passed through the dark imagination of Augustine."[32] It is a legal, ancestral view that says humankind inherited a depraved sinful nature through Adam, who had irreversibly fallen from a perfect state.

During the Reformation, Calvin expounded on this doctrine and taught that humankind's image was marred beyond recognition so that we are trapped in total depravity. No one is capable of choosing goodness or salvation without God's sovereign intervention, according to Calvin.

On the other hand, Eastern Christian theology teaches that humans are born spiritually immature not totally depraved. Our spiritual eyes may be damaged, but they were never destroyed. We still retain God's beautiful image and have what we might call "original innocence." We are capable of drawing on God within us to heal any damaged connection. We are not in some reprobate state destined for hell unless God chooses to save us (Calvinism) or unless we choose Christ as Lord and Savior before we die (Arminianism). We are destined to grow into maturity and wholeness from our immature spiritual state. Everyone is worthy of redemption. No one is wretched and beyond hope.

The doctrine of original sin paints believers as "regenerated" when coming to Christ and unbelievers as depraved, "unregenerated" lost souls. It is a doctrine that divides humanity into "saved" and "lost" and perpetuates the destructive "us vs. them" mentality.

The doctrine also justifies violence against depraved souls. During the Spanish Inquisition, heretics were tortured to force them to repent. Violence was justified for the greater good of turning a lost soul back to the truth and preventing them from going to hell. If they didn't repent and then died, the church had saved others from hell who would have been deceived by their false teaching.

Violence, final judgment, destruction, and eternal damnation for "them" are all justified when popular theology demonizes or dehumanizes other human beings. This is how violent sacrificial religion works. If people are depraved, rebellious, and impenitent, a theology of violence and retribution is acceptable.

To be sure, there is a "doctrine" of sin in the historical Christian narrative. But it's not one of default depravity and wretchedness. It is simply a recognition that every human being fails to measure up perfectly to a God of love. No one is without "sin." Every person is spiritually immature by default and is susceptible to committing grave acts of evil. But they aren't destined for hell. Everyone needs to grow up spiritually (develop values) as well as physically and emotionally.

The refreshing reality is that according to the gospel of the kingdom taught by Jesus, human beings are not depraved and wicked at birth due to some ancestral inheritance but are merely spiritually childish. From birth, and throughout life, although we are capable of evil, we are worthy of unconditional love as image-bearers of God. Even science bears this out. Recent studies are confirming that humankind is prone to cooperation and kindness to other humans, despite our history of war and violence.[33]

7 – THE PENAL SUBSTITUTIONARY ATONEMENT MYTH

Early Christians did not believe that Jesus' death on the cross was a substitute for the judgment of humanity's sin. They did not believe that God could redeem humanity (nor any individual) only if Jesus took the punishment they deserved in their place as a way of satisfying the demands of God's justice. They didn't believe that only if someone formally accepted this saving act, by "receiving Jesus as Lord and Savior," would a person be forgiven.

In other words, the penal substitutionary atonement theory taught by most conservative Christians today was completely foreign to the earliest followers of Christ. History shows that it didn't grow roots until Anselm's teaching in the 11th century and didn't mature as an atonement belief until the Reformation, and, in particular, through Calvin.

Eastern Orthodox theology sees the cross as a transformative phenomenon, not a legal requirement as if God can't forgive unless someone is punished. Jesus' death by crucifixion was not a way to appease God's sense of righteousness but rather an historical exhibition of a non-sacrificial way of ending sacrifice.[34] Despite being scapegoated by an angry mob—including Jewish leaders, Gentiles, a Roman Procurator who couldn't bring himself to overrule the mob, and weak disciples who scattered rather than defend him—the innocent victim Jesus chose to forgive, not to retaliate. No strings attached. That's transformative. And it proves that sacrifice is not necessary to move God. When God, through Jesus, forgives His most violent enemies, there is no reason to continue sacrificial religion.

The Western Church has largely perpetuated a sacrificial, or payment, view of the cross. Marcus Borg names it a "deeply destructive notion." It continues the human religious tendency to see salvation as what Michael Hardin calls, "an economy of exchange." You're saved or healed or delivered *only if* something is given in exchange. In this case, what's given or required is a torturous death of an innocent man.

When we realize that the doctrine of hell is a myth, we can also see that Jesus does not save humanity from hell. He saves humanity from death and the cycle of violence. He saves us from ourselves and our self-seeking, retributive, violent tendencies, when we embrace his way of love.

We will address the problems with *penal substitutionary atonement* in more depth later when we look more closely at the "fraud of the transactional God," which I summarize below.

8 – THE "END TIMES" CRAZE

Jesus did not believe, or teach, that he would return to earth thousands of years in the future to set up his kingdom. No early followers believed this. "The idea of a second coming of Christ in a far distant future was alien to early stages of Christian thinking."[35] Jesus taught the kingdom, or more accurately, *the reign of God* was at hand, already in our midst, and in fact, within us (Luke 17:21).

Nor did he teach that he would physically return within the lifetime of his followers. Jesus used very common cosmic imagery from the Jewish prophets to describe the end of the Jewish sacrificial age (Second Temple Judaism). He was not speaking about the end of the world as we think we know it but rather the end of an era. His language describing the "coming of the son of man" was not about some far-off futuristic-yet-primitive form of space travel in which he would embark upon his return to earth (nor a "rapture" of believers who would join him in the sky). Instead, it was a statement that he and his good news of peace would be vindicated.[36]

If this notion flies in the face of what you have been taught or think you have read as obvious in the New Testament, it is because Western Christianity (both conservatives and sometimes liberals, with notable exceptions) has ignored historical context. This includes the figurative language and nature of apocalyptic literature, the original meanings of certain Koine Greek words and phrases, and, in some cases, the plain words of Jesus himself. For example, when he said, *"This generation shall not pass away until all these things take place"* (Matthew 24:34). "These things" were the catastrophic events before and during the destruction of the Temple and Jerusalem—what the New Testament calls the tribulation at the end of the age.[37]

It has also ignored the clear confirmation that these events occurred in 70 CE as recorded by the first-century Jewish historian Flavius Josephus in his book *The Jewish War*. It's fascinating to read Josephus' account and how it dovetails with the sayings of Jesus on "the coming tribulation." It wasn't some far-off, end-of-the-world scenario that televangelists and "biblical prophecy experts" insist is playing out today. It was a coming disaster within a few decades for the corrupt Jewish Temple cult, the violent Zealot movement, and anyone who refused to love their enemies. A good study of Jewish and first-century history proves that today's popular "end times" theology is a crock. One of the popular variations of it—Jesus will "rapture" true believers to heaven before the seven years of tribulation and his final return—wasn't even conceived until 19th century Plymouth Brethren preacher John Nelson Darby created it.

Current popular theology is obsessed with the end times. It always declares every generation is probably in the time of "the end" and on the cusp of the return of Christ. Every contemporary crisis—in 2020, it was Covid-19—becomes proof of the looming judgment.[38] It loves to warn the masses—telling the church they better re-commit and pray and fast and give and go to reach the last of the unreached tribes of the earth (what I believed I was doing in Africa) in order to bring an end-time revival before Jesus' return. It loves to preach to unbelievers that judgment is coming, so they better repent. It fuels a fear-based religion not really concerned with the future of our planet. The world is ending, we better be doing more to prepare, and the coming judgment on humanity will vindicate true Christians. But this judgment of God is violent and retributive, punishing those who don't accept the right interpretation of Christ, and destroying the unrepentant and consigning them to eternal damnation.

9 – THE MISOGNY FRAUD

There is a deep prejudice against women in Western Christianity. No big surprise there. Evangelicals, of course, claim it's not prejudice but "complementarianism," or God's ordained roles for men and women. Equal worth but different roles, as they say. Women can't be pastors or leaders because they were created to submit to men's leadership. Wives must submit to their husbands, etc. God has assigned men the headship roles and women the *supportive* roles.

The fraud is how a study of New Testament-era history turns this notion on its head. History is full of solid evidence of men changing the translations of Greek terms or even inserting biased commentary to bolster the patriarchy of the era. The woman, Junia, in Romans 16:7 was called an apostle by Paul. Her name was changed to a male form in English translations for centuries.[39] The original Greek states that Phoebe, in Romans 16:1–2, was a "presiding officer," a leader, at a church.[40] That was changed by translators to terms like "deacon" (NIV) or "servant" (KJV).

The passage in I Corinthians 14 which teaches that women should be silent in churches—a direct contradiction to what Paul says in other passages—has been revealed to be either a scribal scam or grossly mistranslated and misunderstood. One theory is that two of the verses were inserted by a biased copyist trying to ensure the male superiority of the day, according to leading biblical scholars, even two of the most respected evangelicals, Gordon D. Fee and F. F. Bruce.[41] The passage does not fit with the context, and some versions of the extant text have it in different locations in the chapter. The other theory—a literal acceptance of the passage as genuine is fraught with irreconcilable problems—is based on the evidence of two missing words not found in modern English Bibles. Greek lexicographer, Ann Nyland, says the passage has been "terribly mistranslated." Paul was quoting from the letter sent to him and was actually condemning the statement that women should remain silent. The two words left out (twice) are "Utter Rubbish!"[42] In other words, Paul thought the view is garbage, or I daresay, bullshit!

In I Timothy 2:12, Paul said, "I do not permit a woman to teach or to have authority over a man; she must be silent." Yet, modern biblical scholars (except for conservative ones who can't get their heads out of the inerrancy box) are in consensus that what is called the "pastoral epistles"—I & II Timothy and Titus—were not written by Paul.[43] The statement contradicts what Paul stated earlier.

It's indisputable that Jesus set an example of honoring and equalizing women like no Jewish Rabbi had done before with this new egalitarianism teaching.[44] Women were leaders in the first organic gatherings of Jesus followers, and Paul's writings, although at times twisted by copyists or mistranslated, still retain a most revolutionary statement: There is no male or female in the Anointed One of Nazareth (Galatians 3:28).

Except when Jewish or Roman patriarchy tried to influence Christian thought, male privilege had little place in most ancient gatherings of Jesus' followers. Today, this misogyny leads to violence against women, either through sexual harassment or abusive husbands using Bible narratives to justify their abuse or pastors using biblical narratives to teach against women divorcing their emotionally or physically abusive husbands (i.e., "wives submit to your husbands" or "women are to stay silent"). Later, we'll see a clear example of this.

10 – THE MORALITY MYTH

French theologian Jacques Ellul forcefully makes the case that "God's revelation has absolutely nothing to do with morality. Nothing. Absolutely nothing."[45] Neither is there a moral system in the teachings of Jesus. In fact, Ellul tells us that "the revelation of God in Jesus Christ is against morality."[46] The whole point of Jesus', and later Paul's teaching, is that the rationality or will of God can never be fixed in a set of commandments or morals. Rather, it must be born from a pure and loving heart. Jesus proves this by attacking the most nit-picking, legalistic moralists of his day: the teachers of the Law (Scribes) and Pharisees.

This is the exact opposite of what Western Christianity and modern evangelicalism has taught us. They use (or more accurately misuse) the Bible as a set of commandments on what is righteous and what is sinful. But a set of rules that tell us what is right and wrong is doomed to fail because it can never predict every scenario, know every person's inner motivation, or adapt to the ever-changing requirements of love. This is why Paul explains to us that engaging in loving behavior fulfills any commandments of the law (Romans 13:8-10). It is also why he says everything is lawful to those who follow the way of love even though not everything is helpful. What counts is not to be moral but to be loving. And true love must have freedom. But with constraints.

> This freedom does not mean doing anything at all. It is the freedom of love. Love, which cannot be regulated, categorized, or analyzed into principles or commandments, takes the place of law. The relationship to others is not one of duty but of love.[47]

Thus, modern evangelicals and fundamentalists cannot accept as equals practicing lesbians, gays, or transgender people in the church. They stumble over real or contrived prohibitions in the Bible against homosexual behavior. Authentically following the way of Jesus (the way of love), however, demands fully accepting the LGBTQ community and not imposing any moral system or commandments on them, except the admonition to live a life of love. Sexual orientation or sexual behavior cannot be condemned by religious taboos. Like all other orientations or behaviors in life, it can only be constrained by love. As long as anyone—whether heterosexual or not—commits to living a life of love (to not harm others by their behavior), they are equals in a community of faith.

Not to mention the fact that there are critical problems with traditional interpretations of homosexual references in the Bible that are laid out in books like *Unclobber: Rethinking our Misuse of the Bible on Homosexuality*. Female homosexuality is not even addressed in the Old Testament at all! And male homosexuality refers to shrine prostitution, idolatry, and sexual exploitation. Other New Testament references are in the context of a Jewish culture surrounded by sacred prostitution and Roman temples that practiced rites consisting of paid intercourse (homosexual and heterosexual) performed as religious worship to appease pagan gods. And a Greek culture that winked at the practice of pederasty—men sexually using mentored prepubescent boys. Moreover, the Old Testament "clobber" passages about prohibiting "males from lying with males as with women" call it an "abomination." But they also call things like mixing two types of cloth, two types of seeds, or eating pork and shellfish an "abomination."[48] Something else is obviously going on in these passages.

This principle is also why both liberal and conservative misogynists stumble over how to treat women, as evidenced by the uncovering of myriads of sexual harassment cases in recent years and the resultant MeToo movement. Modern morals have loosened, which is not necessarily bad when those morals are legalistic. But modern sexual freedoms are too often practiced without fully embracing *love for neighbor* as the ultimate guide—an equal fraternal, unconditional love for both women and men. Sexual "immorality" isn't really the problem. Treating all people, particularly women, with love and respect is.

11 – THE MYTH OF THE TRANSACTIONAL GOD

When I was in the evangelical movement, I spent a few years trying to navigate the theology of charismatic churches. I know, that's a tall order. The churches I attended taught the notion that God wanted to bring revival to society, as He did in the revivals of history—i.e., the Great Awakenings of the 18th and 19th century, the Azusa Street Revival of 1910, the 1960s Charismatic Renewal, and the Jesus Movement of the 70s. A new revival in our day was always described as a precursor to the end-times return of Christ.

These revivals were also described in a way that denoted an economy of exchange. 2 Chronicles 7:14 was an oft-used verse to spur on the faithful: "If my people, who are called by my name, will humble themselves and pray and seek my face and turn from their wicked ways, then I will hear from heaven, and I will forgive their sin and will heal their land." Also, Joel 2 was quoted frequently, in which the Israelites were told to declare a fast and assemble to get God's attention. In other words, if we do things—show humility, pray, fast, seek, and repent—then God will forgive and heal.

Lou Engle, my old friend from my days in a People of Destiny (Sovereign Grace Ministries) church (mid to late 1980s), is the founder of The Call ministry. During the many years when it was active, The Call organized 12-hour-long mass assemblies of evangelicals and charismatics in churches and stadiums to fast and pray to turn America back to God "believing that God is wanting to release another great awakening that will bring transformation in this nation." Other purported goals are to defeat abortion, fight the homosexual agenda, foster racial and generational reconciliation (not a bad idea!), and raise up young people "to live as John the Baptist lived."

As part of the New Apostolic Reformation (NAR) dominion theology movement, The Call also plays into their goal to have Bible-believing Christians take dominion over the "seven mountains" of society: religion, education, family, business, government and military, arts/entertainment, and media. Once control of a significant portion of these institutions is gained, as the dominion theology rationalization assumes, the doors are opened for Jesus to return to fully establish his kingdom.[49]

Long periods of fasting (sometimes 40 days), prayer, and "consecration" were encouraged by The Call ministry in exchange for God bringing "revival." Supposed prophets and apostles in this movement have predicted mass conversions and "miracles" if the faithful obey. Once, Lou Engle told a crowd he dreamed of "100,000 gay and lesbian men and women converting and leaving behind their homosexuality" and then told people to pray to that end for a "divine breakthrough."

Despite being grossly misguided, I believe these people are well-meaning. The trouble is, among other problems, they are perpetuating a sacrificial religion—something that Jesus and Paul vehemently opposed. In this version of charismania, God won't act unless you gather in large numbers and pray and fast for 12 hours or several days—or, in some cases, for 40 days! Since revival hasn't come yet (The Call began in the year 2000), they had gatherings every year at large venues and stadiums. At one time, 23 past events were displayed on the map on The Call website. One planned five-day event in 2018, described a call for "intensive prayer and fasting to shift history...we believe that our prayers can turn this nation back to God." This kind of reasoning is all about what amounts to divine arm twisting. People do intensive, multi-day prayer, fasting, and other religious activities, and God eventually responds by bringing some kind of supernatural revival to turn the nation back to him, which really means, as the website says, "restore the foundations of Christian faith in America and revive the nations."[50]

Today, The Call has morphed into another version of stadium-Christianity called The Send. The focus now is on "activating believers to evangelism and mobilizing missionaries all over the world."[51] This was the common call when I was a young evangelical in the 1980s and 90s. In Chapter 6, I will share more about how the modern evangelical missionary movement that I was a part of for more than 12 years is based on a transactional view of God that makes him into a disinterested, discriminatory, judgmental divinity who won't help, forgive, or save (from hell) "unreached peoples," unbelievers, or homosexuals, unless conservative Christians pray, fast, give money, and go to them and preach what they claim is the gospel. And, of course, the recipients have to accept this brand of Christianity.

Remember what turning back to God, revival, and accepting the gospel means to evangelical, fundamentalist, or charismatic Christians. It means getting "saved" from depravity, joining an evangelical church (for The Call and The Send movements, preferably charismatic), believing in the two-faced God of the whole Bible, being saved from eternal damnation because of Jesus' tortuous punishment that appeased God, starting to obey a moral system of commandments (including on homosexuality), and engaging in sacrificial transactions with God. Not to mention the political changes expected like embracing the goals of outlawing abortion (while ignoring a more reasonable strategy like trying to minimize the need for abortion through empowering the poor and encouraging men to practice responsible birth control), over-turning the homosexual and "woke" agenda, gaining religious rights, and supporting conservative Christian politicians.

Rather than putting their full focus on making the world a better place by spreading love, aiding the poor, working to change the conditions that drive women to choose abortion, actively engaging in racial/class/cultural reconciliation (the ancient way of peace), and sharing the character of a kind and forgiving God who doesn't need his arm twisted to act, people in this movement put personal sacrifices on a religious altar—time, travel, fasts, pleading prayer, public gatherings, consecration, going to the unreached—expecting revival and miracles in exchange.

Meanwhile, Jesus taught his followers to pray privately with very few words (since Abba God knows what you need before you ask) and avoid public displays of prayer because that's what hypocrites do (Matthew 6:5-8). When he mentioned fasting, he said do it without drawing attention to yourself. He never insisted it was mandatory to practice in order to move God to act and care for people. Later in the book, we will go through why this transactional faith, or "economy of exchange," was not the message of ancient Christianity, why it's dangerous, and how it fueled the popular penal substitutionary atonement theory.

12 – THE FRAUD OF GLORYING WAR AND VIOLENCE

In 1979, when first becoming a "born again" Christian in college, I read the Gospel accounts completely and almost immediately became a pacifist. To me, it was clear that Jesus taught his followers to love their enemies and to not resist an evil person, movement, or conquest with violence. Jesus taught and exemplified non-violent resistance to evil, or as Paul put it, he demonstrated how to "overcome evil with good." I thought this was the most revolutionary message in the world.

But the evangelical churches and ministries I attended told me that pacifism was not mandatory or even a wise choice for Christians. Most of them claimed Jesus' commands to love one's enemies didn't apply to governments and countries.

I was told of a "just war" theory that justified most, if not all, of the wars that America had engaged in, particularly World War II, but even Vietnam. Churches regularly honor the military, especially on Veterans Day, and enthusiastically support Christians who enlist. To my shame, I ultimately gave up being a pacifist because in my circles, I was apparently the only one. I was "addicted to approval" and couldn't stand alone.

What I wasn't told were the historical facts. For at least the first two centuries of the faith, followers of Jesus were taught to disavow military service.[52] It was exceedingly rare, if not unheard of, for Christians to be in the military. During this period, "one simply never finds evidence that Christians justified military service as a possibility..."[53] That's two hundred years of Christian pacifists! Early church fathers Tertullian, Cyprian, Clement of Alexandria, Origen, and Lactantius "have the common opinion that violent retaliation was foreign to the spirit of the gospel."[54] Even into the early fourth century, the first Christian historian Eusebius's early editions of Church History proved him to be a pacifist. It wasn't until the fourth century through the "Christian" emperor Constantine that waging war via military service began to be justified. Finally, Augustine provided a foundation for what came to be known as the just war theory.

When this happened—the fourth century church's rejection of non-violence and peace to justify violent opposition or part of what Robin Meyer calls "The Great Reversal"—the church was no longer persecuted by the Roman Empire. Ironically, this is when it began persecuting its own—those whom it deemed heretics. Michael Hardin reminds us of this astounding fact: "In the hundred years following the ascension of Constantine more Christians died at the hands of Christians than had died the previous 250 years at the hands of Empire."[55]

OTHER FRAUDS, MYTHS, AND FAITH CLAIMS

There are other frauds and myths I could cite, such as the requirement of church members to tithe (give 10 percent of one's income before taxes) to the church they attend or the rituals built around taking communion. Tithing was an Old Testament practice for an agricultural society (most was giving produce or livestock, not money) and was never practiced by the early church. There was only encouragement to give to the poor or those who needed sustenance on their journeys while spreading the way of peace. Also, regarding communion, it was originally a love feast, a common meal for the gatherings of followers, at which people drank wine and ate bread to remember Jesus. It was not an ongoing ritual required for believers to receive or retain forgiveness of sins.

Or, as was already briefly mentioned, the myth that divorce was always condemned by Jesus and the New Testament. In fact, Jesus was stating his opposition to casual divorce and what was called "any reason" divorce, not a narrow range of justifiable divorces. His exception clause ("except for marital unfaithfulness") was not meant to be a hard and fast rule that covered the only acceptable reason to get a divorce.[56]

Some may be surprised that I didn't include more traditional, miraculous faith claims in the list of major myths—namely the virgin birth, the deity of Christ, and the resurrection. There is a reason for this. Although these are debatable based on history, in my opinion, they are not beliefs that cause major harm to society. The scams listed above do.

These three miraculous doctrines (the virgin birth, Christ's deity, and the resurrection) are so removed from modern society that one finds both conservative and liberal Christians often coming to similar conclusions even when they disagree. For example, a conservative Christian will say *one must believe* in the resurrection to be a true Christian, even though they have to admit they have never seen the risen Christ or any other person actually resurrected. They trust that because of the resurrection, the spirit of Christ is among us in the world. Yet this is the same conclusion that liberals like the late Marcus Borg came to—that the spirit of Christ is among us in the world, that Christ rose metaphorically—even though he didn't believe in an historical physical resurrection of Jesus three days after the crucifixion. Likewise, liberal Christians like Borg, and even Bishop Shelby Spong, believe in the afterlife—which is really the hope to which the resurrection points.

The truth is Jesus' followers did not believe in any of these phenomena when they first began to follow Christ. And we know the original disciples (not just the Twelve, but women and others) did not believe in the resurrection *until* they actually saw the risen Christ, even though the gospels record Jesus telling them he would be resurrected. In other words, we are all naturally doubting Thomases. We shouldn't be pointing fingers at each other over these three doctrines, whether you believe in them or not. I happen to believe all three. However, I don't really care where your thoughts lie regarding them. What I do care about is how you treat others and how you love your neighbor as yourself.

Now it's time to look at the four foundational beliefs that have led to the harmful myths I listed above.

Four

THE TWO-FACED GOD OF POPULAR THEOLOGY

THE FIRST FOUNDATIONAL TENANT that leads to an array of myths is the belief that God is two-faced. It comes from a literal reading of the Bible. In evangelicalism, fundamentalism, Catholicism, and most of Western Christendom, people are taught to view the Bible as a divinely ordained, definitive collection of books that are the authoritative Word of God. They are inerrant (without error) and infallible (incapable of being wrong). The result of this view is that people believe everything they read in the Bible as historically and theologically accurate. So, in reading passages in the Bible that include both retributive narratives (the flood story, eye-for-eye and capital punishments in the Law, the Canaanite conquest by Israel) and restorative narratives (the Genesis story of Joseph and his brothers, the prophets on restorative justice, and Jesus' teachings), they are forced to believe in a god that is both violent and loving. A god of war and a god of peace. A god who is not wholly good because of his violent streak. A two-faced, or Janus-faced god, as we noted earlier.

There are three huge problems with this view of the Bible and this view of God.

First, when practically applied, this view of the Bible and God is irrational. It is a complete contradiction to the linguistic, cultural, and historical facts, not to mention a contradiction in logic.

Second, as I've already said and can't say enough, Jesus and the earliest Christians, not to mention Jewish people of antiquity, never viewed the Bible this way!

Third, Jesus and his teachings never portray God as two faced. Jesus' "heavenly Father" is principled, consistently righteous, and loving to all—friends and enemies alike. Jesus' Father does hold people accountable for sins and what they do to harm fellow human beings. But He does it in a way that is remedial and restorative, not retributive, much the same way God restored the first human murderer, Cain, in the book of Genesis (as we will see below). He doesn't destroy His lost sheep. He goes out of his way to find them and bring them back to the fold.

THE TWO FACES OF GOD IN SCRIPTURE

One can start seeing the two faces of God in the Bible's first book of Genesis. This is where we first see the story of Cain, which has elements of God's mercy. Cain (a farmer of the land) was the first murderer of the world. He killed his brother Abel (a keeper of flocks), of whom Cain was jealous because God found favor with Abel's offering but not with Cain's. God encouraged Cain to improve and do what is right, and he would be accepted. But Cain harbored resentment and later attacked and killed Abel.

What does God do to this first murderer in all of human history? Does He exact capital punishment on Cain like the later Torah would proscribe? No! He does not proscribe eye-for-eye retribution but instead institutes consequences. He declares Cain is under a curse and will no longer be able to work the land and yield crops. Cain complains that he will be driven from God's presence and whoever finds him will kill him. God says that won't happen and spells out a plan to save Cain from having his life taken. God puts a mark on Cain that protects him from being killed. God had mercy on the first murderer.

The outcome was that Cain went to live in a new land, came to build a city, and had a family that ultimately contributed to humankind's development. His lineage produced Jabal, the father of those who were nomadic keepers of livestock; Jubal, the father of those who played the harp and flute; and Tubal-Cain, who forged tools out of bronze and iron.

Then Genesis pivots to the time of Noah, many generations later, and we start to see the violent, retributive god. God said He was grieved when He saw how great man's wickedness, corruption, and violence had become. So, He decided He would destroy all people except Noah and his family. He said He would bring floodwaters on the earth to decimate all living creatures and all humankind. He's a God of retribution. He responds to man's violence with divine violence.

We all know the story of Noah building an ark as God commands and taking his family inside, as well as two of every animal on the earth, male and female. As popular evangelical Francis Chan admits, God drowned everyone on the planet. Or, for Christians who say science and the original language only supports a local flood, He drowned everyone living in the Mesopotamian basin, which the Genesis text tells us was all of humankind (except Noah and his family). God's response to wickedness in humans was not to try to restore them but to destroy them, except for select favorites. It is a violent narrative of God killing everyone for being wicked, not only responsible adults, but children, infants, and the unborn as well.

Fast forward to Genesis 37 for another opposing view of God. Here, Jacob (also called "Israel") has a favorite son, Joseph, who is betrayed by his jealous brothers. At first, they want to kill him and throw him in a cistern and claim a ferocious animal devoured him. However, one sympathetic brother, Reuben, convinces the rest not to shed any blood and instead throw Joseph into the cistern alive, thinking he would return later to rescue his younger sibling. The other brothers relent, thinking that he would eventually die anyway. Yet when a Midianite caravan comes by on the way to Egypt, they decide to sell him as a slave for twenty shekels of silver. Upon returning to their father, the brothers stick with the ruse that Joseph was killed by a wild animal.

Years later, after many trials as a slave and prisoner in Egypt, Joseph is ultimately made an officer of the Pharaoh, put in charge of the palace, and, later, of all storehouses of Egypt's grain. By that time, a famine had spread to Jacob's country, and he sends 10 of his sons to Egypt to buy grain from the Pharaoh. Joseph recognizes his brothers but does not let on. He sells them grain and puts the silver they used to pay for it back in their grain sacks. The brothers take the grain to their father, and eventually return back to Egypt with their youngest brother, Benjamin.

Time passes before Joseph reveals himself to his brothers. He embraces and kisses them and instructs them to bring their father back. Joseph promises them land so that they don't have to endure the ongoing famine in their own country. He tells them God has used him to save his family from famine despite their betrayal.

In this narrative, God does not take revenge or tell Joseph to do so. Joseph is a forgiving victim. Beyond a three-day confinement ordered by Joseph that helped the brothers see the error of their ways, they were not punished. God is merciful and generous to Jacob's wicked sons and blesses them in the end. Can this really be the same God as the one in the flood story?

In fact, throughout the Torah there is a strange combination of wrathful, unforgiving, and violent characteristics of God juxtaposed with compassion, concern for the marginalized, and love. In Exodus 22–23 and Leviticus, one single list of stipulations for capital crimes punishable by death and destruction of anyone guilty of sorcery, bestiality, and sacrificing to other gods is combined with laws that forbid oppression of foreigners, widows, and orphans. Additionally, there are laws supporting distribution of equal justice, laws against favoritism in lawsuits and denial of justice to the poor, and a requirement to help your enemy or someone you hate when their ox or donkey has wandered off or fallen under its load.

These examples, and others like them, in the Torah are the most obvious way we see the dueling voices in scripture. God often punishes the guilty with violence and death and commands his people to do the same. But He also wants an equal playing field for the marginalized, poor, and anyone who needs help. Even for one's enemy, whose donkey has fallen under its load. In Genesis, God restores Cain rather than executing him. In Leviticus, God orders murderers and other disobedient Jews to be executed. In Genesis, God forgives Joseph's brothers (as does Joseph) for betraying him and leaving him for dead. He then uses Joseph to bless them and the whole family. As we will examine more closely below, in Joshua, God is revealed as the epitome of divine violence. He orders what amounts to be genocide of a whole population of peoples.

And then, as we shall also examine shortly, when the Galilean Rabbi, Jesus of Nazareth, comes on the scene almost 1,300 years later, his teaching aligns with the compassionate narratives of the Torah and the prophets and contradicts the violent narratives. He tells people to love their enemies because that is the character of God. God loves his enemies. "[God] is kind to the ungrateful and wicked" (Luke 6:35). He sends the blessings of rain and sun on both the righteous and unrighteous. Jesus tells people to be merciful to all because their heavenly Father is merciful. He harkens back to the prophet Hosea and says to his hearers, "But go and learn what this means: 'I desire mercy, not sacrifice'" (Matthew 9:13). His words echo the Proverbs that say, "If your enemy is hungry, feed him; if he is thirsty, give him something to drink. In doing this, you will heap burning coals on his head" (Proverbs and Romans). He teaches people to pray for those who persecute them, to actually wish them well, rather than wish for retribution. "If someone forces you to walk a mile and carry their load, walk for them two miles," he instructs. He taught people to turn the tables on their enemies through loving action, not by punishment. He contradicted the "eye for an eye, tooth for a tooth, life for life" commandments in the Torah and said not to retaliate towards those who are evil. Later, we'll look at this merciful side in more depth, but for now, let's dive deeper into the violent side of the God of much of the Old Testament.

THE RETRIBUTIVE GOD OF MOSES AND JOSHUA

Let's uncover this violent side of God of the Canaanite conquest and how the God of Joshua is portrayed. This is what God supposedly said to the Israelites regarding their driving out the inhabitants of the land He promised them after bringing them out of Egypt:

> When the LORD your God brings you into the land you are entering to possess and drives out before you many na- tions—the Hittites, Girgashites, Amorites, Canaanites, Per- izzites, Hivites and Jebusites, seven nations larger and stronger than you—and when the LORD your God has delivered them over to you and you have defeated them, then you must de- stroy them totally. Make no treaty with them, **and show them no mercy**. Do not intermarry with them. Do not give your daughters to their sons or take their daughters for your sons, for they will turn your children away from following me to serve other gods, and the LORD's anger will burn against you and will quickly destroy you. This is what you are to do to them: Break down their altars, smash their sacred stones, cut down their Asherah poles and burn their idols in the fire. For you are a people holy to the LORD your God. The LORD your God has chosen you out of all the peoples on the face of

the earth to be his people, his treasured possession (Deuteronomy 7:1–6). [Emphasis added]

Rather than telling the Israelites to "love your enemies" and "be merciful as your heavenly Father is merciful," God told them to "destroy them totally" and "**show them no mercy**." Later, as the drama of taking the land played out, this is also what happened to the enemy city of Jericho. The scene is set as Joshua and the Israelites were about to take Jericho after six days of marching around the city.

> On the seventh day, they got up at daybreak and marched around the city seven times in the same manner, except that on that day they circled the city seven times. The seventh time around, when the priests sounded the trumpet blast, Joshua commanded the army, "Shout! For the LORD has given you the city! The city and all that is in it are to be devoted to the LORD. Only Rahab the prostitute and all who are with her in her house shall be spared, because she hid the spies we sent. But keep away from the devoted things, so that you will not bring about your own destruction by taking any of them. Otherwise, you will make the camp of Israel liable to destruction and bring trouble on it. All the silver and gold and the articles of bronze and iron are sacred to the LORD and must go into his treasury."

> When the trumpets sounded, the army shouted, and at the sound of the trumpet, when the men gave a loud shout, the wall collapsed; so everyone charged straight in, and they took the city. They devoted the city to the LORD and destroyed with the sword every living thing in it—people, young and old, cattle, sheep and donkeys (Joshua 6:15–21).

> So the LORD was with Joshua, and his fame spread throughout the land (Joshua 6:27).

But the Israelites were unfaithful in regard to the devoted things; Achan son of Karmi, the son of Zimri, the son of Zerah, of the tribe of Judah, took some of them. So the LORD's anger burned against Israel (Joshua 7:1).

Notice one of the themes is to devote the city to the Lord as they destroy everyone with the sword. This is part of Israel's violent sacrificial religion. Devoting something to the Lord is sacrificial. The people and livestock were sacrificed to God. The silver, gold, bronze, and iron were also devoted to God and, in this case, were not to be scavenged. After Jericho fell, Joshua led the Israelite army to the city of Ai for the next battle. There the men of Ai routed Joshua's army and chased the Israelites away. All the people were discouraged by this loss.

Then Joshua tore his clothes and fell facedown to the ground before the ark of the LORD, remaining there till evening. The elders of Israel did the same, and sprinkled dust on their heads. And Joshua said, "Alas, Sovereign LORD, why did you ever bring this people across the Jordan to deliver us into the hands of the Amorites to destroy us? If only we had been content to stay on the other side of the Jordan! Pardon your servant, Lord. What can I say, now that Israel has been routed by its enemies? The Canaanites and the other people of the country will hear about this and they will surround us and wipe out our name from the earth. What then will you do for your own great name?"

The LORD said to Joshua, "Stand up! What are you doing down on your face? Israel has sinned; they have violated my covenant, which I commanded them to keep. They have taken some of the devoted things; they have stolen, they have lied, they have put them with their own possessions. That is why the Israelites cannot stand against their enemies; they turn their backs and run because they have been made liable to destruction. I will not be with you anymore unless you destroy whatever among you is devoted to destruction.

Go, consecrate the people. Tell them, "Consecrate yourselves in preparation for tomorrow; for this is what the LORD, the God of Israel, says: There are devoted things among you, Israel. You cannot stand against your enemies until you remove them."

"In the morning, present yourselves tribe by tribe. The tribe the LORD chooses shall come forward clan by clan; the clan the LORD chooses shall come forward family by family; and the family the LORD chooses shall come forward man by man. Whoever is caught with the devoted things shall be destroyed by fire, along with all that belongs to him. He has violated the covenant of the LORD and has done an outrageous thing in Israel!"

Joshua gathered all the tribes of Israel to determine who was guilty of plundering the "devoted things." Achan was confronted.

Then Joshua said to Achan, "My son, give glory to the LORD, the God of Israel, and honor him. Tell me what you have done; do not hide it from me."

Achan replied, "It is true! I have sinned against the LORD, the God of Israel. This is what I have done: When I saw in the plunder a beautiful robe from Babylonia, two hundred shekels of silver and a bar of gold weighing fifty shekels, I coveted them and took them. They are hidden in the ground inside my tent, with the silver underneath."

So Joshua sent messengers, and they ran to the tent, and there it was, hidden in his tent, with the silver underneath. They took the things from the tent, brought them to Joshua and all the Israelites and spread them out before the LORD.

Then Joshua, together with all Israel, took Achan son of Zerah, the silver, the robe, the gold bar, his children, his cattle, donkeys and sheep, his tent and all that he had, to the Valley of Achor. Joshua said, "Why have you brought this trouble on us? The LORD will bring trouble on you today."

Then all Israel stoned him, and after they had stoned the rest, they burned them. Over Achan they heaped up a large pile of rocks, which remains to this day. Then the LORD turned from his fierce anger (Joshua 7:1–26).

Here, Achan confessed his sin of ignoring the command, coveting the treasure, and stealing it. According to the Lord, the reason Israel cannot now stand against their enemies is because of Achan's disobedience. God ordered that the culprit, and all that belonged to him, be destroyed by fire. Correction and mercy were not an option. Only destruction by fire.

Joshua and "all of Israel" carried out the order. Despite Achan's quick confession and acknowledgement of his sin, there was no mercy. They took Achan, along with his sons and daughters and livestock, and stoned them to death. Then they burned them. Only then did the Lord "turn from his fierce anger." Achan and his family became the scapegoats. Even if one allows for God's punishment for direct disobedience, the fact that God also orders his innocent children be executed stretches the limits of credulity. God only turns away his "fierce anger" when people are killed and burned and some of them are innocent.

Moreover, bear in mind that this is what God orders on His people who disobey (regardless if they confess and repent of their sin). Let's take a closer look at how the God of Joshua was portrayed in the case of His enemies. After this incident, Joshua went back to the city of Ai with renewed confidence that they had fixed the problem in the community and could resume their victorious pursuits with God at their side.

Then the LORD said to Joshua, "Do not be afraid; do not be discouraged. Take the whole army with you and go up and attack Ai. For I have delivered into your hands the king of Ai, his people, his city, and his land. You shall do to Ai and its king as you did to Jericho and its king, except that you may carry off their plunder and livestock for yourselves. Set an ambush behind the city" (Joshua 8:1–2).

Part of the Israelite army laid in wait to ambush the city from behind. The other part marched up and encamped in front of the city to draw out the king of Ai and his army. Sure enough, the Ai army came out to confront them and the Israelites allowed the Ai army to pursue them and lured them away from the city. Then, per God's promise to Joshua to deliver the city to them, the rear-facing Israelite army attacked the city, captured it, and set it on fire. The Ai army turned and saw the smoke of the fire rising. Then both halves of the Israelite army attacked the Ai army from each side, and it fell. This is how the extent of the taking of the city is described:

> Israel cut them down, leaving them neither survivors nor fugitives. But they took the king of Ai alive and brought him to Joshua. When Israel had finished killing all the men of Ai in the fields and in the wilderness where they had chased them, and when every one of them had been put to the sword, all the Israelites returned to Ai and killed those who were in it. Twelve thousand men and women fell that day—all the people of Ai. For Joshua did not draw back the hand that held out his javelin until he had destroyed all who lived in Ai. But Israel did carry off for themselves the livestock and plunder of this city, as the LORD had instructed Joshua (Joshua 8:22–27).

In this scene, God ordered the Israelites to "do to Ai and its king as you did to Jericho and its king," but this time allowed them to carry off the plunder for themselves—the very thing that Achan was stoned for doing in disobedience to God at Jericho. During the ensuing battle and conquest, not only did the Israelites kill the soldiers they ambushed, but they returned to the city and killed all the people of Ai, both men and women. The command from God was kill every living thing in the cities that He was giving them as an inheritance (Deuteronomy 20:16–17).

Joshua's army went on to do this same thing to many other cities of the Canaanites—Makkedah, Libnah, Lachish, Eglon, Hebron, Debir, from Kadesh Barnea to Gaza to the region of Goshen to Gibeon. The battles were attributed to God giving each city and its king into Israel's hand. This was a recurring statement in the record: "They took the city, its king, and its villages, and put them to the sword. Everyone in it they totally destroyed. They left no survivors." (Joshua 10:39). The record also reported that Joshua hung the king of Ai on a tree and left him there for hours. He also killed five Amorite kings in the same manner: "...Joshua struck and killed the kings and hung them on five trees, and they were left hanging on the trees until evening." (Joshua 10:26)

If there is any doubt about how comprehensive the violence was toward even non-combatants, a story in I Samuel makes it even more clear. Here, about 300 years after Joshua's time, the prophet Samuel told Israel's king Saul what God wanted:

> "I am the one the LORD sent to anoint you king over his people Israel; so listen now to the message from the LORD. This is what the LORD Almighty says: 'I will punish the Amalekites for what they did to Israel when they waylaid them as they came up from Egypt. Now go, attack the Amalekites and totally destroy all that belongs to them. Do not spare them; put to death men and women, children and infants, cattle and sheep, camels and donkeys'" (I Samuel 15:1–2).

So, at Jericho, Ai, Amalek, and all the other Canaanite cities cited here and in the rest of the Joshua narrative (Joshua 11 and 12), the God of Joshua ordered the destruction of all living things—not just soldiers—but including soldiers who would have surrendered, non-combatants, and in-nocent women and children, which would have included the unborn. In other words, God ordered the destruction of prisoners of war and "civilians." Today we would call that a war crime. Or murder. Or terrorism. Or even genocide if it was on a large enough scale.

Let that sink in.

So, ask yourself, how does this square with the character of God portrayed by Jesus, who taught that we should be merciful as God is merciful? Does it correspond with the character of God found in the story of Joseph in Genesis or many of the prophets? Does a view of the Bible as a completely trustworthy account of God's ways make sense in light of this stark contrast? Or does it show there are two voices in scripture? A voice of violence and retribution and another of non-violent love and restoration?

THE VIOLENT NATURE OF ONE VERSION OF ANCIENT ISRAEL'S GOD

In another story in the book of Numbers, God's anger burned against the Israelites because they worshipped and sacrificed to false gods. Men were led to fall away from the God of Israel by Moabite women.

> While Israel was staying in Shittim, the men began to indulge in sexual immorality with Moabite women, who invited them to the sacrifices to their gods. The people ate the sacrificial meal and bowed down before these gods. So Israel yoked themselves to the Baal of Peor. And the LORD's anger burned against them.

> The LORD said to Moses, "Take all the leaders of these people, kill them and expose them in broad daylight before the LORD, so that the LORD's fierce anger may turn away from Israel." So Moses said to Israel's judges, "Each of you must put to death those of your people who have yoked themselves to the Baal of Peor."

> Then an Israelite man brought into the camp a Midianite woman right before the eyes of Moses and the whole assembly of Israel while they were weeping at the entrance to the tent of meeting. When Phinehas of Eleazar, the son of Aaron, the priest, saw this, he left the assembly, took a spear in his hand

THE TWO-FACED GOD OF POPULAR THEOLOGY   63

and followed the Israelite into the tent. He drove the spear into both of them, right through the Israelite man and into the woman's stomach. Then the plague against the Israelites was stopped; but those who died in the plague numbered 24,000.

The LORD said to Moses, "Phinehas son of Eleazar, the son of Aaron, the priest, has turned my anger away from the Israelites. Since he was as zealous for my honor among them as I am, I did not put an end to them in my zeal. Therefore, tell him I am making my covenant of peace with him. He and his descendants will have a covenant of a lasting priesthood, because he was zealous for the honor of his God and made atonement for the Israelites."

The name of the Israelite who was killed with the Midianite woman was Zimri, son of Salu, the leader of a Simeonite family. And the name of the Midianite woman who was put to death was Kozbi daughter of Zur, a tribal chief of a Midianite family.

The LORD said to Moses, "Treat the Midianites as enemies and kill them. They treated you as enemies when they deceived you in the Peor incident involving their sister Kozbi, the daughter of a Midianite leader, the woman who was killed when the plague came as a result of that incident" (Numbers 25:1–18).

Here we see a similar theme to what we read in Joshua. When someone disobeys God, His anger burns against them. God's solution to the problem was not to try to correct the disobedient person. Nor was it to have mercy on them and try to restore them to right standing. Nor was it to challenge them to leave their errant ways. No, the solution was simply to kill them. God ordered Moses to kill the leaders and put to death all those guilty of idolatry.

Phinehas complied. He saw an Israelite bring a Midianite woman into the camp, grabbed a spear, followed them into a tent, and impaled both their bodies in one thrust. One person is judge, jury, and executioner.

The taking of the life of the guilty by the obedient who are "zealous for the honor of God" turns God's anger away and "makes atonement for the Israelites." It appeases God, who only "then turns from his fierce anger." Once scapegoats are sacrificed, the relationship with God is restored. Going forward, after the human sacrifice is made, God ordered Moses to "treat the Midianites as enemies and kill them" (Numbers 25:17).

This is *violent sacrificial religion.*

One last narrative on the Canaanite conquest is recorded in Judges. Judah took over for Joshua to lead the Israelites against the remaining Canaanites. He attacked many cities, including Jerusalem. For each city, the narrative reads that "they put the city to the sword and set it on fire," and "they totally destroyed the city." In Bezek, they chased down the king and cut off his thumbs and big toes (Judges 1).

Finally, let's take a brief look at David, the warrior, prophet, and king of Israel who founded Israel's dynasty in Judea and united all the tribes under a single monarch. He started his "career" by slaying Goliath—a great story about a small, weak Israelite boy defeating a powerful, enormous adversary. Yet, he used violence to conquer rather than wisdom and love. Later, when he became an adult warrior-king, it appeared that God was behind his warring exploits. II Samuel 5:19-20 tells us, "so David inquired of the Lord, 'Shall I go and attack the Philistines? Will you deliver them into my hands?' The Lord answered him, 'Go, for I will surely deliver the Philistines into your hands.' So, David went to Baal Perazim, and there he defeated them." In another reference to war with the Philistines, it says, "[a]nd there was war again. And David went out and fought with the Philistines and killed them with a great slaughter" (I Samuel 19:8). Later, I Samuel tells us of other battles: "Now David and his men went up and raided the Geshurites, the Girzites and the Amalekites...Whenever David attacked an area, he did not leave anyone alive, but took sheep and cattle, donkeys and camels, and clothes" (I Samuel 27:8–9).

On how pervasive this violent streak is in parts of the Jewish scriptures, Derek Flood quotes the late Swiss Catholic theologian, Raymund Schwager, "Approximately one thousand passages speak of Yahweh's blazing anger, of his punishment by death and destruction, and how like a consuming fire he passes judgment, takes revenge, and threatens annihilation...No other topic is as often mentioned as God's bloody works."[1]

JUSTIFYING VIOLENCE

One of the characteristics of *violent sacrificial religion* is the claim that the violence is always justified. Supposedly, there's always a good reason to condemn, attack, and kill. So, we notice that God drowned the whole planet because "[t]he Lord saw how great man's wickedness on the earth had become and that every inclination of the thoughts of his heart was only evil all the time." The victims were demonized or dehumanized. Therefore, God was justified in killing everyone. He spared Noah and his family because "Noah was a righteous man, blameless among the people of his time and he walked with God" (Genesis 6:5–9). Except for those on the ark, humankind was irredeemable.

We can also see this in the Joshua narrative. In Deuteronomy, God told Israel not to make a peace treaty with the nations that He was giving them. So, even if the enemy wanted to broker a peace, the Israelites were commanded to conquer them. In Joshua, that was rationalized. "Except for the Hivites living in Gibeon, not one city made a treaty of peace with the Israelites" (Joshua 11:19).

Now, you would think more cities would try to make peace rather than risk the destruction that was happening all around them. And, in fact, one did. The Hivites. They pretended to be from another country and fooled the Israelites into a treaty on the grounds they were an exception by not being one of the tribes of Canaan. Once Israel realized the deception, it was too late because the Israelite leaders had vowed before the Lord to maintain the peace with them. The Law said they could not break a vow. To punish them for the deception, Joshua ordered they be made slaves for the Israel community as wood cutters and water carriers (Joshua 9). But why didn't other cities try to sue for peace?

> ...not one city made a treaty of peace with the Israelites. For it was the Lord himself who hardened their hearts to wage war against Israel, so that he might destroy them totally, **exterminating them without mercy**, as the Lord commanded Moses (Joshua 11:19–20) [Emphasis added].

This is a major theme of violent sacrificial religion. It seems incredible that no one could be that bad or unreasonable until it becomes justified because God Himself hardened their enemies' hearts to act a certain way for His purposes. In this case, for the purpose of destroying them all without mercy!

To avoid any confusion, it's important to remember, as noted above, that God supposedly ordered the Israelites to never make a treaty with the nations that He was giving them. That is, the seven nations of the Hittites, Girgashites, Amorites, Canaanites, Perizzites, Hivites, and Jebusites. However, when the Israelites did encounter enemies in a city outside their divinely appointed area, they were told to offer terms of peace. If that city accepted peace, the terms were that all the people of the city would become their slaves. If they refused to make peace, they were to take the city and put to the sword all the men. The women, children, and livestock left would become plunder for them. In other words, they would take them as property—slaves, servants, and animals (Deuteronomy 20).

Defenders of one voice in the Bible will try to justify the flood story and the Canaanite conquest by saying these people were terribly wicked and practiced despicable evil, immoralities, and violence. They also say God has a right to judge the world because He is just and confronts evil with righteousness and force. But this too flies in the face of the Father of Jesus who is merciful and kind to the ungrateful and wicked and tells us to overcome evil with goodness. Violent sacrificial religion justifies violence because of the wickedness of the people who they attack or sacrifice. But it only perpetuates a cycle of violence as the punisher becomes just like the punished, practicing the same acts—in this case, murder and terrorism—that they claim their enemies do.

Another defense of the *one voice* position is the notion that since God is sovereign over all, governs all, and ultimately controls all—everything is in His hands—and whatever He wills or decides is always right. John Piper, a Calvinist, "reformed" preacher is a popular defender of this view. He minces no words in his flat pronouncement of God's sovereign right to kill:

> It's right for God to slaughter women and children anytime he pleases. God gives life and he takes life. Everybody who dies, dies because God wills that they die... God is taking life very day. He will take 50,000 lives today. Life is in God's hand. God

decides when your last heartbeat will be, and whether it ends through cancer or a bullet wound. God governs...[2]

As shocking as this statement is, for people who truly believe there is a one-faced God in scripture—who believe that God's Word, the Bible, is altogether inerrant and wholly reflective of God's character—this really is the only rationale one has. There are narratives of God ordering the slaughtering or enslaving of non-combatants, women, and children in the Bible side-by-side with narratives of mercy and love for all including His enemies. For both to be true, God must be caring and kind one day or era and uncaring and violent the next. He must love all of humanity one day or era and order a human agent or circumstance to snuff out or enslave a portion of humanity the next. God can commit genocide and enslave anyone at will and do what modern society and most Christians would condemn and still be righteous. He can indiscriminately kill, taking the life of anyone. He can both love and kill His friends or His enemies. He can have mercy and be unmerciful to whomever He wants and still be worthy of worship.

Of course, this is non-sensical. For this to be true, God has to be arbitrary, capricious, and unprincipled. If the Mercy Code is right and to be obeyed—be merciful as God is merciful—and Piper's view of God is right—that God can rightfully slaughter women, children, infants, and the unborn, then Jesus is either telling us to be better than God or he's telling us this violent view of God is wrong. Which makes the most sense to you? Peter Enns adds this implication:

> More practically speaking—and without intending to implicate Piper—history bears witness that those who envision God the way Piper does are only one small step away from forming their own Christian Taliban to be God's agents of wrath in this life. Some kill abortion doctors and gays, but more commonly the end result of such thinking is a brand of Christianity that is agitated, judgmental, suspicious, and ready to draw blood whenever a perceived offense to God is committed.[3]

Aside from the above problems with Piper's view (and that of his many evangelical and Calvinist followers), there are claims underneath that are not logically or scripturally self-evident. Piper and Joshua's God wills all death. How is that necessarily true? His sovereignty means He "takes life every day." That is not logically established. It is a theological leap. The Joshua narrative, for which Piper is defending, is suspiciously aligned with the ancient practice of justifying one's military conquests in the name of one's god. Finally, there is now overwhelming archaeological evidence that "the systematic slaughter of the population of Canaan around 1,200 BC did not happen."[4]

The case for one consistently righteous voice in scripture is hanging by a thread. It's time to contrast it with the alternative and come to a conclusion: There are two distinct voices in the Bible, and it's necessary to reject the violent one and choose the peaceable one.

THE RESTORATIVE GOD: JONAH, JESUS, AND THE ENEMY-LOVE, ANTI-WAR ETHIC

Now, let's go even deeper to contrast the voices above about a retributive god with other voices of the Old Testament and in Jesus' teachings, i.e., the voice of the restorative God. We've already mentioned the examples of a restorative God in the stories of Cain and Joseph. Now let's look at Exhibit C: the story of Jonah. Its portrayal of God is admittedly not the perfect example of unconditional, non-transactional love for enemies, but it's a far cry from the violent God of Joshua. Jonah was told to go to the city of Nineveh (in the Assyrian Empire and an enemy of Israel that was known for its cruel and ruthless warriors) and preach against it because its wickedness had come before God. He refuses to go, but three days in the belly of a whale changes his mind.

Once in Nineveh, Jonah went through the city claiming that because of their wickedness, the city had forty days before it would be overthrown. The Ninevites believed the message and repented of their sin. The king proclaimed a fast to show their seriousness and said, "Let everyone call urgently on God. Let them give up their evil ways and their violence" (Jonah 3:8).

That's exactly what happened. God relented. But Jonah was not happy because he hated the Assyrians and wanted them punished. He didn't want to go to Nineveh because he feared that God would relent. He said, "That is what I tried to forestall by fleeing to Tarshish. I knew that you are a gracious and compassionate God, slow to anger and abounding in love, a God who relents from sending calamity" (Jonah 4:2).

In depression, Jonah told God he would rather die than go on, apparently because his enemies were spared. He was even saddened over a plant that died overnight that had been providing him shade. Now, here's the clincher. God gave him perspective: "You have been concerned about this plant, though you did not tend it or make it grow. It sprang up overnight and died overnight. And should I not have concern for the great city of Nineveh, in which there are more than a hundred and twenty thousand people who cannot tell their right hand from their left—and also many animals?" (Jonah 4:10–11).

This is a narrative of God's concern for the enemies of Israel and the theme—found in other parts of the Old Testament—that God is "gracious and compassionate, slow to anger and abounding in love. He will not always accuse, nor will he harbor his anger forever" (Psalm 103:8). It does not go as far as the narratives of Jesus and Paul, as we shall see, but it does provide a stark contrast to the Canaanite conquest where God has no concern for the enemies of Israel, gives them no time or warning to repent, hardens their hearts so they can't change, and doesn't differentiate from innocent civilians and combatants. Or, in contrast with the cities outside Canaan, where God does tell the Israelites to offer peace, but if they accept, they are enslaved. Additionally, we can see the repentant Nineveh that was spared contrasted with Achan, who, despite his confession and remorse, was still killed along with his innocent children (Joshua 7).

We saw earlier how King David became a warrior in addition to being a prophet. In a curious twist to the violent narratives when God ordered and empowered Israelite armies to go to war and slaughter their enemies (including combatants, non-combatants, and sometimes even children and infants), we catch a glimpse of the nonviolent face of God when He tells David his plans for building a temple. David explained to his son, Solomon, that God wouldn't allow David to build the temple. He elaborated why and instructs Solomon to build it instead.

> But this word of the Lord came to me: 'You have shed much blood and have fought many wars. You are not to build a house for my Name, because you have shed much blood on the earth in my sight. But you will have a son who will be a man of peace and rest, and I will give him rest from all his enemies on every side. His name will be Solomon, and I will grant Israel peace and quiet during his reign. He is the one who will build a house for my Name (I Chronicles 22:8–10).

So, since David had shed much blood in the sight of God, he was not allowed to build the house of God. Again, we see here another example of this strange duplicity of the Old Testament. God orders the Israelites to conquer and slaughter their enemies and says He will "deliver them into their hands," but He will not allow ones who have "shed much blood on the earth" to build His house. Despite being the one who ordered, approved, and helped them to "shed much blood on the earth."

When God Sides with The Victims

We see the compassionate voice of the God of Israel when He sides with the victims of punishment, abuse, and oppression. We saw this when God favored the Israelite slaves and raised up a way for them to be freed through Moses. The problem with that narrative is that once the slaves were freed, the oppressed Israelites became the oppressors when they attacked, killed, and burned Canaanite cities without mercy. When they did have "mercy," they enslaved their captors rather than kill them.

The stronger victim-siding narratives are ones like the story of Joseph we examined earlier, where Joseph was saved, vindicated, and used to extend mercy to the ones who betrayed him and had him captured. We also see this in the sufferings of Job, who was scapegoated by his "friends" as the cause of his own suffering because of something he did to deserve it. But Job is vindicated by God who sides with him in the end. Moreover, God sided with the victims in the book of Psalms "which contains the first sustained outcries in world literature of the single victim who is persecuted by enemies."[5]

Yet another example is in Isaiah (52:13-53:12) when "the suffering servant" was scapegoated by his community in Babylon and did not resist. God honored this victim and servant who was like a "lamb led to the slaughter."

But the most striking way to see the two voices of scripture is to compare the teachings of Jesus, and his citations of the prophets with many of the commandments and stories in the Old Testament. Let's look at the ones specific to violence and enemies. Jesus said:

> You have heard that it was said, "Eye for eye, and tooth for tooth." But I tell you, do not resist an evil person. If anyone slaps you on the right cheek, turn to them the other cheek also. And if someone wants to sue you and take your tunic, let him take your cloak as well. If someone forces you to go one mile, go with him two miles (Matthew 5:38–39).

Bear in mind, when Jesus says, "do not resist an evil person," the word "resist" is the Greek word, *anthistemi*, which in this case does not refer to any resistance, but the kind that is violent. In the context of what Jesus is contrasting—the violent "eye-for-eye" justice system spelled out in the Torah—he tells us, "Don't use violence to resist evil," as N.T. Wright translates this phrase.[6] Jesus goes on:

> You have heard that it was said, "Love your neighbor and hate your enemy." But I tell you, love your enemies and pray for those who persecute you, that you may be children of your Father in heaven. He causes his sun to rise on the evil and the good, and sends rain on the righteous and the unrighteous. If you love those who love you, what reward will you get? Are not even the tax collectors doing that? And if you greet only your own people, what are you doing more than others? Do not even pagans do that? Be a whole person, therefore, as your heavenly Father is whole[7] (Matthew 5:43–48).

> But to you who are listening I say: Love your enemies, do good to those who hate you, bless those who curse you, pray for

those who mistreat you. If someone slaps you on one cheek, turn to them the other also. If someone takes your coat, do not withhold your shirt from them. Give to everyone who asks you, and if anyone takes what belongs to you, do not demand it back. Do to others as you would have them do to you. ...love your enemies, do good to them, and lend to them without expecting to get anything back. Then your reward will be great, and you will be children of the Most High, because he is kind to the ungrateful and wicked. Be merciful, just as your Father is merciful (Luke 6:27–31 and 35–36).

In the context of history, Israel's enemies were the Gentiles and disobedient Jews. In the Torah, both the enemies and the disobedient typically were to be either killed by obedient Israelites or struck down by God by a plague (Numbers 25). Those who harmed others were to be harmed equally (Exodus 21:24, Leviticus 24:20) and shown no pity. "Show no pity: life for life, eye for eye, tooth for tooth, hand for hand, foot for foot" (Deuteronomy 19:21). Murderers, blasphemers, those who curse their parents, and adulterers (defined as all women who have sex outside of marriage and men who have sex with a married woman) were to be put to death.

Could Jesus only have been talking about disobedient Jews as enemies? Absolutely not. The evidence is overwhelming that his love ethic extended to the Gentiles, the hated Samaritans, the Romans, and other pagans. His reference to "go a second mile" was about officials or soldiers, including Roman soldiers, who had special passes and, by law, could conscript someone to aid them, often by carrying their load for a mile. In Capernaum, Jesus healed a Roman centurion's servant from afar and initially offered to come to the centurion's home. Afterward, he told the crowd that many such Gentiles (form the east and west) would have a place at the feast in the kingdom.

He cited Elijah helping a pagan widow during a famine (rather than an Israelite widow), who was from Sidon, an area known for idolatry and pagan practices. He cited Elisha healing Naaman the Syrian of leprosy, even though there were many in Israel with leprosy who Elisha did not heal. He made a Samaritan the hero in the Good Samaritan parable. He talked approvingly to a Samaritan woman and offered her the water of life. He traveled to the region of the Decapolis, ten Greco-Roman cities, mostly east of the Sea of

Galilee and the Jordan River, where he healed a deaf mute and a man with unclean spirits. Matthew records that great crowds of people from Decapolis followed him.

A Syrophoenician pagan woman once begged Jesus to deliver her daughter from an evil spirit. He rebuffed her at first telling her, "First, let the children eat their fill. It's not fitting to take the children's bread and throw it to the little dogs." But she replied by continuing his theme, "Sir, even the little dogs under the table eat the little children's little crumbs." Jesus conceded that she had a great reply and proceeded to heal her daughter. Interestingly, Jesus chose the word for "little dogs" or puppies, a softer expression from the common term, dogs, the Jews used to describe Gentiles.[8]

Finally, whereas Jesus originally told his disciples he came for the lost sheep of Israel and that they were only to go to the Israelites when he sent them on their own, after his resurrection, he told them to go to the heathen (the nations) and then to the whole world. By the time of Paul, Gentiles were so common in the gatherings of followers that the Jewish leaders had to decide whether they should follow the Law of Moses or not (Act 15). They decided they didn't have to, except for four concessions, which they were encouraged to do (not commanded)—to refrain from food sacrificed to idols, consuming blood, eating strangled animals, and *porneia*.[9]

Jesus' theme of God's mercy to enemies is grounded in God's merciful character to both the righteous and unrighteous. Moreover, his theme of non-retaliation was grounded in the non-retributive nature of God. Jesus' God is marked by mercy rather than self-righteous anger and retribution. Jesus introduced a Mercy Code (be merciful, just as God is merciful), rather than a Holiness Code (be holy, just as God is holy), and was opposed to the unmerciful Eye for Eye Code (show no pity: life for life, eye for eye, tooth for tooth, hand for hand, foot for foot in Deuteronomy 19:21).

Later, the Apostle Paul explained how God's character had always been merciful to both the Israelites and the Gentiles when they were disobedient or became his enemy:

> As far as the gospel is concerned, they [the Jews who opposed Gentile followers of Jesus] are enemies for your sake; but as far as election is concerned, they are loved on account of the patriarchs, for God's gifts and his call are irrevocable. Just

as you who were at one time disobedient to God have now received mercy as a result of their disobedience, so they too have now become disobedient in order that they too may now receive mercy as a result of God's mercy to you. For God has bound everyone over to disobedience **so that he may have mercy on them all** (Romans 11:28–32) [Emphasis added].

This enemy-love ethic does not take revenge on the disobedient or the wicked. It aligns with the story of Joseph in Genesis and the mercy he showed his brothers along with other scriptures we've seen. But it is in serious conflict with the destructive flood narrative and the God of Moses, Joshua, Phineas, Judah, Saul, and at times, David.

Don't Destroy Human Lives

To solidify this point about the two voices in the Bible—one of violent wrath and one of genuine love for humanity—we need to look at one more story in the Old Testament, a few New Testament narratives, and the Mosaic law on capital punishment.

In 2 Kings, the prophet Elijah brought a message to the King of Israel in Samaria, Ahaziah, who "did evil in the eyes of the Lord" and "served and worshipped Baal." When the king wanted to consult Baal-Zebub, the god of Ekron, about an injury he had sustained, Elijah prophesied he would die as a result. Later, the king sent a captain with a contingent of fifty soldiers three times to Elijah to inquire about this prophecy. Two of those times, this is what happened:

Then he sent to Elijah a captain with his company of fifty men. The captain went up to Elijah, who was sitting on the top of a hill, and said to him, "Man of God, the king says, 'Come down!'" Elijah answered the captain, "If I am a man of God, may fire come down from heaven and consume you and your fifty men!" Then fire fell from heaven and consumed the captain and his men (2 Kings 1:9–10).

A total of 102 men were killed and destroyed by fire.

Fast forward to Jesus going through Samaria on his way to Jerusalem perhaps 900 years later. When the people of Samaria did not welcome him—an insult to his standing as a representative of God—two of his disciples responded, "When the disciples James and John saw this, they asked, 'Lord, do you want us to call fire down from heaven to destroy them, even as Elijah did? But Jesus turned and rebuked them'" (Luke 9:54–55).

In some Greek manuscripts of Luke, Jesus elaborated his response by saying, "You do not know what kind of spirit you are of, for the Son of Man [a title Jesus gave himself] did not come to destroy men's lives, but to save them." This echoes the words in the gospel of John that "God did not send his Son into the world to condemn the world, but to save the world through him" (John 3:17). Here we have Jesus rebuking the very idea of emulating the prophet Elijah calling down fire to "consume" Samaritans. Samaritans were the enemies of the Jews with a running feud between them having roots going back to the separation of Judah and Israel around the time of Elijah.

Another narrative is when Jesus was arrested by the Temple police in the Garden of Gethsemane. Peter lashed out with a sword to protect Jesus and cut off the ear of the high priest's servant. Jesus then told Peter to put away the sword and added the warning, "for all who draw the sword will die by the sword" (Matthew 26:52). In Luke's version, it says, "Those around Jesus saw what was about to happen and said, 'Lord, should we strike with our swords?'" Impetuous Peter apparently didn't wait for the answer before he struck the man. Then Jesus says, "No more of this!" and healed the man with a touch, thereby reversing the violent act.

The disciples still had not learned "what kind of spirit one is of" who resorts to violence and destruction of human lives in response to hostility, idolatry, or disobedience. Jesus rebuked this voice that was still speaking to his followers through the Jewish scriptures. And the voice was very loud.

Take the Law of Moses, for example. It is filled with commands to administer violence on the disobedient or idolatrous. The list of those guilty of capital crimes deserving death, usually by stoning and sometimes burning, include sorcerers, idolaters, false prophets, adulterers,[10] women who have sex before marriage, murderers, a person who strikes one of their parents, a person who curses one of their parents, kidnappers, prostitutes who are a daughter of a priest, anyone who blasphemes God, false witnesses in a capital crime, and male homosexuals who are shrine prostitutes (Leviticus 20 and 21). After the stipulation was made in these narratives, the author recorded Moses as saying things like, "So you shall purge the evil from your midst; and all Israel will hear and be afraid." And again, for other crimes: "Show no pity: life for life, eye for eye, tooth for tooth, hand for hand, foot for foot (Deuteronomy 19:21).

In the one instance in the gospels where Jesus was challenged to comment on one of these capital crimes as proscribed in the Torah, he rejected the punishment and advocated for mercy. When an adulterer was brought to him who the crowd wanted to stone, according to the law of Moses, he refused to condemn her and deftly had her released by saying only an accuser who is sinless may throw the first stone (John 8:1–11). There is no violent retribution in Jesus' ethics. He has removed it from the character of God. He rebuked his disciples for calling for fiery judgment and those zealous for carrying out Mosaic death sentences. He called for people to not retaliate against evil people and to love their enemies and pray and bless them, rather than hate, fight, and kill them. All while still holding people accountable for their sins by calling for contrition, change, and, as we will see, at times warning of judgment that is corrective rather than retributive.

To try to harmonize these two voices of God in the Bible is to burst the bounds of credulity. It makes no sense.

A MIRROR OF VIOLENT ZEAL

It's illuminating to compare these Jewish violent narratives in scripture with the behavior of the some of the Jews in Jesus' time. According to the Gospels, some Jews frequently called for the death of Jesus and, later, his followers. In my evangelical experience, we were told this is because the Jews could not accept Jesus as Messiah and God in the flesh. That would make Jesus a "false Messiah" like a false prophet or blasphemer and worthy of death. This is only partly true.

First, there was no unified concept of a Jewish Messiah in the first century. There were a wide variety of Messianic expectations in the various streams of Judaism. Some of them perceived the Messiah as a priestly reformer, others a political king, and others as a military conqueror. Second, the Jews of second Temple Judaism were largely practicing violent sacrificial religion. They were serving the two-faced God who was violent toward His enemies and anyone who was disobedient to God or the Mosaic law. Their heroes were people like Moses, Joshua, Judah, Elijah, Phinehas, and David who were "zealous for God's honor" and would punish and kill their enemies: idolatrous Gentiles, especially ones who oppressed the Jews, and Jews who violated the Torah. They saw Yahweh as one who punishes His enemies, "exterminating them without mercy" (Joshua 11:20).

In fact, you begin to see this early on when Jesus went to his childhood synagogue in Nazareth and was rejected by his hometown community (Luke 4:14–30). He stands up and recites Isaiah 61:1–2, one of the most popular passages in Judaism and one which everyone would know. It is the Jubilee passage that says God will deliver the poor and oppressed, proclaim the year of the Lord's favor, and exact revenge on Israel's enemies.

But Jesus leaves off the last sentence of the passage: "...and the day of vengeance of our God." Some Bible translations inaccurately portray the scene, saying the people spoke well of him at first before getting angry at him. But the King James simply states, "all bore witness to him," and the Greek does not stipulate whether it is a negative or positive reaction. The scene makes more sense if people's immediate reaction to his leaving off the retribution of God phrase to the Jubilee announcement is one of shock.[11] Jesus says the passage is fulfilled as they heard it.

Jesus then cited those two stories in the Torah we saw earlier where Elijah and Elisha went to the Gentiles to help and heal them rather than judge them. Elijah assisted a widow in Sidon and Elisha healed a Syrian leper. The text is not ambiguous here: "All the people of the synagogue were furious when they heard this." They then physically forced Jesus out of town and tried to throw him off a cliff! Jesus made a serious breach of the popular violent sacrificial theology of the day. The people's rejection of Jesus had nothing to do with a Messianic claim but rather his declaration that God is merciful to Gentiles and doesn't take revenge on Israel's oppressors.

As his ministry continued, there were several times when the Jewish leaders react to Jesus as a disobedient Jew. One day, Jesus challenged the popular teaching of the day on the Sabbath. He questioned the Pharisee's interpretation of what was unlawful on the Sabbath, cited the prophet Hosea that God desires mercy, not sacrifice, and declared the son of man is "Lord of the Sabbath." He then declared it is lawful to do anything on the Sabbath that helps a human being, the same way it is lawful to lift a sheep that falls into a pit on the Sabbath. Then the text states, "But the Pharisees went out and plotted how they might kill Jesus." Again, at this point, the reason for their rejection of Jesus is not because he declared himself the Messiah but because he challenged the Law on the grounds of it being harsh. And the reasoning to initiate a plot to murder him was because that's what any sacrificial Jew who read and believed Leviticus, Joshua, Numbers, etc., would do.

The gospel of John also records the chief priests and Pharisees calling a meeting of the Sanhedrin (the governing assembly of elders in Jerusalem) in which they decided to plot to kill Jesus. They were worried because his influence on the masses was so great, all the people might believe in him and his "false" teaching on the Mosaic law, the Temple, and how to treat Gentiles. They were also afraid the Romans would take over their Temple and their religious national existence.

This is also recorded in a similar way in the gospel of Luke. "The chief priests and the scribes were seeking how they might put Him to death; for they were afraid of the people" (Luke 22:2 NASB). They were afraid the people would so follow Jesus in droves that their violent sacrificial religion would be effectively quashed, and Jesus would so disturb the social order that the Romans would retaliate. E.P. Sanders elaborates, "The leaders of Jerusalem were not physically afraid of Jesus and his few followers, nor would they have believed that he knew what God would do. They were probably anxious lest his prediction of coming upheaval and the intervention of God [that the Temple would be destroyed] should touch off riots."[12]

Their fears were completely misplaced. History tells us that the opposite ultimately happened. Later, riots occurred but not as a result of a peace movement such as the Jesus Movement. They were the result of the increasingly violent Zealot movement. A Jewish violent uprising led by the Zealots and fueled by the violent sacrificial faith found in the dark voice of scripture led to the destruction of Jerusalem and the Temple within a mere 40 years. Riots over the claim of a coming attack on the Temple didn't cause the Romans to destroy Jerusalem. It was the Zealots leading their Jewish brothers to stage a violent revolt against their arch enemies, the Romans.

Finally, the Sanhedrin presided over the trials of both Jesus and Stephen. They condemned Jesus for blasphemy, a charge that would merit death in Mosaic Law. They ask the Roman procurator Pilate to crucify him,[13] which he ultimately did, although he did not technically find Jesus guilty of Roman law. Pilate was all too agreeable to join in with the Jewish leaders to scapegoat Jesus and torture and murder him in order to keep the "peace" in Jerusalem and avoid a riot—always a concern for Roman procurators who didn't want any word of civil unrest to get back to Rome.

The Sanhedrin had Stephen stoned for speaking words of blasphemy against Moses and the Temple. Paul, who at the time was known as Saul, approved of this scapegoating and began to persecute followers of Jesus for their supposed blasphemy. Saul breathed "murderous threats" against them and sought to imprison anyone who belonged to "the Way."

The Nazareth synagogue, the chief priests, the scribes, the teachers of the law, the Pharisees, the Sanhedrin, the crowds wanting to stone an adulterer and pre-converted Paul were following the examples of Moses, Joshua, Phinehas, Elijah, Judah, Saul, David, and the ancient Israel community: kill the enemies of God and serious violators of God's law, foreign or domestic. Popular theology overlooks this connection. The reason Jewish leaders persecuted and murdered Jewish followers of the Rabbi Jesus and Jesus himself was because they followed the violent God portrayed in portions of the Old Testament. They carried out the orders of this violent God, who commands them, not to "love your enemies" as Jesus taught, but to "kill them" (Numbers 25:17). They would have perceived the pursuit of this divine violence as being "zealous for the honor of God" and as "making atonement for the people of Israel," by purifying their ranks from disobedient Jews and God's enemies.

Most Christians today still consider the violent narratives in the Old Testament to be the Word of God that accurately portray the character of God in Jewish history. But, when Saul was changed into a disciple of Jesus and renamed Paul, he realized he had been wrong about the character of God. He gave up his wrathful image of a violent god for the loving image of a nonviolent God. He didn't convert to Christianity. He converted to a peacemaking Judaism, where God is no longer favoring the Jewish people and hating and killing their enemies, but rather a God who consistently sees both the oppressed and oppressor as needing love and redemption. *A God who does not make victims but rather defends the victims.* In order to do that, Paul had to give up his belief in the God found in passages Genesis, Joshua, Numbers, Judges, and others. He also had to reevaluate and reinterpret the Torah and the prophets to decide what was of the way of love and nonviolence and what was not. He had to reject the violent, retributive passages in scripture and only retain the compassionate, restorative passages.

The question is, why don't Christians give up this belief too? Or why don't Christians recognize this distinction and pave a new way of equitable mercy for all like Jesus did?

FIVE

THE ERRONEOUS WAY PEOPLE VIEW THE BIBLE

THE SECOND TENANT THAT leads to myths is the belief that the Bible is the divinely ordained definitive collection of books that are the authoritative Word of God throughout. Everything you read in it is absolutely true and can never be questioned, so people say. As we have already touched on, evangelicals and fundamentalists insist this collection is inerrant (without error) and infallible (incapable of being wrong) in its original writings. Practically speaking, the way most people quote it, this means it's considered inerrant in our modern English translations as well. Your average reader or teacher does not make this qualification: our English translations cannot be inerrant because no one has access to the original extant texts to compare translations and confirm translation accuracy. The originals have been lost. Yet, the everyday reader will still insist their preferred translations are without error. So, the final consensus is that this sacred text of sixty-six books must be accepted as altogether true, historically accurate, entirely trustworthy, theologically consistent, and "the supreme authority in all matters of faith and conduct." There can be no middle ground or gray areas when it comes to the Bible. Sadly, this view is written in countless churches' statements of faith as a supposed self-evident, historically supported, and orthodox Christian doctrine.

There are two huge problems with this view of the Bible. One, as we have already seen, when practically applied, this view of the Bible is not rational. It is a complete contradiction of the linguistic, cultural, and historical facts and logic. And two, as was stated earlier (this needs to be said over and over), Jesus and the earliest Christians, not to mention Jewish people of antiquity, never viewed the Bible this way! The Bible itself never claims each of its 66 books or even one of its books are without error. Let's first look at whether this traditional view of the Bible even makes sense. And then we'll look at how the Bible was derived and who put it together. This will shed light on how Jesus, his early followers, and the Jews in general viewed "the Bible" in their day and show us a better way to view it in modern times.

THE CONTRADICTIONS

We have already gone through many of the contradictions in the Bible regarding the two-faced God. We don't have to revisit those here. There is a clear depiction of a retributive, violent god in many passages of the Old Testament and even a few in the New Testament (i.e., the books of 2 Thessalonians, 2 Peter, and Revelation). As we will learn below, there are contradictions in books like I Samuel and I Chronicles as it appears a later writer was correcting mistakes in numbers, historical details, and theological statements. Moreover, there are many contradictions in the New Testament. They are not necessarily sweeping contradictions that change the overall narrative or character of God (although sometimes they do), yet they at least shed serious doubt on the inerrancy doctrine.

I outlined some of these in my first book, *Confessions of a Bible Thumper*. For example, there's the chain of events between the crucifixion of Jesus and the resurrection. The book of John lists only one woman going to Jesus' tomb, Mary Magdalene. Matthew mentions two women, Mary Magdalene and another Mary. Mark says three women went to the tomb, adding a woman named Salome. Finally, Luke states more than three women went to the tomb adding Joanna and others.[1]

I also cited a few of the 142 contradictions found in various passages of the Bible and New Testament. In Matthew, Jesus said John the Baptist was the "Elijah who is to come." But in the book of John, John the Baptist denied he is Elijah. Matthew says Jesus got two donkeys and sat on both of *them*. The other Gospel writers say there was only one donkey. Matthew, Mark, and Luke say the Last Supper was the feast of the Passover. John says it was the night before Passover.[2] Historians have no trouble spelling out what is contradictory, as historical narratives are often like that, since various witnesses and their memories will often contradict each other in minor ways. In some cases, we can tell which narrative is probably the correct one, as historian Garry Wills explains that Matthew got it wrong with two donkeys as Matthew was misunderstanding Hebrew parallelism found in Zechariah

9:9, a passage he claimed Jesus was literally fulfilling. Similarly, John was most likely the only one that got the timing of the Last Supper right as it couldn't be the night of Passover because the Jewish leaders would not have had their trial of Jesus on such an important holiday.

These examples of contradictions teach us that the traditional way of viewing the Bible doesn't make sense.

HOW JESUS AND HIS EARLIEST FOLLOWERS VIEWED THE BIBLE

Earlier we made the case that the Apostle Paul would have had to give up his belief in the violent God found in passages in Genesis, Deuteronomy, Numbers, Joshua, Judges, 2 Kings, 1 Samuel, etc. in order to become a follower of Jesus. How could he have done this so easily? Most modern Western Christians who choose to disavow huge swaths of the Old Testament would be deemed heretics. It would not be so easy for them to do it. What was it like for Paul?

When a person studies how the Jewish people and later the followers of Jesus through the fourth century compiled and created a canon (definitive list) of the scriptures that would become what we call the Bible, they discover how different our modern view of the Bible is. It was easy for Paul to condemn Old Testament stories of a violent God in the Bible because there was never a definitive list nor a strict definition of what "scripture" was in that day. Moreover, neither was there a rigid rule that one had to accept all ideas about God within scripture as accurate. In fact, as we shall see, many of the prophets in scripture rejected other claims in scripture. And all of the four major divisions of Judaism in the era of Jesus (Sadducees, Pharisees, Essenes, and Zealots) had their own take on scripture and their interpretations. Moreover, the most popular Jewish scholars of the period whose influence remained for decades, Rabbis Hillel and Shammai and their followers, were known for their vigorous debates.

Whose Bible Is the Right One?

The priestly and aristocratic sect of the Sadducees refused to go beyond the Torah—the first five books of our Old Testament—in their beliefs and teaching about the ways of God. They did not recognize the Jewish oral, legal traditions, as the Pharisees did, or the rest of the Jewish scriptures that most Jews had (the Prophets and the Writings in addition to the Torah). These made up what became known as the Tanakh.

Greek Jews had the Septuagint as their scriptures, the Old Testament version which the New Testament quotes, and which contains an additional 14 books called the Apocrypha that are not within the traditional Prophets and Writings. We know from history they were revered as holy scripture, even by the earliest Christians, and today are within the Roman Catholic and Eastern Orthodox Bibles.

The Essenes had their own additional scriptures, as evidenced by the Dead Sea Scrolls, that included many books like I Enoch, an apocalyptic text quoted in the New Testament book of Jude. The Qumranites, most likely a distinct Essene sub-group, had developed their "perfect" way within their interpretation of their scriptures, which included many of the intertestamental books.

Whereas there is no wide-spread consensus among scholars, evidence suggests the present-day Jewish canon was not closed until sometime between 150 to 250 C.E. In addition, the rise of Christianity probably had a role in influencing Jewish authorities to define a canon.[3] In other words, there was never a universally recognized definitive list of books that made up the Jewish scriptures until at least 120 years after Jesus lived! The boundaries of the Bible of the first century were fuzzy. The content of this Bible was as well and continually needed someone to bring it into focus.

How the New Testament Was Compiled

In my second book, Craft Brewed Jesus, and in my Religious Deconstruction Workshop, I go through how the New Testament was compiled. In other words, how did the Western Church decide on a definitive list (canon) of books recognized as authoritative? This wasn't completed until the fourth century, 300 years after Jesus! Before it was canonized, there were a variety of sets of scriptures, or what some scholars call "local canonicity," where different regions would have their own set of writings they deemed inspired or just preferred. Books like Revelation, Hebrews, James, Jude, 2 Peter, 2 John, and Paul's letters of Titus and I and II Timothy were some of the common books disputed by "orthodox" Christian leaders and not found in many lists of scriptures before the fourth century. Revelation and the book of Jude were probably the most suspect and outright rejected likely by half of the communities. Although all four gospels, Matthew, Mark, Luke, and John, were generally acknowledged, they weren't all preferred. Roman Christians resisted the gospel of John because gnostic heretics made use of it. Eastern Christians used John and didn't necessarily use Matthew, Mark, and Luke.[4]

When we look back on Paul's writings, we find not all of them found in today's New Testament were universally accepted. Today, historians are in near universal agreement that the only authentic books attributed to Paul are I Thessalonians, Galatians, Philippians, Philemon, 1 and 2 Corinthians, and Romans. The pastoral epistles of Titus and the Timothies were probably not written by Paul but someone trying to relay his sentiments and were among the disputed or rejected texts. Historians are in dispute about whether Colossians, Ephesians, and 2 Thessalonians should be attributed to Paul.[5]

Then, there are many books that were never canonized into the New Testament that many orthodox leaders thought should have been considered holy scripture (i.e., the Shepherd of Hermas, the gospels of the Hebrews, the Egyptians, and Matthias, and the letters of I Clement, Barnabas, the Didache, a composite gospel called the Diatessaron, the Apocalypse of Peter, and the Wisdom of Solomon).[6] When we talk about the New Testament being authoritative and inspired writings to define our faith and practice, which New Testament is the right one?

Moreover, bear in mind that most followers of the way of Jesus for hundreds of years did not have what we call the New Testament. In the beginning all they had was the oral tradition passed down by those who knew or were close to Jesus and his original followers. Later, they may or may not have had a handful of Paul's letters (50s to 60s CE). Later still, they had maybe one or more of the four gospels (68 to 90s CE). Most likely, they eventually would have had one or more of the several books mentioned above that were never accepted into the New Testament. The movement survived 300 years without a New Testament or definitive list of scriptures. Finally, what today we call the Old and New Testaments had initially been decided in 363 CE at the Council of Laodicea (a group of men bishops and representatives). This council listed all the books we have today excluding the book of Revelation and the Apocrypha, the 14 books that were part of the Greek Septuagint (Old Testament) and accepted by the early Greek followers of Jesus. The Council of Carthage, which Augustine attended in 397 CE, had the same list but added the book of Revelation. It also made an exclusionary statement that these books should be read in the church to the exclusion of all others. This last council was generally accepted as authoritative in the West but not unanimously. It was also not entirely accepted in the East.[7]

The Bible Critiques Itself

Another thing to keep in mind is that the Bible is cited by historians as the only sacred text that critiques itself.[8] Just two examples would be: (1) how the prophets and the Psalmists continually critiqued the Mosaic sacrificial system and (2) how the writings would make corrections to earlier historical narratives.

Isaiah declared that God had no need of sacrifices:

> "'The multitude of your sacrifices—what are they to me?' says the LORD. I have more than enough of burnt offerings, of rams and the fat of fattened animals; I have no pleasure in the blood of bulls and lambs and goats. When you come to appear before me, who has asked this of you, this trampling of my courts? Stop bringing meaningless offerings!" (Isaiah 1:11–13).

The Psalmist concurs:

> "For You do not delight in sacrifice, or I would bring it; You take no pleasure in burnt offerings. The sacrifices of God are a

broken spirit; a broken and a contrite heart, O God, You will not despise" (Psalm 51:16–17).

Jesus often cited the prophet Hosea who said, "For I desire mercy, not sacrifice, and the knowledge of God rather than burnt offerings" (Hosea 6:6). He told his audience once, "If you had known what these words mean, 'I desire mercy, not sacrifice,' you would not have condemned the innocent" (Matthew 12:7). The prophet Micah summed up what was really on God's mind rather than making sacrifices:

> "With what shall I come before the LORD and bow down before the exalted God? Should I come to Him with burnt offerings, with calves a year old? Will the LORD be pleased with thousands of rams and ten thousand rivers of olive oil? Shall I offer my firstborn for my transgression, the fruit of my body for the sin of my soul? He has shown you, O mortal, what is good. And what does the LORD require of you? To act justly and to love mercy and to walk humbly with your God" (Micah 6:6–8).

In Micah and Hosea, we see the mercy theme that Jesus taught, that we have called "The Mercy Code" in contrast to "The Holiness Code." Jesus never taught people to be holy as God is holy but rather "be merciful as your Father is merciful." Finally, in a normally ignored and glaring contradiction, the prophet Jeremiah said that God never even gave the Israelites the sacrificial system to begin with!

> "Thus says the LORD of hosts, the God of Israel, 'Add your burnt offerings to your other sacrifices and eat flesh' [offerings to other gods by Israelites described in verse 18]. For I did not speak to your fathers, or command them in the day that I brought them out of the land of Egypt, concerning burnt offerings and sacrifices. But this is what I commanded them,

saying, 'Obey My voice, and I will be your God and you will be my people'" (Jeremiah 7:21–23 New American Standard).[9]

Jesus Critiques the Torah and Picks and Chooses Scripture

One of the most common critiques that the Bible is not inerrant or infallible, goes something like this: "Michael, you foolish man, you can't cherry pick what you want from the Bible. You have to accept it all."

The problem with this critique is twofold. First, as we have seen above, we got the Old and New Testaments we have today because someone else picked and chose what books should be in it. In the time of Jesus, there was no definitive list of Old Testament books that everyone accepted. The Jewish people did not finalize a list until more than a century or more after Christ. Western Christians did not finalize an Old Testament nor the New Testament until the fourth century. So, why could a group of men in the fourth century get to pick and choose and we can't?

Second, keep in mind that before this, the common practice was for everyone to pick and choose one's preferable scriptures (i.e., as previously mentioned, the Sadducees, the Pharisees, the Greek Jews, and the Essenes). Jesus entered into this practice and contrasted the retributive narratives of much of the Old Testament with his enemy-love ethic. He instead chose the restorative narratives and rejected the others. He rejected the "eye for eye, tooth for tooth, and life for life" philosophy. He was very selective in which scriptures to quote. He sometimes left out verses in a passage to make a point (i.e., the way he quoted Isaiah 61:1–2 as recorded in Luke 4:18 and left out the phrase, "and the day of vengeance of our God"). He added the word "mind" to the daily "Shema" prayer found in Deuteronomy 6:4–5, calling people to love God with not only their whole heart, soul, and strength but also their whole *mind* (compare Deuteronomy 6 with Matthew 22, Mark 12, and Luke 10). He only selected passages that reinforced his neighbor-enemy-love, restorative, and egalitarian ethic. So, why can't we follow this same practice that Jesus did?

The answer is simply we can and should. We should think for ourselves and allow the example of Jesus and most of the prophets guide us into how we read and view the Bible.

The Bible Revised

As for an example of changing historical narratives, a most glaring and descriptive one compares I Samuel to I Chronicles in one of the stories of David. In I Samuel 24:1, the text says God caused David to commit a particular sin. In the later, revised narrative of the same exact story in I Chronicles 21:1, it says *Satan* caused David to sin. One theory is that this is a correction to the earlier story and is evidence of evolving human moral development inside biblical narratives. Generally, the later texts probably reflect a higher understanding of divine revelation or were written in order to clarify and correct earlier texts.

There are several other examples of this changing of historical narratives in the Jewish scriptures. The book of Chronicles, written later in chronological order than the books of Samuel and Kings, varies many times with Samuel and Kings on numerical details. Here are just two examples: (1) II Kings 8:26 says King Ahaziah was twenty-two years old when he began his reign while II Chronicles 22:2 says he was forty-two; (2) II Kings 24 says King Jehoiakim was eight years (most Hebrew manuscripts) when he became king, reigned for three months, and was succeeded by his uncle, but II Chronicles 36 states King Jehoiakim was eighteen years when he became king, reigned for three months and ten days, and was succeeded by his brother.

Some translations of these passages "correct" the words or numbers in the text but in the footnotes the original translation is retained. So, in II Chronicles the NIV footnotes say in the first instance that the Hebrew word is *forty-two* and in the second that the Hebrew word is *brother*. These are clearly cases where the writer of Chronicles is both correcting an earlier depiction and adding some more detail (in the case of the length of the reign). But it's also an indication that the translators are not being entirely honest. They end up citing the minority view or make it appear that there was no discrepancy to begin with.

This is all to say that there was always an ongoing debate about God's revelation and its own history within Jewish communities. The concept of biblical inerrancy or infallibility was not present. If the writer of II Chronicles thought he found a mistake in an earlier narrative, he would simply correct it or add detail to make it more accurate. Yet, both narratives were retained as scripture. The prophets and psalmist were free to critique the sacrificial system going so far as to say God doesn't delight in sacrifices at all (Psalms), He takes no pleasure in the blood of sacrificial animals (Isaiah), He desires mercy, not sacrifice (Hosea), He only requires his people to act justly, love mercy, and walk humbly; He does not require sacrifices (Micah), and that He never gave the command to sacrifice to begin with! (Jeremiah)

Jesus enters into the debate, claiming he has come to fulfill the Law and the Prophets. This doesn't mean, as most of popular theology asserts, that Jesus completely agrees with everything stated in the Torah and scriptures. The Greek word "fulfill" can mean to complete and even to *perfect*.[10] Jesus makes an audacious claim. He's going to clear up the debates. He's going to reflect what God is really like. In Jesus' first formal teaching (the Sermon on the Mount) he kept comparing Old Testament narratives with his revelations.

For instance, you've heard in the Law, he says, "love your friends and hate your enemies." Although hating one's enemies is not a direct command in the Law, this is obviously taught in the Numbers, Joshua, and Judges narratives we discussed. Joshua spared his friends (Rahab the prostitute and her family because she helped the Israelites) and hated and killed his enemies. God spared His friends (Noah and his family) and drowned His enemies. In the Essenes' scriptures found in the Dead Sea scrolls, there was a daily pledge that the faithful would make. They pledged to "love all the sons of light, each according to his lot in God's design, and hate all the sons of darkness, each according to his guilt in God's vengeance." Their apocalyptic beliefs, similar to today's popular theology and view of the coming Judgment Day at the return of Christ, embraced the militaristic version of the coming Messiah. "They were ticking down the days until the Messiah would arrive to start the war on evil and slay all the wicked on earth."[11]

But Jesus tells us to love our enemies and even wish them well (pray for them), not destroy them. He rejects what you've heard in the Law, "an eye for an eye and a tooth for a tooth" (Exodus). He tells us to not violently resist an evil person but rather challenge their violence with kindness. Do not retaliate with reciprocal violence. The Apostle Paul picks up on this theme when he wrote to the followers of Jesus in Rome, "Do not be overcome by evil, but overcome evil with good" (Romans 12:20).

Many have suggested Jesus' command of non-retaliation is another example of moral development in the Bible. In Genesis there were narratives of supposed justice that entailed revenge seven times the violation and even up to 77 times (Genesis 4:24). The eye-for-an-eye directive in Exodus was a way of controlling escalating retribution to a balanced tit-for-tat—a retaliation in kind. Jesus comes along and says even equal retribution is wrong.

Jesus ultimately reduces the Law to love—being a loving person, loving our neighbor as ourselves, including our enemy, and doing to others what we would want them to do to us. This summarized the Law and Prophets. Later, Paul, made similar statements that also simplified the Law into living a life of love: "...whoever loves others has fulfilled the law. The commandments, *You shall not commit adultery, You shall not murder, You shall not steal, You shall not covet*, and whatever other command there may be, are summed up in this one command: *Love your neighbor as yourself.* Love does no harm to a neighbor. Therefore, love is the fulfillment of the law" (Romans 13:8–10 and Galatians 5:14). Jesus "fulfilling" the law is about his way of love trumping the law. Paul says, "we have been released from the Law" (Romans 7:6). Paul also offers his interpretation of Jesus' teaching compared to the Torah and the Law: "Christ is the end of the Law" (Romans 10:4).

Jesus and Paul followed the Jewish tradition of faithful questioning of the scriptures as a way of weighing in on the ongoing debates about God's ways. Their conclusion was that God was not violent, not retributive, and not sacrificial. Jesus is inclusive of all—not just Jews—and not beholden to the Temple or even the Torah.

The Bible Itself Does Not Claim It Is Inerrant

Another point is that the Bible does not claim to be inerrant. In the Bible, no writer claims a revelation that God dictated which books should be in the Bible, let alone that all the books are inerrant. The verse 2 Timothy 3:16 that says, "All scripture is God-breathed and is profitable," is often used to prove all of the Bible is inspired and, therefore, one hundred percent trustworthy. But when that was written (probably by a follower of Paul not by Paul himself), there was no New Testament! And, when it was written, the Old

Testament had not been formalized but was a loose compilation of writings. A more logical meaning of that verse is found in several translations that say "all scripture inspired by God is profitable." In other words, when scripture, or literally 'writings,' are inspired by God, they are profitable.[12]

A further point is how evangelicals love to call the Bible "the Word of God" or simply "the Word." Yet, the Bible itself never claims to be the Word of God. The New Testament makes it clear that the "Word" (logos in the Greek, which means the *rationale* of God) is Jesus Christ, not the Bible. The "Word" is personified in the person of Jesus. It is not every word, verse, passage, chapter, or book of the Bible.

The Jewish Tradition of Questioning

History tells us that the Jewish community throughout their existence had a tradition of disputing their sacred texts and even what God had said. From the Hebrew Bible to the Talmud to the Midrash, one can find countless examples of questioning and protest. It is a collection of dissenting views. Rabbi Anson Laytner lays out many such examples in his book, *Arguing with God: A Jewish Tradition.*[13] Abraham argued with God over destroying Sodom and Gomorrah (something Joshua never did). He questioned the justice of destroying everyone. Later in the story, the text revealed God spared Lot and his family because "God remembered Abraham" (Genesis 19:29).

Moses questioned God over and over about his mission. When God was exasperated with the disobedience of the Israelites, He said, "I will strike them down with a plague and destroy them" (Numbers 14:12). But Moses argues against God's plans and appeals to Him saying if the people are put to death the nations will mock God's reputation, for He would have failed in his plan to bring His people into the promised land. He then quotes God's own words saying, "The Lord is slow to anger, abounding in love and forgiving sin and rebellion," and then pleads for Him to forgive the people. God relents and forgives them with the qualification that the disobedient ones would not see the promised land (Numbers 14:10–23).

The book of Job is perhaps the best example of a debate over many of the things that Yahweh was recorded as saying. Job continues to question the conventional wisdom that since he has suffered, he must have committed some great sin. This "wisdom" can find roots in the "blessings and curses" narrative that Yahweh gave to Moses, that if the Israelites obey the Law, God would bless them. But if they didn't, they will be cursed. In the end, Job is vindicated.

All of these examples, from the Torah, the Prophets, the Writings is a record of what Derek Flood calls "faithful questioning" of the scriptures. This was a longstanding tradition from the beginning of Jewish history that the prophets and Jesus carried on. It is juxtaposed to the legalistic practice depicted in other narratives—from Joshua to the Pharisees and teachers of the law—that is, the practice of "unquestioning obedience" of the scriptures.

Peter Enns explains how Jesus practiced faithful questioning. "He [Jesus] didn't stay inside the lines...He wasn't a Rulebook reader of the Bible." In other words, he didn't take the "unquestioning obedience" approach. And he wasn't the first to read the Bible this way. The Jewish scriptures themselves make it imperative that its readers prod, probe, and debate its contents.

> ...the Old Testament Law is surprisingly ambiguous and diverse—it's begging to be debated and deliberated over, which is exactly what we see happening in the Old Testament and also in some of Jesus' teachings.[14]

> Debating the Bible, especially the Torah, and coming up with creative readings to address changing times was a mark of faithful Judaism.[15]

Although there are plenty of examples of "unquestioning obedience" in the Bible, the mere existence of the "faithful questioning" narratives makes an irrefutable claim that the Jews welcomed debate over their own scriptures. And they didn't necessarily try to harmonize any contradictions they saw in their scriptures. We saw how the prophets critiqued parts of the Torah and how some historical writings corrected mistakes they saw in other historical depictions.

As this former biblical inerrantist concluded, always trying to explain away contradictions and conflicts in the Bible is not a being faithful to the text.

Sure, I could scrutinize the wording of these verses, dig into the Hebrew, and come up with some way to force an agreement. But would that really be faithful to the texts? These aren't just single verses that appear contradictory; they represent vastly opposing viewpoints—a debate going on within the pages of the Old Testament.[16]

REJECTING A FLAT READING OF THE BIBLE

A flat reading of the Bible is when people read it as if every word, verse, passage, chapter, and book is equally inspired. This way of reading ignores two critical distinctions. First, Jesus told us there are "more important matters of the law": justice, mercy, and faithfulness (Matthew 23:23). Not everything is equally important. Some content is inferior to "weightier" matters. Following the more important admonitions matters more than following the less important. This is why Jesus accused the teachers of the law of "straining out a gnat and swallowing a camel." They legalistically applied things that didn't matter a hill of beans (e.g., not healing on the Sabbath) and ignored the things that really mattered a hell of a lot (caring for someone who urgently needs help).

Second, the Bible, like any book, needs to be read in its own literary context. Some passages are not meant to be read in isolation otherwise one misunderstands what is being said. But by reading the whole context of a verse or passage one can better understand the point of the text or the conclusion to which the writer comes. That is what is important. One good example of this is Romans chapters 1 through 13. Here, Paul writes a long argument that leads to some major conclusions. All of those chapters should preferably be read in one sitting, otherwise the reader may misconstrue the points Paul is making. So, for example, Paul comes to critical conclusions like, "For God has bound everyone over to disobedience so that he may have mercy on them all" (Romans 11:32). And "hence love is the full totality of the Law"[17] (Romans 13:10). These are like final verdicts that are often casually ignored by Bible readers who are so caught up in a flat reading of the Bible that they miss these golden nuggets. If they don't like the face value of these statements, they can find some other "infallible" Bible verse earlier in the passage to counter these important conclusions Paul makes.

REJECTING CERTAIN BIBLICAL NARRATIVES TO FOLLOW THE PRINCIPLES OF LOVE

Finally, Derek Flood makes the case that a faithful reading of the Old Testament should not only include our own questioning, but after we question, prod, and probe it, we must choose what we see as truth in the scriptures and reject what we don't.

> Because the Old Testament is a record of dispute, it calls us by its very nature to enter into that dispute ourselves as we read. In fact, because of its multiple conflicting narratives we simply have no choice but to choose; we must take sides in the debate; we are forced to embrace some narratives while rejecting others.[18]

It makes sense this is true of the New Testament as well. The Bible has mysteries within its pages and there is nothing wrong with questioning it, coming to conclusions about misinterpretations, mistakes, mistranslations, or copyist insertions when we have good, literary, historical, and linguistic reasons to, or simply saying we just don't know.

This is vitally important because when people believe the Bible is infallible and can't be questioned, they ultimately end up harming others. They may take some passage out of context, ignore the conclusion or the main point of that passage, and apply a verse or idea to a situation that is not comparable. They may follow the "command" of the Bible even though in some circumstances it contradicts the principles of love. They may admonish others with "instruction from the Word of God" when those admonitions are abusive, harmful, and unloving.

One example happened in 2002 but came to light in 2022. Evangelical pastor John MacArthur and his congregation, Grace Community Church, shamed a woman and put her under church discipline (based on Matthew 18:15–20) because she refused to take back her child-abuser husband. She had filed a legal separation and a restraining order against him after he repeatedly abused her children (physically and later sexually). The church told her to drop the protective order and return to her marriage because it violated I Corinthians 7:10, which says "a wife must not separate from her husband." They also said she must "model for her children how to suffer for Jesus" and submit to her husband as the "scriptures" teach (Ephesians 5:22–24).

This was spiritual abuse—admonishing someone to obey a biblical imperative that doesn't fit the person's circumstances and violates the overriding law of love. It was done by her own church and pastors while her husband was physically abusing their children and even once threatened to kill all of them. The wife eventually reported it to the police who, unlike the church, took her seriously (it is common for evangelical churches to teach that such conflict should not be reported to police but be handled "biblically" by the church).

Within three years her husband was convicted in court of "corporal injury to a child, child abuse, and aggravated child molestation." A church that preached biblical infallibility did nothing to protect a desperate woman and abused children from a dangerously abusive man. It accused her of disobeying the "Word of God" and shamed her publicly with "church discipline," all in the name of fidelity to an "inerrant" Bible.[19]

SIX
THE PROBLEM WITH A TRANSACTIONAL GOD

THE THIRD MAJOR TENANT that leads to upholding Christian myths is believing the notion that God is essentially a transactional god. Sacrificial religion only works if you have a transactional God—a God who insists on lots of quid pro quos. Being transactional is not bad in and of itself. It's how capitalism and free market societies work. It's an economy of exchange. If I give a vendor a specified amount of money, I'll get the goods and services I want in exchange. It's a win-win.

The problem comes when the transactions are corrupt, or, in the case of religion, when you have a god, or you think you have a god, who is wrathful, conditional, petty, demanding, and retributive. In religion, the payment has several "advantages," such as social control of a religious community, the enforcement of religious taboos or laws, and appeasement to a demanding god.

Most of the stories we've told here are reflective of ancient, sacrificial, sacred violence. In the story of Achan, when the Israelite army broke the agreement that they had with God on how to execute the conquest of Jericho, God got very angry then refused to aid the army in their next conquest of Ai. Only when Joshua found the guilty party and punished him, stoning and burning him and his possessions and even his children, did God "turn from his fierce anger" and lend his assistance in the next battle. Divine punishment was the payment that controlled the masses from further violating the divine contract and appeased the anger of Yahweh.

In the story of Phineas, the Israelites had broken covenant with God by sacrificing to foreign gods after being seduced to do so by foreign women. God burned with anger as a result. In response, God sent a plague on the land that killed 24,000 people. In exchange, Israelite judges had all the men who were guilty of idolatry to the god of Baal killed. Phineas became the hero who set the example of zealous, righteous anger by impaling a guilty man and woman, who were particularly brazen in their capital crime. Once the guilty parties were destroyed per the Law of Moses, God ended the plague, and the relationship was restored. Here, punishment of the guilty is the payment to stop another punishment (the plague) and appease Yahweh, e.g., turn away his anger and restore religious harmony.

As we learned above, revivalism in American Christianity operates in an economy of exchange with a belief in a transactional God. Do "this" for God and get "that" from God. Evangelical Christians claim they believe in the unconditional grace of God, but because many or most of them have bought into a transactional view of God, they actually practice conditional grace and forgiveness. True agape love, unconditional love that the New Testament claims is divine, does not require quid pro quos. It is "a flow of energy willingly allowed and exchanged, without requiring payment in return."[1]

Something conditional is transactional. Grace or forgiveness or even blessings are not extended or sustained unless the recipient does something in return—get right with God, accept the evangelical view of Jesus as Lord and Savior, read and obey the Bible, commit to a church and its leadership, tithe, give money, pray, fast, worship, attend prayer assemblies, or some other condition. I know this from my personal experience in the evangelical movement where this mentality was commonplace.

THE TRANSACTIONAL GOD AND SACRED VIOLENCE

The transactions are not violent, per se, except when you look under the hood at conservative Christian theology. Most evangelicals have a violent sacrificial view of God. They may not directly engage in violence, but they approve of it and applaud a God who practices it. The transactional violence in evangelical theology focuses on beliefs such as: They believe God really did drown the planet and commanded the Israelites to commit genocide; they endorse capital punishment based on the Mosaic law; they support most if not all of America's wars; many justified the torture of Al Qaeda detainees; some Trump-supporting Christians justified storming the capital and violence to "stop the steal;" they believe Jesus' excruciating death on the cross appeased

God's anger over sin—and if Jesus did not die on the cross, we could not be forgiven, the same way that God would not have forgiven the Israelites unless Joshua had Achan killed (and his children); they believe certain calamities in the world are God's punishments for sin; they expect the return of Christ will usher in a final judgment of humankind and destruction of unbelievers; and they believe that unbelievers will experience eternal conscious torment in hell.

Popular modern theology is based on sacred violence. The reason being that modern Christians, with some notable exceptions, have largely failed to grasp the revelation of the Rabbi Jesus that God does not operate under transactions, especially violent ones. That it wasn't God who instituted a violent, sacrificial, religious system for Jews, but rather it was a natural reflection of ancient sacred sacrifice that you can trace throughout human cultures of antiquity. Moreover, Jesus did not take the punishment that humankind deserved to appease God's anger and satisfy his justice system of violent retribution for sin.

This notion that God is not transactional or sacrificial at His core is backed up by a study of history and theology in Judaism and Christianity starting in the first century through the time of "The Great Reversal." The Great Reversal, according to Robin Meyers, is when Christianity took a final turn away from its roots of universal love and peacemaking when the emperor Constantine Romanized the faith and later when the emperor Theodosius made it the official religion of the Empire in the fourth century.

This is also supported by social science anthropologist and philosopher Rene Girard, who some describe as "the Darwin of the human sciences." His seminal theories on sacred violence shed light on our topic. For example, the historical trajectory of violent sacrificial religious rituals and beliefs ultimately leads to the Gospel narrative of the crucifixion of Jesus. Girard found, when objectively observed outside the lens of popular modern theology, Jesus' death turns sacrificial theology on its head:

> Girard's theory of sacred violence takes its most controversial turn when he claims that biblical religion, especially Christianity, is a radical attack on the whole logic of religious violence. After all, according to the Gospels, Jesus was killed by the Jewish high priests and by the Romans as a scapegoat and

as a sacrificial victim. That God himself became the victim of both scapegoat murder and sacrificial killing demonstrates, says Girard, that the central message of the Gospels is to overturn once and for all the whole machinery of scapegoat murder and sacrificial violence. Of course, Christians themselves have notoriously participated in scapegoat persecution of Jews and heretics, so Girard has conceded that many if not most actual Christians have failed to grasp what he takes to be the central teaching of Christianity.[2]

Through Jesus, God overturns the sacrificial ideology of the Jews of second-Temple Judaism. Most early Christians understood this. Most modern Christians don't. As we learned earlier, the notion that Jesus' death reflected the Mosaic, sacrificial system and that he was a substitutionary sacrifice for humankind to satisfy God's demand for justice for sin is a fraud first foisted on the church by Anselm in the 13th century (his "satisfaction" theory) and later by Calvin in the 16th century when he introduced the notion that the satisfaction was penal substitutional atonement for human sin. In reality, the earliest followers of Jesus recognized that what happened at the cross was actually inverting the traditional meaning of sacrifice. In traditional, religious sacrifice, the victim is unwilling. He or she is a scapegoat, whether they are guilty or not and whether they admit their guilt or not. Achan was guilty, and admitted his guilt, but was unwilling to submit to stoning. His children were not guilty and unwilling to submit to stoning. They were unwilling to sacrifice themselves.

Jesus was innocent but voluntarily submitted to the violence of the cross. His was a self-sacrifice. He was an innocent, willing victim. "The ethic is flipped. It is to endure suffering rather than inflict it."[3] Jesus was not taking on the sacrifice because God's anger with human sin demanded it but because humankind's anger with Jesus demanded it, despite him being an innocent, righteous victim. And he was willing to let it happen, willing to refrain from defense or retaliation, and still forgive.

Richard Rohr spells out how this is the mark of divine love stating "there is no room for human punishment, vengeance, rash judgment, or calls for retribution. We certainly see none of this small-mindedness in the Risen Christ after his own rejection, betrayal, and cruel death..."[4]

If Jesus is a reflection of the true God of mercy, then Jesus becoming a sacrifice to atone for humankind's wickedness and appease God's anger makes no sense. The Father of Jesus does not demand appeasement, whether religious or sacrificial. He is merciful by nature, Jesus taught. The God of Jesus doesn't need an innocent victim or scapegoat to be tortured and murdered in order to have mercy on people. Neither does He advocate for people of faith to resort to violence to either punish their enemies or balance the scales of justice so they might be forgiven. Jesus said he had authority to forgive anyone's sins without having to go through the religious, sacrificial system (Luke 5:17–26).

Jesus' willingness to stand up to religious and imperialistic corruption and bear the brunt of human brutality—the crucifixion being one of the cruelest methods of capital punishment ever known—isn't about God being angry at humankind enough to sacrifice Jesus to pay for sins, but rather about humankind's anger and violence against God. God, in the form of an innocent, peacemaking, righteous victim. In the light of that violence, Jesus said, "Father, forgive them for they know not what they do" (Luke 23:34). He didn't say, "Father, forgive them now that I've appeased your wrath and your demand for justice." Brad Jersak puts it this way:

> God-in-Christ is literally given over to the wrath, to our sin, to that murderous death. He suffers our defiant, violent rejection. Because that sin is directed against him, he can do one of two things: he can avenge it, or he can forgive it. He can either pay us back with wrath or he can forgive us freely with grace—he can react in kind with punishment or respond with mercy. For love's sake, God opts for mercy and forgiveness on Good Friday. God chooses restoration over retribution. He does this for us; he does it for love. Amazingly, this forgiveness extends beyond the conspirators and agents of his crucifixion—beyond Pilate and Caiaphas and their cronies. He applies forgiveness to all humankind for all time.[5]

In fact, Jesus' revelation and the record of his death, his forgiveness of his accusers, betrayers, and torturers, and his resurrection, in which he takes no revenge, proves God is not transactional. As we will see, it also proves that Jesus' most profound contribution to humankind is his radical way of peace.

Unfortunately, when popular theology embraces penal substitutionary atonement—that Jesus appeases God's wrath over sin with his death and takes the punishment upon himself that we deserve—it opens the door for just the opposite of peace. Brad Jersak explains:

> I would submit that by viewing substitution as mollification or wrath-appeasement by means of violent punishment, we impose a gross projection of our own twisted demands for retribution onto divine justice, reducing it to carnal vengeance.[6]

In other words, if we believe God demands violent punishment of sinners or lawbreakers, and the only way for God to forgive humankind is if Jesus becomes a substitute and take the violent punishment we deserve (and we have to "accept" that interpretation in order for God to forgive us), then we believe in divine violence. Then we believe in violent sacrificial religion. Then we believe that God is violent. He either punishes sinners or lawbreakers with violent acts (Joshua killing Achan, Phineas spearing the idolatrous couple, the first century Jewish leaders convincing the Romans to torture and murder Jesus, Paul encouraging the stoning of Stephen, the punishment of war in the Joshua narrative or in modern warfare), with stern punishments (today's penal justice system with prolonged prison terms, solitary confinement, and capital punishment) or, in popular theology, if they don't become Bible-believing Christians, we say God punishes them in hell, itself a violent, abusive consignment with no way of escape.

Moreover, if the traditional view of the cross and substitutionary atonement is true, then there really is no such thing as real forgiveness. The debt of humanity's sin was never really forgiven. It was paid for by someone else. It was a conditional transaction. God is appeased and relents from implementing severe punishment on us only if Jesus pays, only if he is tortured and murdered, and only if individuals accept this transaction. As Garret Higgins says, "It fundamentally contradicts the notion of a loving God."[7]

WAYS MODERN EVANGELICALS BELIEVE IN A TRANSACTIONAL GOD

When I was in the evangelical missions movement in the early 1980s through the early 2000s, I studied at institutions like the U.S. Center for World Mission, Fuller Seminary's School of World Mission, and William Carey University (all in Pasadena, CA). The evangelical mission objective was to fulfill "The Great Commission"—that is to complete the task that Jesus gave to "go and make disciples of all nations" (Matthew 28:19) and that "this gospel of the kingdom will be preached in the whole world as a testimony to all nations, and then the end will come" (Matthew 24:14). Evangelicals picked up on the Greek word for "nation," or *ethnos*, and started to teach this verse meant missionaries needed to go to every ethnic and linguistic group in the world in order to fulfill this command of Jesus (even though the word is also shorthand for "Gentiles," that is any non-Jews.) They called the ethno/linguistic groups of the world, where fewer than 1 or 2 percent of their population were evangelical Christians (there were also some that had no believers at all), *hidden* or *unreached*. Only when we missionaries reached all these groups with the gospel (that is, a significant number had converted to evangelical Christianity) would the world be ready for "the end to come," meaning Christ would return in final judgment. And, only by going to the unreached would we really obey the command and fulfill the task, as going to others that were already "reached" would be counterproductive.

In a part time volunteer job I had for a brief time at the U.S. Center for World Mission at the Zwemer Institute, I used ethnologies to compile a database of the Muslim people groups of the world that were not sufficiently "reached" and should be considered "unreached." The idea was to have mission agencies know who these groups were and send missionaries to them. In fact, later in the 1990s, my wife and I and another family did go to an unreached Muslim group called the Yao in Malawi, East Africa, with a goal to plant sufficiently evangelical but culturally relevant churches or communities of believers.

The mentality of this movement can be summed up in the message of an Annual Report brochure of an agency I worked for later on, called Mission to Unreached Peoples.[8] With a photo of a Muslim or Hindu woman and man on the cover and inside cover, the message said, "I will never meet a Christian, hear the gospel, see a Bible, know forgiveness, or find salvation *unless* someone prays, *unless* someone gives, *unless* someone comes to my people, *unless* someone does something different."

This is a transactional view of reaching people for Christ. Unless evangelicals pray and give money and send evangelical missionaries to unreached peoples to preach the gospel, these lost ethno/linguistic groups will not know the good news that God loves them. They won't find forgiveness. They will never be saved. They will remain lost and wind up in eternal perdition. This world view is that God is dependent on "believers" to do something (pray, give, and go) before God can save people and restore them to good standing. This is actually a pagan view of god. God can't act, love, forgive, redeem, restore, or save unless a transaction is made or goods are exchanged. Unless people do something to convert them, these people are damned. God is powerless and uncaring to save whole swaths of humanity unless someone appeases him through prayer, donations, and religious deployment.

The refreshing reality I discovered in my historical research is that this is a completely warped way of looking at "The Great Commission." The "end to come" Jesus referred to was the coming tribulation he clearly spoke of, that is the destruction of the Temple and Jerusalem in 70 CE (by the Romans) and the end of the age of Temple worship. Going to make disciples of all nations is declaring the good news of the restorative God of love to the nations (Gentiles) wherever one finds themselves. Making disciples is about encouraging all people to follow Jesus' love ethic. Jesus didn't say drop what you're doing and travel to every ethno-linguistic group on earth. Before departing, he told the disciples "So then, off you go."[9] In other words, wherever you go, share the good news with everyone.[10] The good news that we don't need to appease God with religious prayers, donations, sacrifice, or violent retribution, in order to get Him to bless humanity. The reign of God Jesus taught tells us he is already merciful to all without us doing a damn thing. If we do go to a foreign land to share the good news, it's not a transactional message of retribution—you are in danger of going to hell unless you accept [our] Christ and God can't really bless you with his love until you become an evangelical Christian or follower of Jesus. The good news is about sharing the universal love of the always-merciful God that Jesus demonstrated. This God cares for the oppressed, calls the oppressors to account, and promises a day is coming, and has already come, when the playing field is being leveled and all is being restored.

SEVEN

VIOLENCE IN POPULAR THEOLOGY AND AMERICAN CULTURE

THE FOURTH MAJOR TENANT that leads to upholding Christian myths is believing the notion that God justifies violent punishment for sins and advocates for war under certain circumstances. The Old Testament teaches us that God drowned the planet (except for one family) in response to people being evil, that God ordered the Israelites to go to war with the Canaanite tribes and kill every man, woman, child, infant, and animal that breathes in each city without showing mercy at all. The Torah teaches that God commands capital punishment for a variety of religious and immoral sins, including homicide, cursing one's parents, striking one's parents, kidnapping, witchcraft and divination, bestiality, worshiping other gods, violating the Sabbath, child sacrifice, sexual relations outside of marriage for a woman or with another man's wife for a man, incest, and male homosexual intercourse in the context of idolatry or shrine prostitution (by the way, the Torah has no such punishment or any punishment at all for lesbian sexuality). God also commands retributive justice. "And a man who injures his countryman—as he has done, so it shall be done to him, namely, fracture for fracture, eye for eye, tooth for tooth. Just as another person has received injury from him, so it will be given to him" (Leviticus 24:19–21). God is routinely portrayed as using death and retribution to weed out evil influences and as a type of appeasement toward him to bring about divine justice and equilibrium.

Faith in such a God makes it easy for believers to justify violent punishment, death sentences for crimes, and the act of war in various circumstances, even the pettiest. In stark contrast, Jesus teaches people to not reciprocate but rather turn the other cheek, go the second mile (to turn the moral tables on one's adversary), love one's enemies, be kind to the ungrateful and wicked, and have mercy on them just as our heavenly Father does. Despite those admonitions, most modern Christians do not apply Jesus' teachings. Psychological (inhumane imprisonment) and/or violent punishment, death penalties, and war is routinely justified and even applauded.

A BRIEF HISTORY LESSON
ON AMERICAN WARS

We Americans—whatever our religion—tend to routinely justify violence and war as part of a righteous American tradition. We may at times come to realize that not all wars are justified and that in fact some of our wars of history were not good. The Vietnam War, the Iraq War, and the extension of the War in Afghanistan are three that immediately come to mind in this generation. We may also admit that many of our violent conflicts with Native Americans were not exactly righteous. At the end of the day, Americans believe that there are good and bad wars, and we just need to work at ensuring we don't pursue bad wars. There is little passion or conviction to work towards abolishing war.

American historian, social critic, and activist Howard Zinn once gave a talk at Boston University on the three "holy" wars of our country. Author of the best-seller *A People's History of the United States*, Zinn reviewed the popular conceptions of The Revolutionary War, The Civil War, and World War II. He offered a series of historical facts on each that led people to rethink popular support for these wars.[1]

At first glance, it seems outrageous to question the legitimacy of these wars. Each is considered good because they each achieved tremendous advances for our society and the world: independence from colonialism and the emergence of the first modern democracy, the emancipation of slaves and the abolition of slavery, and the defeat of fascism and militarism in Europe and Japan.

Zinn starts to unravel these achievements by inserting some often-ignored facts that bring perspective. First is the human cost. The Revolutionary War killed a relatively small number of Americans, 25,000, compared to today's population and demographics. In proportion to today's numbers, however, it was more around 2.5 million people.

Next, he relayed what John Adams had written that exposed there really wasn't widespread support for this war. It's generally accepted that a third of the country supported it, a third were against it—that is they were *loyalists*—and a third were ambivalent. As a result, it was hard to recruit soldiers for the Continental Army. "People don't naturally rush to war. You have to seduce them; you have to bribe them, coerce them," said Zinn. Soldiers were promised land and compensation, but officers, who were mostly affluent, were treated much better than ordinary foot soldiers. There were several mutinies in George Washington's army as a result. Washington put one down in New Jersey by executing the mutineers.

Not everyone benefited from the war nor the independence that was won. Slaves certainly didn't. Western Native American tribes certainly didn't, as the winning of the war opened up American expansionism that had been checked by British territorial restrictions (although admittedly not put in place for the benefit of indigenous peoples).

Finally, why is it that Canada gained independence from Britain without resorting to a bloody war? Why couldn't American colonists have done the same? The answer is probably because we are too committed to quick fixes that wars and violence promise. We are not naturally inclined to do the slow work of non-violence and peacemaking. Zinn made this case: "Canada is independent of England. They did not fight a bloody war. It took longer. But, you know, sometimes it takes longer if you don't want to kill. Violence is fast. War is fast. And if you don't want killing, you may have to take more time in order to achieve your objective. And actually, when you achieve your objective, it might be achieved in a better way and with better results..."[2]

The Civil War raises the same questions with even more bloody and devastating costs, Zinn explained. Except for the United States, every country in the Western Hemisphere ended slavery without a bloody civil war. Couldn't we have done the same?

Could a slower path of activism, abolitionism, a 19th century Civil Rights Movement, and non-violent strategies have prevented our nation's Civil War and much of the destruction it brought? The war killed 750,000 soldiers from battle or disease (2.5% of the total population) and claimed 55,000 amputations without anesthetic. It was the bloodiest, most brutal war in our history. Proportionally, if 2.5% of the American population died today, 8 million people would be dead.

Good came out of the war, no doubt. Most slaves were freed and slavery abolished, at least on paper. Yet after the war, most former slaves were still under the control of former slaveholders. In other words, they went from slaves to serfs to sharecroppers. "The same white plantation owners who had been their masters when they were slaves were now their masters when they were serfs."[3]

Post-war Reconstruction (rebuilding the South in an equitable way) started fairly well. But in time, there was a great betrayal that went on, explained Zinn. Eventually, the federal government ignored inequalities and stopped enforcing the policy of reconstructing the South to equality. Segregation, Jim Crow laws, and the practice of lynching arose. Presidents violated their oath of office. They did not enforce the 13th and 14th Amendments (ending slavery and bringing equality) and collaborated with southern politicians. The war did not resolve the root problems.

Again, the question must be asked. Why is it that England ended slavery without the need for war? In fact, slavery was ended in every other country in the Western Hemisphere without a bloody civil war. Abolishing slavery without the Civil War would have assuredly taken much longer and required a larger, sustained, and coordinated abolitionist and political movement, but that is what happened in most countries. "Partly due to the sheer size of the Atlantic slave trade and the enormous volume of capital and human energy expended in maintaining the trade, the abolition movement took over a century to complete. A complex web of humanitarian, economic, and political factors, each supporting the others, served to put an end to the slave trade and then to slavery itself outside of Africa by the end of the nineteenth century."[4]

Finally, there's World War II. Much good came out of World War II—the defeat of a crazed, diabolical dictator and mass murderer, Adolf Hitler, and the eradication of European fascism. But as Zinn explains, whereas that is true, it's also not that simple. We did terrible things too. "In the course of a war, the good guys become the bad guys. War poisons everybody. War corrupts everybody."

Both sides, Nazis and Allies committed atrocities. We are routinely taught about the atrocities of the Nazis. What we don't know and are not taught is that the Allies bombed the hell out of combatants and non-combatants alike, which of course includes the elderly, women, children, and the unborn.

Howard Zinn himself was a bombardier in the U.S. Army Air Corps and admits his naivety during his service, not examining who he was bombing. It is very impersonal to bomb at 10, 20, or 30,000 feet (roughly the cruising altitude of a commercial plane or jet). Soldiers are not trained to think but only to obey. Zinn explains:

> I dropped bombs on Germany, on Hungary, on Czechoslo-vakia—even on a little town in France three weeks before the war was to end, when everybody knew the war was to end and we didn't need to drop any more bombs, but we dropped bombs. On a little town in France, we were trying out napalm, the first use of napalm in the European theater. I think by now you all know what napalm is. One of the ugliest little weapons. But trying it out, and adding metals. And who knows what reason, what complex of reasons, led us to bomb a little town in France, when everybody knew the war was ending? And yes, there were German soldiers there, hanging around. They weren't doing anything, weren't bothering anybody, but they're there, and it gives us a good excuse to bomb. We'll kill the Germans, we'll kill some Frenchmen, too. What does it matter? It's a good war. We're the good guys.[5]

Another example is the Allies raid on Dresden, Germany in early 1945 (of which Kurt Vonnegut wrote in his book, *Slaughterhouse-Five*) that resulted in 35,000 civilian deaths in one night. Altogether during the war, a total of 400,000 or more German civilians perished by Allied bombing. In Japan, the U.S. Army Air Corps in one long night in March 1945, firebombed Tokyo and killed up to 100,000 people, mostly civilians. One million people were left homeless becoming "the most destructive single air attack in human history."[6] Altogether, up to 330,000 Japanese civilians were killed by U.S. air power.

The two atomic bombs the U.S. dropped on Hiroshima and Nagasaki in August 1945, killed around 110,000 people, of which only around 20,000 were Japanese military. This is not counting the harmful effects and death by radiation that impacted bomb survivors in the form of increased rates of cancer, leukemia, and chronic disease over the generations.

After the war, researchers discovered the Japanese were ready to end the war even before Hiroshima and Nagasaki. Historians surmise it might have taken only a few months but would have happened fairly quickly. Zinn also cited this fact. "We didn't have to invade Japan in order for Japan to surrender. Our own official investigative team, the Strategic Bombing Survey, which went into Japan right after the war, interviewed all the high Japanese military, civilian officials, and their conclusion was Japan was ready to end the war. Maybe not the next week, maybe in two months, maybe in three months."

> Based on a detailed investigation of all the facts, and supported by the testimony of the surviving Japanese leaders involved, it is the Survey's opinion that certainly prior to 31 December 1945, and in all probability prior to 1 November 1945, Japan would have surrendered even if the atomic bombs had not been dropped, even if Russia had not entered the war, and even if no invasion had been planned or contemplated.[7]

Did World War II rid the world of totalitarianism and fascism? No. In fact, the introduction of the atomic bomb led to an arms race during the Cold War between the greatest super powers and then globally. At the peak of tensions, the total number of nuclear weapons based in Europe reached 7,300 in 1971.[8] And of course, we know that the second world war did not rid the world of militarism, racism, and fascism. Winning a war only pushes these evils below the surface, it does not eliminate them.

Zinn concluded, "This notion of violent revenge and retaliation is something we have to get rid of... Every war is a war against children."[9]

What could have been an alternative way of addressing the Axis threat without war? Prior to and during the war, there was a German resistance movement. They leaked information about ill treatment and deportations of Jews to garner public support. Anti-Nazi activist and Lutheran pastor, Dietrich Bonhoeffer, was among those who uncovered this information and helped lead an underground campaign to launch a coup against Hitler and to end the war. There was a coalition of civil servants, trade union officials, and German military prepared to carry out this plan.

Their goal was to gain support from Western Allies as well as assurances the Allies would negotiate a peace with the German government once Hitler and his influence was squelched. The "resistance" needed to be certain of this before attempting any coup.[10] But Winston Churchill and President Roosevelt did not back this regime-change plan.

Starting in January 1943, they and the Allies insisted that Germany surrender unconditionally.[11] They remained committed to a military solution to stop Hitler. But what if the Allies had supported such a coup instead? Could the war, or at least much of it, have possibly been averted by a non-military movement to disrupt the Nazi threat from within? Later, in Chapter 11, we'll look at some concrete examples of successful nonviolent and non-military tactics of fighting violent oppression, one being the Danes who fought Nazism without taking up arms.

HOW CHRISTIANS ENDORSE VIOLENCE

A theology of violence leads to endorsing acts of violence or becoming violent. In the risk of being overly redundant, this point can't be made enough: If one believes God once drowned all of humanity (sparing only one family), ordered Israelite armies to kill their enemies (including non-combatants, the elderly, women, children, and the unborn), instituted capital punishment for various sinful and evil acts, praised people who obeyed the stipulations to "treat the Midianites as enemies and kill them" (Numbers 25:17) or who punished the disobedient or idolators with violence (Joshua 7 and Numbers 25), then it's easy to justify violence in the name of God today. It's easy to justify our country's "holy wars" and other forms of violence. It's easy to attribute violent events that happen in our country to God's punishment of us for abandoning the faith, disobedience, or support for gay marriage and/or abortion.

If one believes God could not forgive humanity for their sins unless an innocent, first century Palestinian Rabbi named Jesus was tortured and murdered through crucifixion as a substitute for what sinful humanity deserved and that one has to believe in that atonement narrative in order to avoid eternal damnation, then it's easy to rationalize violent acts of punishment today.

In 1991, as the U.S. entered the Gulf War, Brian Zahnd recalls how "America's pastor (Billy Graham), had prayed with America's president (George H. W. Bush), and assured him all of this was keeping with God's purposes."[12] As an evangelical pastor at the time, Zahnd excitedly watched Operation Desert Storm on CNN (complete with friends and pizza) as it presented the bombing of Baghdad in retaliation of Saddam Hussein's invasion of Kuwait. Years later Zahnd confessed he felt God whisper to him saying, "That was your worst sin."[13]

In 2001, evangelical Christian President George W. Bush called for war on Al Qaeda as retribution for 9/11 and eventually called for war with Iraq, which had nothing to do with the attack on New York. He later justified torture techniques, including waterboarding (a form of torture), of suspected Al Qaeda detainees.[14] Many evangelical Christians did not object. A violent retribution mentality reigns in most of evangelicalism.

> "If more good people, had conceal carry permits, then we could end those Muslims before they walked in and killed..."
> — Jerry Fallwell, Jr.[15]

> "Jesus is not Mother Teresa, he is William Wallace. He is a hell raiser, he started arguments and fights everywhere he went."
> — Jimmy Meeks of Sheepdog Seminars[16]

> "In Revelation, Jesus is a prize-fighter with a tattoo down His leg, a sword in His hand and the commitment to make someone bleed. That is the guy I can worship. I cannot worship the hippie, diaper, halo Christ because I cannot worship a guy I can beat up." — Former Mars Hill Church pastor Mark Driscoll[17]

Decades-long war correspondent, Chris Hedges, made the following observation about evangelical chaplains who serve in the military in war time: "Military chaplains, a majority of whom are evangelical Christians, defend the life of the unborn, tout America as a Christian nation, support the death penalty, and eagerly bless the wars in Iraq and Afghanistan as holy crusades. The hollowness of their morality, the staggering disconnect between the values they claim to promote, is ripped open by war."[18] Evangelical chaplains would justify a soldier spending a military tour killing people in a war zone as a god-ordained pursuit but condemn the same soldier for finding comfort from the horrors of war by spending a few minutes with a prostitute.

Many Christians believe the right to bear arms, to own modern weapons such as handguns, rifles, and semi-automatic firearms, is a God-given right. Wayne LaPierre of the National Rifle Association once said the Second Amendment was a right "granted by God to all Americans as our American birthright."[19] In 2015, after a shooting in San Bernardino, California, then Liberty University president Jerry Falwell, Jr., made that statement cited above: "I've always thought that if more good people had concealed-carry permits, then we could end those Muslims before they walked in..."[20] Shane Claiborne couldn't help but make the following observation: "The irony is you can't have a beer at Liberty [University], but you can have a gun." After a 2017 shooting in a Southern Baptist Church near San Antonio, Texas, the pastor of the First Baptist Church of Dallas, Robert Jeffress, confessed on *Fox and Friends* that he knew his congregants were carrying weapons which made him feel more secure.[21]

Perhaps an extreme example, yet fitting the sentiment of many Second Amendment Christians, is The Sanctuary Church near Scranton, Pennsylvania, led by Pastor Sean Moon, son of the late Reverend Sun Myung Moon. After the elder Moon died in 2012, his Unification Church split. Two of his eight sons began a new church. A Washington Post profile, entitled "Locked and Loaded for the Lord," explains how the younger Moon's followers "are eagerly awaiting the end times. And they are armed." By cleverly attributing the book of Revelation's depiction of Christ and his eventual rule of the kingdom "with a rod of iron," Sean Moon justifies the importance of believers owning a gun.

Although Revelation was written long before the invention of firearms, Pastor Moon concluded that the "rod of iron" was Bible-speak for the AR-15 and that Christ, not being a "tyrant," will need armed sovereigns to help him keep the peace in his kingdom. As a result, a recent Sanctuary Church news release had noted that "blessed couples are requested" to bring with them to the upcoming Book of Life ceremony an AR-15 semiautomatic rifle "or equivalents." This was unfortunate timing for the Church: The next day a young man walked into Marjory Stoneman Douglas High School in Parkland, Florida and killed 17 people with an AR-15. Additional mass shooters used that same model rifle to carry out mass murders in Las Vegas, Orlando, San Bernardino, California, and other cities.[22]

> That latest tragedy was freshly imprinted on millions of minds, among them Pastor Sean's. He eased into his hour-long Sunday morning sermon by reminding everyone of what President Trump had pointed out after the Parkland shooting: "He said if the teachers were armed, they would have shot the hell out of that guy. This is the first time we've heard a president talk like that. This is God's grace, folks.[23]

AMERICA'S VIOLENT RHETORIC AND JUSTIFICATIONS

Violent and war-mongering rhetoric is common in our leaders' political discourse. At the Republican National Convention in 2016, Donald Trump confidently proclaimed, "We are going to defeat the barbarians, and we are going to defeat them fast." On August 8, 2017, after North Korea successfully tested intercontinental ballistic missiles, Trump responded, "North Korea best not make any more threats to the United States. They will be met with fire and fury like the world has never seen." At the United Nations a month later, he reiterated that "the United States has great strength and patience, but if it is forced to defend itself or its allies, we will have no choice but to totally destroy North Korea. Rocket Man is on a suicide mission."[24]

Of course, this war-rife rhetoric is not just among conservatives and Republicans. At the 2016 Democratic National Convention, the audience heard these words from General John R. Allen, "And to our enemies, we will pursue you, as only America can. You will fear us."[25] Excluding some calls for opposing "unjust" wars like Vietnam, both political parties generally support the concept of America going to war, whether it's our country's "holy wars," the Revolutionary War, the Civil War, and World War II, or recent wars such as the Gulf War (under George H.W. Bush), Iraq (under George W. Bush), Afghanistan (under George W. Bush and Barak Obama), or the attack on Libya (under Barak Obama and Secretary of State Hillary Clinton).

Our modern American religion, whether fueled by conservative theology or merely nationalistic ideals, leans toward violence. The justification? The major one is the myth that America is raised up by God for special purposes. That America is being used by God to both bring the gospel to the nations, and to protect the world and democracy through militaristic means. As Brian Zahnd observes, therefore, although it is not directly preached, it is logically surmised where "[i]n the Christian mind, a trillion-dollar military is also connected to the purposes of Christ in the world."

Preston Sprinkle, a conservative biblical scholar who believes in the infallibility of the Bible, wrote the book, *Fight: A Christian Case for Non-Violence*. Although I disagree with his view of the Bible (in which he downplays the Joshua narrative of the destruction of whole cities as either hyperbole or partly figurative but still accurate in telling what God commanded the Israelites), he makes a strong case for pacifism as the proper response to Jesus' teachings. He also admits that his own evangelical tradition is dangerously militaristic. He cites Hal Lindsey (author of the Left Behind series), Jerry Falwell, Jr., William Boykin (an evangelical military general), and Wayne Grudem all supporting the notion that "America's military [is] an extension of God's fight against evil."[26] In addition, he admits that although the Iraq war was the most opposed war in America's history (even more so than Vietnam), "churchgoers were more supportive than non-churchgoers and evangelicals were the most supportive of all."[27]

When you think, by default, God is always on your side as a church or a country, you develop a type of theology or nationalistic mindset that becomes absolute. Rather than searching for truth with humility, people begin to speak for God with arrogance. They make the sovereignty of God their own. Especially with militant nationalism, whose goal is protecting a country or region from its enemies, violence is justified to keep things in order and remain superior as people think they are doing God's will. People will rally around a common enemy or scapegoat—something or someone to blame for our problems—and its destruction brings us peace and security.

Such was the plight of detainees in the "War on Terror." Human Rights Watch reported scores of violent abuse against them. Since 2002, at least 780 people from around 40 countries (mostly Afghanistan, Saudi Arabia, Yemen, and Pakistan, but also a variety of countries in the Middle East, Africa, Europe, and Asia, including China) have been imprisoned at Guantanamo Bay. At least 40 of those have been for more than 10 years. Most of them were never charged or brought to trial. About 540 were released to home or third countries under the Bush administration, almost 150 under Obama, and one under Trump.[28]

In 2004, CBS News reported on abuse of prisoners at the US-run section of the Abu Ghraib prison in Iraq. These are some of the abuses they and other US-held prisoners endured:

> Detainees in US-run facilities in Afghanistan, Iraq, and Guantanamo Bay endured prolonged mistreatment, sometimes for weeks and even months. This included painful 'stress' positions; prolonged nudity; sleep, food, and water deprivation; exposure to extreme cold or heat; and total darkness with loud music blaring for weeks at a time. Other abuses in Iraq included beatings, near suffocation, sexual abuse, and mock executions. At Guantanamo Bay, some detainees were forced to sit in their own excrement, and some were sexually humiliated by female interrogators. In Afghanistan, prisoners were chained to walls and shackled in a manner that made it impossible to lie down or sleep, with restraints that caused their hands and wrists to swell up or bruise.[29]

The Bush administration claimed these abuses were isolated incidents, yet this was disputed by groups like the Red Cross, Amnesty International, Human Rights Watch, and the Research University of Amsterdam.[30]

The Evangelical Jericho March

What could be considered the epitome of accepted violent retribution against military, ideological, political, or criminal enemies, was the reaction of certain evangelical Christian leaders after Trump lost the election in November 2020. Eric Metaxas, prominent Christian author, radio host, former featured speaker at the National Prayer Breakfast, and once a speaker at Christian Seattle Pacific University's business breakfast, was the master of ceremonies at a Christian event in December 2020[31] (Metaxas ironically also wrote a book about Dietrich Bonhoeffer that was criticized by Bonhoeffer scholars).[32]

The event, aptly named Jericho March, had speakers who said Trump had been betrayed and his election stolen. Amidst the pseudo-spiritual prayers of many like Michelle Bachman, who also addressed the crowd, some specifically called for violence to suppress "this insurrection" and the supposed election fraud carried out by the "evil" Democrats and liberals that blocked Trump's re-election. Since many evangelicals believed God had put his stamp of approval on Trump, that "Christian" prophets had prophesized his first election and his re-election, and that God is two-faced, it was easy for them to swallow these types of frauds and calls for violent sacrifice at the Jericho March:

> President Trump has been betrayed at every step of the way ... he needs to invoke the Insurrection Act and suppress this insurrection ... You can be called up as the militia to support and defend the Constitution ... if he does not do it now while he's commander in chief, we're gonna have to do it ourselves later in a much more desperate, much more bloody war. Let's get it on now while he's still commander in chief.[33]

Metaxas can be seen in the background of this speaker quoted above. In retrospect, you can see that the speaker is actually the far-right, anti-government Oath Keepers' leader Stewart Rhodes, who later was convicted of seditious conspiracy for his part in the January 6th attack on the Capital. Other speakers included Alex Jones, who spread the conspiracy theory that the Sandy Hook School shooting of children was staged (and was later found guilty in a lawsuit brought against him by parents), and General Michael Flynn, who pleaded guilty of making false statements to the FBI and pleaded the Fifth when asked by the January 6th Committee if he thought the violence on January 6th was justified. You have to wonder why the evangelical movement is now inviting such people to speak at their events. As for Rhodes, this may have been before he was convicted of seditious conspiracy, but he clearly called for a "bloody war" at an evangelical endorsed public event.

It gets worse. On a related podcast that same month, Metaxas defended the "stop the steal" effort of Donald Trump and continued hyping the lies that Trump's election was stolen, despite having no evidence presented in court. He claimed "stealing" the election was a violent deed, accused those who disagreed with him to be like Germans who didn't stand up to Hitler, and called for fighting this evil "to the last drop of blood."

> It's like stealing the heart and soul of America. It's like holding a rusty knife to the throat of Lady Liberty...This is evil. It's like somebody has been raped or murdered...This is like that times a thousand...Everybody who is not hopped up about this...you are the Germans that looked the other way when Hitler was preparing to do what he was preparing to do. Unfortunately, I don't see how you can see it any other way...So who cares what I can prove in the courts? This is right. This happened, and I am going to do anything I can to uncover this horror, this evil...We need to fight to the death, to the last drop of blood, because it's worth it.[34]

These words were said weeks before a real insurrection occurred on January 6th, when hundreds of Trump supporters stormed the capital using various weapons (clubs, battering rams, etc.) and other modes of attack to break windows and barriers and harm capital police. They were said weeks before they called to hang Vice President Mike Pence for inaction against the formal vote of electors to declare the actual winner of the election, Joe Biden.

Mainstream evangelical Christian leaders like Metaxas and their invited guest speakers alleged the "stealing" of the election of Trump was worse than murder, that not fighting this injustice, despite a lack of concrete evidence, was like appeasing Hitler, and that we need to fight it, not just metaphorically, but "to the last drop of blood." They called for Trump to invoke an emergency act and organize a militia to fight this supposed grave injustice. If he didn't, Christians would have to do it themselves "in a much more desperate, much more bloody war." This dangerous rhetoric was all in the background in the minds of many evangelical Christians and Trump supporters when Trump made his speech on January 6th promoting, "We need to fight like hell or we're not going to have a country anymore."

The Attack on the Capital and Other Justifications

The fruit of January 6, 2021, was a trampling mob of hundreds of Trump supporters storming the capital. Utilizing pepper spray, flag poles, makeshift battering rams, stun guns, fire extinguishers, baseball bats, and hand-to-hand combat, they violently attacked police and reporters who were protecting the U.S. Capital and Congress. A gallows was erected on the grounds, and several lawmakers were singled out in order to capture and harm them, including Nancy Pelosi. Chants of "Hang Mike Pence!" rang out. The Capital building locked down and lawmakers and staff were evacuated. The mob occupied and vandalized the building for several hours. Over 140 police officers were injured and several from the mob itself. Five people died, including one police officer a day later.[35]

It could have been worse. Placed the night before, pipe bombs were found right outside the offices of the Democratic National Committee and the Republican National Committee. Moreover, Molotov Cocktails were found in a vehicle near the Capital.

As of this writing 727 people were charged with federal crimes, including assaulting and impeding law enforcement officers, engaging in physical violence, unlawful and violent entry, obstructing an official proceeding, and disorderly conduct. Seventy-five of these were charged with "using a deadly or dangerous weapon or causing serious bodily injury to an officer."

Two Capital Police officers and two DC Metropolitan Police officers testified before Congress. Capital Police Sgt. Aquilino Gonell reported, "[t]he physical violence we experienced was horrific and devastating. My fellow officers and I were punched, kicked, shoved, sprayed with chemical irritants, and even blinded with eye-damaging lasers by a violent mob. I was particularly shocked at seeing the insurrectionists violently attack us with the very American flag that they claimed they sought to protect."

DC Metropolitan Police Officer Michael Fanone reported he had been "grabbed, beaten, tased, all while being called a traitor to my country...[I] was at risk of being stripped of and killed with my own firearm as I heard chants of 'Kill him with his own gun.' I can still hear those words in my head today."

Even after the January 6th insurrection, many evangelical and conservative Christians continued to support Trump, believe the Big Lie about the election, and backed retributive narratives. Known for being a prominent national leader in the charismatic, evangelical movement, pastor Che Ahn (my pastor when I lived in Pasadena, California in the 1980s and who presided at my wedding) still advanced support for Trump despite all that transpired. Trump's appointment of conservative Supreme Court justices (in the hopes of overturning *Roe v Wade*) is all that mattered to people like Ahn and most evangelicals. In a sermon he delivered just eleven days after January 6th (*All Lives are Sacred*, January 17, 2021), Ahn praised Trump. He believed Trump won the election and that God had raised up Trump to extend mercy to our nation. He also said that Christians who voted for Joe Biden were spiritually deceived (read: demonic deception) and needed to repent.

Regarding abortion, there are no gray areas with people like Ahn. If you aren't one hundred percent "pro-life" and if you don't support only politicians that say they are pro-life, including supporting those who don't allow exceptions for rape and incest, then you are directly supporting murderers. In his sermon, Ahn warned (citing the theology of the violent God of the Old Testament) that those "murderers of the unborn" would have to be executed in order to right the injustice and prevent our land and nation from being cursed. Ahn states, "Whoever sheds the blood of man by man shall his blood be shed, for God made man in his own image. Here's the penalty if you shed innocent blood—life for life. Here we have the foundation of capital punishment coming into our legal system. If you shed innocent blood, [it's] so heinous to God that your blood will have to be shed. If it doesn't happen, then justice will not be met. He's a God of justice...But look what he says, and this is what's really stunning here. It's not just to meet justice, but you see, if this does not go punished, it leaves a curse on the land. The whole nation is cursed."[36]

Ahn continues, "There's no sacrifice [that] can be made for the land, for the blood that is shed on it [from abortion]. Except by the blood of the man who shed it. In other words, there's going to be a curse on the land, polluting the land, talking about a curse on the land [from America legalizing abortion]. The only way that could be done [sacrifice the guilty for the land] is by justice, by the man who committed murder has to be executed. There has to be capital punishment. Today we say put them in the electric chair."[37]

Evangelicals like Ahn ignore the violence of January 6th, Trump's complicity in it, his failure to try to stop it, his blatant lies about the election being stolen, and the calls for revenge by Trump supporting insurrectionists, in order to carry on their crusade against abortion.

In a Master's thesis for Georgia State University, David Sharp evaluated this very sermon of Ahn's to make the point how certain evangelical leaders twist both scripture and political facts to push their grievances and religious agenda.

> Ahn's sermon is arguably the most constitutive out of the entire corpus, using victimage, grievance, and rhetorical questioning as the catalyst for engaging his audience into action more than any other pastor. Ahn is also far more likely to spread falsehoods and mischaracterize his political targets. He constantly paints believers as victims and dehumanizes the non-believers that grievance them.[38]

In that sermon, Ahn quoted Proverbs to make the case for God's hatred of abortion. Proverbs 6 states that there are seven things that God hates, but Ahn only cited one: "hands that shed innocent blood." He took the verse out of context and failed to mention the other detestable items. The entire passage states, "There are six things the Lord hates, seven that are detestable to him: haughty eyes, a lying tongue, hands that shed innocent blood, a heart that devises wicked schemes, feet that are quick to rush into evil, a false witness who pours out lies and a person who stirs up conflict in the community" (Proverbs 6:16–19).

It's ironic that the other six personas on the list—the prideful, liars, evil schemers, those quick to do evil, false witnesses, and those who stir up conflict—are all character traits one could easily argue of which Trump is guilty. Ahn filters out scripture that weakens his case that the former president was a blessing for the country. He was so fixated on the abortion issue that he couldn't see the forest for the trees. Trump regularly committed all those detestable sins. And nearly 1,000 of his supporters on January 6th, just eleven days before this sermon, had taken part in or contributed towards violence that "shed innocent blood" of capital police officers, while Trump sat on his ass for 187 minutes not lifting a finger to stop them.

This reveals that the anti-abortion crusade includes elements of violent sacrificial religion. In other words, "prolife" evangelicals scapegoat anyone who remotely sides with or is pro-choice on abortion, call them murderers, and threaten to back capital punishment for perpetrators, even while ignoring other abominable sins that God hates when they are committed by their own.

An Important Word About Abortion

In the late 1980s, I became involved in a "pro-life," anti-abortion movement called Operation Rescue (OR). It recruited members by claiming abortion was the same as murder. Its leader, Randall Terry, kept saying repeatedly, "If you believe abortion is murder, act like it's murder." I heard him speak at The Church of the Nazarene in Sierra Madre, California (at the time James Dobson's church). OR promoted non-violent sit-ins at abortion clinics to be the appropriate action to take. This is how I was persuaded to take part in "rescues" and risk arrest, which happened when I was a member of Che Ahn's first church in Pasadena, California. Granted, OR taught non-violent techniques at these sit-ins. Yet, at the same time, they accused abortionists, women who had abortions, or anyone who supported abortions as essentially murderers. Pro-life activists routinely called abortion in America, The American Holocaust. They and most of the movement promoted laws against abortion that would make abortion homicide and took no notice of those repercussions. They agreed that homicide could mean capital punishment and to use existing law to sentence people for murder or accessory to murder. Touting themselves as non-violent resisters to evil, like the civil rights movement, their goal wasn't conducive to non-violence. At the end of the day, they/we wanted abortion made illegal with laws that punished those for getting or performing abortions. This could include imprisonment for women who had abortions, and even, as Che Ahn appeared to support, executions for all convicted abortion providers.[39]

Treating abortion as murder is a very dangerous practice. It motivates those who claim they are taking "justice" in their own hands while they themselves murder doctors and workers and carry out bomb and arson attacks at abortion clinics.[40] It leads the "righteous" to try to equalize the law, so that suddenly the same punishments for homicide apply to abortion. It leads people to ignore exceptions that harm girls and women, such as rape, incest, serious congenital diseases, and dangerous pregnancies that put mothers at risk of losing their lives. It also pits people against each other and cultivates a culture war where one side is the scapegoat to the other self-righteous side. Moreover, it drives people to reject anyone's ideas on the basis of them being pro-abortion (i.e., all Democrats) and accept or tolerate any ideas as long as they are pro-life (i.e., President Trump).

Gerald Thompson, who is pro-life, makes the case why abortion should not be considered murder in an article entitled, *A Pro-Life Attorney Explains Why Abortion is Not Murder (So Please Stop Saying It Is)*. Analyzing from the perspective of science, law, theology, and scripture, Thompson argues that life begins before conception (sperm and eggs are forms of human life), that there is a difference between "human life" and when that life becomes a fully formed "human being" with legal rights, and that an unborn fetus has potential but not personhood. The fetus does not have the major attributes of what believers call, "the image of God." The fetus has no ability to reason, express thoughts, communicate, be creative, express personality, or have moral awareness. Scripture differentiates between God breathing into a human to create a living being and God creating an animal living thing. With these arguments and the practical legal problems it brings, Thompson eviscerates the claim that by definition abortion is murder.[41]

If you think abortion is tragic, like I (and Thompson) do, there is much you can do to minimize abortions, without saying pro-choice advocates have blood on their hands.[42] Overturning Roe v. Wade was not the answer. Women seeking abortions have only reduced slightly since June 2022. Criminalizing abortion and punishing patients and providers is not the answer. Ironically, abortion numbers have significantly dropped since 1990 during the Roe v. Wade era. Between 1990 and 2016 they dropped by approximately 45%. The abortion rate has declined by about half between 1981 and 2020.[43]

The best way to make abortion rare is to fight its root causes. Most women get abortions because they are economically unable to raise a child and/or they have relationship problems. Economic empowerment of women and more social safety nets would make a huge difference in curtailing abortion rates. You would think that a consistent pro-life ethic would support that politically and socially. Moreover, probably the number one way to minimize abortion is to teach men to be more responsible with how they treat women and by men taking most if not all of the responsibility for birth control. While arguing adoption is not as simple as it seems, Gabrielle Stanley Blair, in her book, *Ejaculate Responsibly: A Whole New Way to Think About Abortion*, makes a persuasive argument "for moving the abortion debate away from controlling and legislating women's bodies and instead direct the focus on men's lack of accountability in preventing unwanted pregnancies."[44] There is an unfair burden placed on women to prevent pregnancy, most birth control for women has painful side effects, and men, who are fertile 100 percent of the time, are largely off the hook for preventing pregnancy and living with its consequences.

Tribal Christianity in The Culture Wars

None of this is really surprising if you step back and look at the history of American fundamentalist and evangelical Christianity over the years. In her book, *Jesus and John Wayne: How White Evangelicals Corrupted a Faith and Fractured a Nation*, Kristin Kobes Du Mez argues that what we're seeing today is a fulfillment of evangelical values that have been around for decades. When I first came into the evangelical church in the 1980s, there was a rallying cry against the evils of *secular humanism* and how it had influenced the widespread acceptance of things like abortion and sexual promiscuity. Prior to that, the looming evil was communism. Gradually, every year or so, another rallying cry would arise from the pulpit that would drive the congregation to fear another threat to the faithful. Feminism, gay rights, radical Islam, Democrats, socialism, liberals, the "attack" on Christmas, and currently threats of Critical Race Theory, "wokeness," and, for many, government-mandated masks and vaccinations that perceived to restrict worship and religious freedom.

Even if one could surmise that some of these concerns are legitimate (historically, we discover they are not with the exception of fascist communism and Islamic terrorism and now domestic terrorism), their answer to these supposed threats is not theological (to love their enemies and overcome evil by building bridges and doing good), but rather aggressively political. The response is to attack and malign one's enemies politically or resort to violence to stop the perceived evil. When Donald Trump came on the scene in 2015 and courted the evangelical movement for votes, he became a perfect tool for many evangelicals to use, in the same way that evangelicals became a tool that Trump used. A symbiotic, political relationship arose that brought a new level of corruption, hatred of the other, violent rhetoric, and in the end, violence itself.

Don't let the fact that this phenomenon of creeping political violence can happen on the secular left as much as the religious right cloud your thinking. This is not the time to run off and list a litany of "What About-isms" to justify these events. This is the time to face the music of a faith gone bad.

To be sure, we should acknowledge and condemn the rioting and violence that stemmed from some of the Black Lives Matter protests (and black leaders, many communities, and top Democrats did), but we must tread lightly. This is not an apples-to-apples comparison. It was wrong when BLM protests of social injustice and police brutality veered off from being peaceful to include bullying, looting, rioting, and violence. By all accounts, the protests were mostly peaceful, but sometimes peaceful movements are hijacked by violence. This is part of the problem with America's retributive tendencies. It always has been. During the 1960s, Martin Luther King, Jr., advocated for peaceful, non-violent strategies for fighting for civil rights. But not everyone was as committed. Not everyone who protests social injustice is committed to peace and non-violence.

Religious leaders need to condemn both the retributive, hateful rhetoric and the violence that stems from these examples and call it what it is: a faith gone bad. The same way that Democratic Representative James Clyburn of South Carolina did in the wake of the BLM protests that went bad. "We have to make sure we do not allow ourselves to play the other person's game. Peaceful protest is our game. Violence is their game. Purposeful protest is our game. This looting and rioting, that's their game. We cannot allow ourselves to play their game. [Our purpose] is to make a better country, a better world, for those who must come after us. Breaking out a window will not contribute to that. Setting a fire, throwing stones at police officers, that's destructive behavior, which will not contribute to anything that will make this a better country and make a better future for our children and our grandchildren."[45]

A Prolife Evangelical Questions the Gun Culture

At some point, pro-life activist Robert Schenk, who had been active in the same anti-abortion organization I was, Operation Rescue, began to see a contradiction in his own worldview much like I did. When 12 people were killed and three injured in a mass shooting at Washington Navy Yard in 2013 (down the street from where he lived), he decided he had to learn more about American gun culture. He met an African American mother who lost her teenage son to gun violence (Jordan Davis in 2012). The shooter was not initially charged because of Florida's Stand Your Ground law, which allows those who feel a reasonable threat of death or bodily injury to "meet force with force" rather than retreat. What constitutes a "reasonable threat" turned out to be entirely subjective. Four black teenagers in a car with no guns but blaring loud music was all it took for the law to at least theoretically apply in the shooter's first trial, which the judge ruled a mistrial.

Schenk's research also revealed that violence directed toward abortion providers had become fairly common. Several murders of abortion providers or workers had occurred in the 1990s and, as of 2015, at least 8 people had been killed by anti-abortion activists, another 17 people were victims of attempted murders, and many others were threatened by 42 bombings and 186 arsons of abortion clinics. He knew his former organization, Operation Rescue, had a nonviolent philosophy, but he wondered if they still had gone too far. A widow of one doctor killed recently publicly declared that she believed the rhetoric of organizations like OR incited violence against her husband. Remember, this is the organization that insists that abortion is murder. Schenk asked himself, "Can good people come together and yet contribute to bad outcomes?"

He also wondered why his own prolife movement was not consistently pro-life. He asked questions like: *Why aren't we also against a lax gun culture and the ease it is to obtain guns, particularly semi-automatic weapons? Why don't we advocate to always err on the side of preserving life? Why don't we trust God to protect us more than having a gun at our side? How can we be both prolife and pro-gun, seemingly without supporting any constraints to owning dangerous guns or at least requiring scrutiny and mandatory training? Why are evangelical Christian leaders absent in the conversation to bring ethical answers to gun violence?*

He discovered that two of his own staff members had conceal-carry permits. When he interviewed a group of fellow evangelical pastors, including the then-president of OR, Troy Newman, he heard a slew of pat, simple solutions to the problem of gun violence that didn't sit well with him. They were answers that took no notice of Jesus' teachings. Most of the pastors were gun owners who advocated for the use of guns to protect innocent human life. They even tied the justification for owning guns to the concept of the Israelites using weapons to take the Promise Land (the story of Joshua). But they were against most gun control measures. "The surest way to stop a bad guy with a gun is a good guy with a gun" was a common refrain. Newman even said we need people in our congregations armed.

What they didn't see were the points that Schenk was making. As Christians, they were called to love the bad guy too. They were ignoring the fact that God's love extends to the bad actor and the criminal. Moreover, it's one thing to own a gun and another to be well-trained in gun responsibility and only own a gun that fits its purpose, something they thought was optional. According to Schenk, it seemed like they were saying, "All you need is Jesus and the gospel to convert people, and a side arm to protect you from evil people." But it was based on fear and self-righteousness.

In January 2023 I interviewed Schenck on my podcast/videocast (The Spiritual Brewpub). To my utter shock and dismay, he shared a new product that has been successfully marketed to conservative Christians. It's a leather-bound Bible cover that is designed, not for protecting a Bible from wear and tear and keeping Bible-study notes, but for holding a semi-automatic handgun and an additional ammunition magazine.[46] The company that sells it, Garrison Grip, calls it the "Holy Bible Gun Case" and brags that it's "a very popular item." It says Holy Bible on the front and has a silver or gold cross embedded on the spine. If your gun won't fit into this cover, you can always buy a larger Bible Case/Day Planner, which also includes a decorative cross on the front and on the zipper handle.[47] This is the prime object metaphor for the two-faced god worshiped by many Christians.

In addition to my interview, you can see Robert Schenk's narrative and many of these interviews and conversations on film. He helped produce a 2015 documentary about his full story of becoming consistently pro-life and joining gun-control safety advocates, like the mother of Jordan Davis. It's called *The Armor of Light*.[48]

Sadly, just seven years later, we know more from other mass-violence incidents like the Uvalde, Texas, Robb Elementary School shooting in 2022, which killed 19 students and two teachers. Uvalde proves the claim that good people with guns stops bad people with guns is a myth. It might happen rarely, but it overwhelmingly fails. At Uvalde, a cadre of trained police-officer good guys had guns, and it took 77 minutes to take down one 18-year-old with a gun. A review of the final report by the Texas House Committee relays how even with training and equipment, the good guys can fail. How much more should we doubt that average citizens with guns can solve gun violence?

> It [the report] explains how the gunman, who investigators believe had never fired a gun before May 24, was able to stockpile military-style rifles, accessories and ammunition without arousing suspicion from authorities, then enter a supposedly secure school unimpeded and indiscriminately kill children and adults.
>
> In total, 376 law enforcement officers—a force larger than the garrison that defended the Alamo—descended upon the school in a chaotic, uncoordinated scene that lasted for more than an hour. The group was devoid of clear leadership, basic communications and sufficient urgency to take down the gunman, the report says.[49]

OTHER CULTURAL AND POLITICAL VIOLENCE IN AMERICAN SOCIETY

One of the unintended consequences (and sometimes intended) of endorsing violence and spouting violent rhetoric is violent outbursts of private citizens toward a manufactured or real evil. That was true for the January 6th insurrection, it happens within the violent streak of the anti-abortion "prolife" movement, and with those who use violence and destruction of property in the name of pursuing civil rights. But it also expresses itself in other arenas.

For example, the LGBTQ community is often scapegoated by right-wing Christians as a bunch of "pedophiles" who are "grooming" children to "sexualize" them and "recruit" them into the LGBTQ community.[50] Despite this being a ridiculous claim, it inevitably leads to a retributive backlash against the LGBTQ community. In 2022, rumors began spreading on social media that providers at Boston Children's Hospital were performing gender affirming surgeries on patients younger than 18, which hospital authorities said was untrue. In 2022, a Texas man was charged for threatening a Boston doctor who provides care to the transgender community. In a voicemail from him, the man threatened to kill the physician and said there was already a group of people on their way to carry it out.[51] This was the same year a mass shooting took place at an LGBTQ nightclub in Colorado Springs called Club Q. "According to a study by the Williams Institute at UCLA School of Law, LGBTQ+ people are nearly four times more likely than non-LGBTQ+ people to experience violent victimization, including rape, sexual assault, and aggravated assault."[52]

Political violence is also becoming more common and can be perpetrated by people from both sides of the aisle. It is usually fueled by the practice of scapegoating and dehumanizing "the other" and justifying violence against them. David DePape was arrested for breaking into U.S. House Speaker Nancy Pelosi's home and severely beating her husband, Paul Pelosi, with a hammer. Mr. Pelosi was knocked unconscious and woke up in a pool of his own blood. DePape was charged with attempted murder and assault with a deadly weapon among other charges. His actual target was Nancy Pelosi. His reason for the attack was to exact retribution on her for her political actions while serving as House Speaker. "DePape told police he wanted to hold the Democratic leader hostage and 'break her kneecaps' to show other members of Congress there were 'consequences to actions,' the criminal complaint alleges."[53] DePape was not acting in a vacuum. Republican Congresswoman Marjorie Taylor Greene, who is a self-described Christian Nationalist, is known for supporting and "liking" posts on social media that call for violence against prominent Democrats. She once announced that Nancy Pelosi was a traitor guilty of treason, including noting that that's a crime punishable by death. She once threatened Pelosi "will suffer death or she'll be in prison."[54]

In June 2022, an armed man went to Supreme Court Justice Brett Kavanaugh's home to kill him. Nicholas Roske's motive was retribution over the school shooting in Uvalde, Texas, a leaked draft of the Supreme Court decision that would later overturn Roe v. Wade, and the possibility of the court striking down a New York State gun control law. He was armed with a pistol with two magazines and ammunition, a knife, pepper spray, zip ties, a hammer, and a crowbar, among other items. He planned to break into the house and kill the justice but was apprehended before he could carry out his plan.[55] This is another example of violence coming from the left side of the political divide. It reinforces how portions of our society often buy into violent revenge as the solution to conflict in the culture war, rather than civil dialogue or the courts. But all these examples show how *hatred of the other* is rampant in our polarized culture, whether towards the "liberal, radical Left" or the "crazy, extremist Right."

Political and Divisive Religion

Evangelical historian George Marsden says evangelical Christianity has become a political religion. People have come to believe certain political positions are deeply Christian. "When Trump was able to add open hatred and resentments to the political-religious stance of true believers, it crossed a line. Tribal instincts seem to have become overwhelming. The result is that many Christian followers of Trump 'have come to see a gospel of hatreds, resentments, vilifications, put-downs, and insults as expressions of their Christianity, for which they too should be willing to fight."[56]

The fruit of this? There is widespread infighting in most of conservative Christianity. In 2021, when Peter Wehner interviewed pastors and other experts about this phenomenon, this is what some of them said: "Nearly everyone tells me there is at the very least a small group in nearly every evangelical church complaining and agitating against teaching or policies that aren't sufficiently conservative or anti-woke. It's everywhere."[57] The point? "The aggressive, disruptive, and unforgiving mindset that characterizes so much of our politics has found a home in many American churches." A sociologist lamented, "The divisions and conflicts we found are intense, easily more intense than I have seen in my 25 years of studying the topic." Some pastors are quitting while others are taking part in "domineering leadership, bullying, spiritual abuse, and a toxic culture."[58]

The point is that violence seeping into popular religion is not just physical. It can be emotional and spiritual violence and just as devastating. And it's been getting worse. Moreover, physical violence has always been justified in popular theology, whether it's in an American "holy" war, a global war on terror, or protecting oneself, one's possessions, and one's country by using firearms or other armaments. And even hiding those firearms inside a fake Bible cover. What's more, it's not just happening among religious conservatives. Although from my research it is much more predominant among the right-wing, sometimes, liberal movements, like the opportunists who hijacked the largely peaceful BLM movement and the man opposed to the conservative influence on the Supreme Court, can resort to destruction and violence.

EIGHT

THE MYTH OF REDEMPTIVE VIOLENCE

THE MYTH OF REDEMPTIVE violence is the notion that you can do evil to create good. Both conservatives and liberals can buy into it. Gareth Higgins put it this way: "The myth of redemptive violence is a term to refer to the idea that we can bring order out of chaos through lethal force."[1] This idea comes from a lot of ancient creation mythologies that begin with a violent battle between gods, includes the creation of humankind, and ends with praise for the winning god. The Enuma Elish Babylonian creation myth is a good example.

Redemptive violence is the hallmark of the examples we saw above from the Torah and from the Joshua narrative. The Canaanites were the enemy that needed to be destroyed to bring Israel into the Promise Land. Without violent conquest, there was no reward. Achan was the scapegoat who needed to be stoned and burned, along with his children and possessions, to restore harmony with God, which allowed the conquest to be successful. Without capital punishment for Achan and his clan, God was not appeased and could not help the Israelites win (Joshua 7). Likewise, Phinehas became a hero when he rushed into a house and drove a spear through an Israelite man and Moabite pagan woman lying together. The woman had led the man astray to follow a foreign god. Phinehas was obeying God's command to destroy the lead idolators among the Israelites, and by doing so, stopped a God-ordained plague that had already killed 24,000 people. God was appeased. But without the death of the man and woman and presumably other "lead idolators," the plague would have continued, and God's fierce anger would still be turned toward Israel (Numbers 25).

The myth of redemptive violence is also the hallmark of the violent sacrificial view of the cross. Jesus had to be tortured and murdered in order to satisfy God's wrath over sin. When people accept this bloody sacrifice that they supposedly deserve, only then can God forgive and bring reconciliation and peace. Without accepting this substitutionary atonement, God's wrath remains, and eternal damnation awaits.

Redemptive violence is transactional. Violent acts lead to an end to chaos and restoration of order. Without violence, there is no help from God (Achan in Joshua 7). Without violence, there is no protection (Phineas stopping the plague in Numbers 25). Without violence, there is no maintaining order or achieving justice. This is seen in the eye for an eye example in Leviticus and in the various punishments of criminals from non-restorative imprisonment to solitary confinement to capital punishment to abusing and torturing terror suspects in the name of stopping terrorism. Without violence (Jesus' tortuous death on the cross), there can be no salvation for humankind. Without violence, the transaction cannot take place. Only with violence is the transaction made.

The notion that violence can be redemptive is the justification for a variety of global and social conflicts, from wars to criminal justice systems, to social protests, to even disciplining children.

A WORD ABOUT VETERANS AND THE MILITARY

Before digging further into why redemptive violence is a myth, I want to unequivocally say how much I admire our veterans and those who serve in the military. Or anyone who sincerely believes they are fighting a just war for a worthy cause. People who join the military knowing that war or combat is a real possibility are worthy of our respect. They are doing what our society has taught them is the only way, or the superior way, to fight evil and protect our country. They are courageous.

The problem is not the people in the military. The problem is a society who refuses to question our view of redemptive violence, look under the hood, and see its inherent problems. For example, the problem of how war is a poor chisel for peace, as Martin Luther King, Jr., said. How war tends to lead to more war, not less. How war severely harms both the combatants who wage it and the non-combatants who suffer from it. How both groups die needlessly. How military solutions to local and world conflicts rarely bring lasting peace.

And when they do—as it did after World War II when we became peaceful allies with the Germans and Japanese—it is not because of war, but in spite of war. In that case, it was largely due to things like the Marshall Plan, which provided economic aid to restore the economic infrastructure in post-war Europe, and later, the occupation of Japan that led to the rebuilding of their entire country. In other words, after World War II, we loved our enemies and helped them rebuild, unlike what happened after World War I when we severely punished our enemies and set the stage for World War II.

Below, we'll see how redemptive violence doesn't work and how, often-times, it's those who have participated in war—our combat veterans—who are calling us to rethink it.

NOT FROM THE PEACEMAKING GOD OF JESUS OR THE PROPHETS

The first reason that redemptive violence can be seen as a myth is because it is not from the peacemaking God of the Jewish tradition. It is from the violent god of both Jewish and pagan traditions. It is the violent side of the two-faced god. Once one can accept that it is perfectly reasonable to expose the two-faced god of the Bible—the peacemaking side and the violent side—and to embrace the peaceful divinity and to reject the violent divinity, it is easy to see that redemptive violence is a myth. And that redemptive compassion is the counter myth. This way of reading the scriptures was practiced by Jesus, the prophets, and many of the Jewish traditions throughout history.

In Genesis, redemptive violence was found in the story of Noah and the flood. Only by drowning the planet and all of the human population except for one family, including every man, woman, child, infant, and the unborn, could God redeem the human race. *Redemptive compassion* is found in the story of Joseph. God turned an evil act done with violent intent by evil hearts into a restorative peaceful reconciliation by blessing the victim of the evil act and having mercy on the perpetrators.

In Joshua, redemptive violence is found in the story of the Canaanite conquest. Only by treating the Canaanites as enemies and either killing them or enslaving them without mercy—could God bless the nation of Israel. This included every man, woman, child, infant, and the unborn except for Rahab the prostitute and her family.

Redemptive compassion is found in the prophets when Hosea told us that God desires mercy, not sacrifice. Or when Micah said that God only requires his people to act justly, love mercy, and walk humbly (not perform violent sacrifice). Redemptive compassion is found when the writer of Proverbs told Israel to feed their enemies if they were hungry rather than kill them. Or when Elijah helped a non-Israelite widow. Or when Elisha healed a Syrian man of leprosy.

Redemptive compassion is found in the Jesus narrative, when Jesus told his fellow Jews to love their enemies and have mercy on them and bless them, or when he taught that God is kind to the ungrateful and wicked. It is seen when he made the hero of one of his parables a Samaritan, who took care of his Jewish enemy after he was attacked by thieves, and when he tore down purity codes that punished the supposed unclean and extended compassion on them without forcing them to go through the transactional religious system of the day. It is seen when he welcomed anyone from the traditional enemy camp—tax collectors, women street workers, Gentiles, Romans, and new enemies, such as Pharisees and teachers of the law—into his entourage with no conditions except to change their mind about what mattered most and then live accordingly. It is seen when he taught that those who don't measure up and love their neighbor (i.e., the poor, the sick, the hungry, and the marginalized) would ultimately be judged and rehabilitated in order to learn repentance. It is seen when Jesus never spoke of eternal torment only judgment that ends in remedial correction.

Redemptive violence is not the character of the true God. Redemptive compassion is.

REDEMPTIVE VIOLENCE DOESN'T WORK

The second reason redemptive violence can be seen as a myth is because it doesn't work, or it only works temporarily. As previously mentioned, Martin Luther King, Jr., said, "War is a poor chisel to carve out peace." Violence only begets more violence and creates a cycle that is difficult to end. Violence and even most forms of traditional punishment have unintended consequences.

As far as violence, retribution, or punishment go as tools for change, if society uses them to try to change a criminal, an evil person, or an enemy, it typically backfires. For example, "The U.S. releases over 7 million people from jail and more than 600,000 people from prison each year. However, recidivism is common. Within 3 years of their release, 2 out of 3 people are rearrested and more than 50% are incarcerated again."[2] This means that imprisonment as punishment does not restore relationships or necessarily change people for the better.

This also applies to children and the mentally ill who resort to crime. Psychiatrist James Gilligan, in his book *Violence: Reflections on a National Epidemic*, relays his years of experience with criminally insane inmates at the Bridgewater State Hospital in Massachusetts. He became convinced the issues these adult inmates faced were the results of misguided, harsh punishment as children, and, rather than redeeming them, the punishment encouraged children to take revenge.[3] "Punishment stimulates violence; Punishment causes it. The more punitive our society has become, the higher our rate of violence both criminal and noncriminal has become."[4] "For children, punishment increases their feelings of shame and simultaneously decreases their capacity for feelings of love for others and of guilt toward others."[5]

Traditional approaches to an evil or disobedient person who is not conforming to the norms of society is to punish them or exact retribution on them. The reasoning is that this will, number one, deter others from doing the same, and number two, bring about a kind of moral balance—the revenge mentality—where justice has now been served. But, as James Gilligan reports, retribution only causes more violence. It doesn't work.

Using violence in war also brings unintended consequences. In September 1940, Hitler began what came to be known as "The Blitz:" an ariel bombing campaign on England that lasted nine months. 80,000 bombs were dropped on London alone. Hitler and his generals fully expected the assault to break the morale of the nation, cause debilitating fear, and deflate the country's will to resist. Instead, almost the opposite happened.

To be sure, there was great grief over the loss of life and wiped-out neighborhoods. Yet, overall, the will of the people was emboldened and unified. "[E]verybody helped each other out and no one cared about your politics, or whether you were rich or poor." A British historian wrote, "British society in many ways became strengthened by the Blitz. The effect on Hitler was disillusioning." Rather than punish the British into submission, the campaign only instilled further resistance. One study concluded "There is no evidence of breakdown of morale."[6]

Despite this, Winston Churchill and his generals held the same view of the effectiveness of bombing and, in retaliation, wanted the Germans to be dealt an even harsher blow. Over the course of the rest of the war, England and the Allies rained hell down on Germany. There were ten times as many casualties as the Blitz, including German civilians, and more than half of German cities and towns were destroyed. Yet, as Rutger Bregman reports, the bombings did not have the intended effect per eyewitness accounts and findings of scientists:

> There was no mass hysteria. On the contrary, in places that had just been hit, inhabitants felt relief. "Neighbors were wonderfully helpful," Panse recorded. "Considering the severity and duration of the mental strain, the general attitude was remarkably steady and restrained."...After the raids, people helped each other out. They pulled victims from the rubble, they extinguished fires. Members of the Hitler Youth rushed around tending to the homeless and injured...The scientists' findings were stark: the civilian bombings had been a fiasco. In fact, they appeared to have strengthened the German wartime economy, thereby prolonging the war...In the twenty-one devasted towns and cities...investigated, [war] production had increased faster than in a control group of fourteen cities that had not been bombed.[7]

The Allied bombing of Germany probably prolonged the war, and the result was much more production of war implements in cities that were not bombed. The same can be said for the American bombing of North Vietnam from 1965 to 1968; the campaign was called Operation Rolling Thunder. It only emboldened the enemy to dig in and retaliate, thus prolonging the war. Secretary of Defense, Robert McNamara, became convinced as early as 1967 that both Rolling Thunder and the ground war in South Vietnam were not working.

This principle can also be seen in the War on Terror. As Claiborne and Martin report, "The same can be said of terrorism or violence—when we return violence for violence, we add fuel to the fire. One soldier in Iraq said he went into the military to fight terrorism but ended up realizing that they were creating it. He said every person killed made the fire of rage and violence even stronger."[8]

THE FAILURE AND CONSEQUENCES OF REDEMPTIVE VIOLENCE

Anyone who has watched Ken Burn's documentary, *The Vietnam War*, or read Robert McNamara's *In Retrospect: The Tragedy and Lessons of Vietnam*, will know that the Vietnam War was not based on, nor followed, any just war theory and was an unmitigated disaster in carrying out what it set out to do: to defend a sovereign nation—South Vietnam—against Communist aggression and contain Communism, supposedly to safeguard the region. McNamara admitted that the U.S was "terribly wrong" to wage war in Vietnam. Today, it is a one-party Communist state, has one of the fastest-growing economies, and is one of the more politically stable countries in Southeast Asia. The human death toll of this war was two million civilians on both sides, over a million North Vietnamese soldiers, up to 250,000 South Vietnamese soldiers, and almost 58,000 American soldiers.

The Iraq War in 2003 has also been cited as a failed enterprise, despite its initial "victory." Anthony Cordesman said the war managed to "snatch defeat from the jaws of victory" three times. Here is his assessment:

> In round one, the United States invaded Iraq in 2003 to meet a non-existent threat of proliferation and drive Saddam Hussein from power. It scored a massive military victory with no plan for what would happen once Saddam was removed. The net impact resulted in crippled Iraqi military forces, deep sectarian conflict and ethnic divisions, the empowerment of Sunni extremists, and the creation of a new war.

In round two, the United States and its allies ended up fighting these Islamic extremists from 2004 to 2010. Although the United States defeated these extremists in western Iraq with the aid of a massive surge of U.S. ground troops and the aid of Iraqi Sunni popular forces, the United States failed to create a stable Iraqi government and economy. The United States effectively abandoned its nation building efforts after 2009 and withdrew its combat forces at the end of 2011—creating a power vacuum that opened up Iraq to ISIS—all the while, it was never able to decide on any active strategy for stabilizing Iraq or dealing with the Syrian civil war. It focused on defeating ISIS—relying heavily on Syrian Kurds in the process—and scored another "victory" in 2016-2018 by disbanding the ISIS 'caliphate.'

However, the United States never developed any meaningful plan for dealing with Iraq's political and economic crises, for dealing with Syria, or even for dealing with the tens of thousands of ISIS prisoners that its "victory" created. In the process, it opened up Syria to Russia, Iran, and Hezbollah...The United States ultimately failed to ensure that most Iraqis saw the critical role that U.S. advisors and airpower played in defeating ISIS, to make any clear efforts to reform a failed Iraq government, or boost the Iraqi economy, or to ensure that the populated areas shattered by the fighting would be rebuilt or receive effective aid.[9]

THE PSYCHOLOGICAL EFFECTS OF VIOLENT ACTS

There is another, more sinister way that war and violence fail us more times than not. Not only does war and violence harm, torture, and kill its victims, it creates severe psychological damage among its participants.

Sadly, Post Traumatic Stress Disorder, or PTSD, (also referred to as *soldiers' heart, shell shock, combat fatigue*, and *war neurosis*) is common among soldiers. Among veterans who served in the Iraq War and the conflict in Afghanistan, 11 to 20 percent had been diagnosed with PTSD. From the Gulf War, it was around 12 percent. Thirty percent of Vietnam veterans have experienced PTSD in their lifetime.[10]

Pastor and former marine, Dwight Ford, laments, "Something leaves a human, I believe, when they have to take life. Even if it is, in their mind, to save their own, or justified. There's a horror that stays with folks."[11]

Why is this? Killing another human being is not an easy task. Modern movies and shows that depict warfare, in whatever time period, lie to us when they portray armed violence carried out by combatants with relative ease and with little to no effects. In the Pacific theater in World War II, Colonel Samuel Marshall once did research on a particular battle where American soldiers didn't fare well. It turned out most of the soldiers never fired their guns. He expanded his study to include other groups of servicemembers in the Pacific and Europe. He found that only 10 to 25 percent of soldiers actually fired their weapons while in battle. And there was no difference between new recruits and experienced ones.

In his book, *Humankind: A Hopeful History*, Rutger Bregman describes this phenomenon and quotes Marshall in his 1946 book, *Men Against Fire*: "...the average and normally healthy individual...has such an inner usually unrealized resistance toward killing a fellow man that he will not of his own volition take life."[12] Marshall concluded that most of us have an inherent "fear of aggression."

Later studies confirmed Marshall's findings. In the Second World War more than half of soldiers never killed anyone. Most casualties were caused by a minority of combatants. Research on Civil War battles uncovered even starker numbers. Out of almost 30,000 muskets recovered after the battle of Gettysburg, 90 percent were still loaded and unfired. A study of the French army had similar findings.[13]

According to Lt. Col. Dave Grossman and most Christians, there's a difference between murder and lawful use of deadly force to protect the innocent. Therefore, there's a need to use guns and armaments to make the world safe. But as we have just seen, people do not naturally kill others.

Committing violence is unnatural. Grossman admits, "Healthy people have to be trained to kill."[14]

"People don't naturally rush to war. You have to seduce them; you have to bribe them, coerce them." — Howard Zinn

The best way to train soldiers to kill is to dehumanize the enemy. After decades of covering war, journalist and former foreign correspondent, Chris Hedges concluded, "The celebration of war is also a celebration of us, the celebration of our virtues, of our prowess, of our goodness, accompanied by the dehumanization and racist attacks against whoever we are fighting."[15] Remember that dehumanization is the way of *violent sacrificial religion*. We dehumanize our enemy in order to scapegoat them and justify violence against them and even celebrate that violence.

Karen Armstrong explains how we do this: "Still, we fight. But to bring ourselves to do so, we envelop the effort in a mythology—often a 'religious mythology'—that puts distance between us and the enemy. We exaggerate his differences, be they racial, religious, or ideological. We develop narratives to convince ourselves that he is not really human but monstrous, the antithesis of order and goodness. Today we may tell ourselves we are fighting for God and country or that a particular war is 'just' or 'legal.'"[16]

How does an army dehumanize the enemy? First, by killing them from a distance. Either across the expanse of an open battlefield or through dropping bombs in the air. If we can't see the people we are killing, it makes it palatable. The other way is to condition soldiers, through training (that includes dehumanization) or giving them intoxicants (the Germans distributed methamphetamines to soldiers in certain battles). After World War II, due to the recommendation of Colonel Marshal, the US Army began conditioning techniques. And they worked. The firing ratio in the Korean War increased to 55 percent and in Vietnam it went up to 95 percent.[17] "Vietnam recruits were immersed in boot camps that exalted not only a sense of brotherhood, but also the most brutal violence, forcing the men to scream 'KILL! KILL! KILL!' until they were hoarse. Second World War veterans (most of whom had never learned to kill) were shocked when shown images of this brand of training."[18]

Bregman asserts that this new conditioning tactic by the army came with a price. PTSD rates jumped to thirty percent for Vietnam veterans. "If you brainwash millions of young soldiers in training, it should come as no surprise when they return with post-traumatic stress disorder (PTSD), as so many did after Vietnam. Innumerable soldiers had not only killed other people—something inside them had died, too."[19] These examples reveal that our culture has been lied to. Violence is not redemptive. And it is nothing to celebrate.

> I think many people, including veterans, who come back [from war], face an existential crisis, in that they realize that everything they've been told by their church, by their schools, by their political leaders is a lie...it's not just that they cope with trauma, they cope with that existential crisis that they've seen behind the mask.[20]

THE MISTAKE OF ADVOCATING FOR HUMANE WAR

In Chapter 11, we will look at the historic peace and anti-war movements that thrived in Europe and America between the Civil War and World War I. Historically, the horrors of war press upon the conscience of people's good will and inevitably raise up anti-war activists who press to abolish war. Unfortunately, they rarely prevail.

But we must also look at another response to war's horrors: the movement to make war more humane. This has led to such international laws as the Geneva Convention, which seek to legislate a more humane way of waging war as well as how non-combatants and prisoners of war are treated. It included the efforts of organizations like The Red Cross that initially staffed hospitals and ambulance companies and recruited tens of thousands of registered nurses to serve the military in order to lessen suffering and death in war. These are all worthy pursuits, but do they minimize war and suffering or only contribute to its acceptance?

In his book, *Humane: How the United States Abandoned Peace and Reinvented War*, Samuel Moyn argues that the pursuit of humane war has only perpetuated war into an endless exercise, as evidenced by America's 20-year War in Afghanistan. It was thought that making weapons of war technologically more precise, remotely controlled, and effective would lessen loss of life and bring a quicker end to wars.

Now let's go back a hundred years to get context. In the lead up to the use of modern weapons of warfare, it was initially thought that aerial combat might be a more humane way of fighting with more precise bombing techniques and a way to lessen the horrors of close-range fighting. An Englishmen named J. M. Spaight had promised in the 1920s "that air power would transform hideous bloodletting into bloodless surgery."[21]

Air warfare was rare in World War I, so we didn't get to test this theory until later conflicts between colonial powers and African "colonies," Japan's war with China in the late 1930s, and finally, World War II.

After several noteworthy attacks that shocked the world—Japan's bombing of the Chinese city of Chongquing in May 1939 and then the bombing of Warsaw, Poland in September of that same year by the Luftwaffe—President Franklin Roosevelt condemned this tactic. He called it a "ruthless bombing from the air of civilians in unfortified centers of population" and a "inhuman barbarism" that "shocked the conscience of humanity." He made a public plea that "'every government" [should] affirm that "in no event, and under no circumstances" would any power bomb civilians or "unfortified cities." The "rules of warfare" prohibited it, [he] insisted."[22]

International observers during World War II, with its relentless string of aerial bombing campaigns by both the Axis and Allies, concluded the notion of a humane aerial war was a pipedream. After the bombing of German cities, and in particular the devastation of Dresden that killed tens of thousands of both the enemy and civilian refugees, the New York Times editorial board summarized its position in March 1944. In light of critique from pacifists like Englishwoman Vera Brittain, they concluded, "Attempts to humanize [war] have utterly failed. Let us not deceive ourselves into thinking that war can be more humane. It cannot. It can only be abolished. Let us resolve that this war shall be so conducted and so concluded that no city shall ever be bombed again."[23]

Later that same year after British and American air forces fire stormed German cities together, Moye laments how "one U.S. officer worried that it would 'absolutely convince the Germans that we are the barbarians they say we are, for it would be perfectly obvious to them that it is primarily a large-scale attack on civilians as, in fact, it of course will be.' As, of course, it was."[24]

Of course, we know that these earlier critiques, condemnations, and pleas to circumvent the barbaric killing of civilians were unheeded. The U.S., under President Harry S. Truman, dropped two atomic bombs on Hiroshima and Nagasaki in August 1945. These bombs killed between 129,000 to 226,000 people, most of whom were civilians.

But even before that, the American's low altitude bombing of Japanese cities, including Tokyo, in March 1945, likely killed even more people. As Samuel Moyn reports, "Scores of cities and hundreds of thousands of civilians were incinerated well before Harry Truman's climatic decision to nuke Hiroshima and Nagasaki."[25]

No one was questioning these decisions on the grounds of law. The boundaries of war had expanded way beyond any international or domestic legal constraints. Roosevelt's plea, that officer's observation, and scores of anti-war and pacifist outcries were all but forgotten.

ISN'T THERE A CASE FOR SELF-DEFENSE?

What about cases of using lethal force in self-defense? To use violence to prevent someone from committing violence? Isn't it redemptive to resort to violence in those cases? When one's life is threatened, or more persuasively, when the life of one's spouse or child is threatened by an attacker at the door, isn't it morally legitimate to use violent force to stop such an evil doer? What if it's someone who is threatening to kill your family?

I don't think anyone should categorically condemn a person who resorts to violence in defense of a loved one. What's more, we certainly want trained police officers who engage an active shooter threatening children or other innocent victims to stop the perpetrator(s) in their tracks; if it means shooting them dead, because that is the only resort, then perhaps we must sadly accept that as the lesser of two evils. Yet the truth is that violence of any kind is problematic and almost always has unintended consequences. Moreover, there is good reason to question or reject this self- or other's-defense theory as a justification for using lethal force as unrealistic and problematic, at the very least in cases only involving average citizens.

As Preston Sprinkle explains about the what-if-you-have-an-attacker-at-the-door scenario, it is often broached to persuade pacificists to conclude their position is unrealistic. Yet, it is always couched as if there are only two options. One, be a pacifist and let the attacker kill a member of your family or use a firearm to take the attacker down. Real life scenarios are not that straightforward.

Will a citizen with a firearm really be a good enough shot to take down or disarm an attacker? Will two guns in such a scenario risk more harm than good because of the heightened risk of a stray bullet hitting someone? What if the attacker's threats of violence are only meant to instill fear (remember, people don't naturally find it easy to shoot or kill). What if he's hoping he doesn't have to use the gun in order to get his way? But you choose to shoot at him, and he gets angry and shoots one of your family in response to your aggression? When U.S. Representative Gabby Giffords and 18 others were shot in Tucson, Arizona, in 2011, someone nearby was legally carrying a firearm. He immediately ran to the scene and took actions to help subdue the killer. Yet he didn't have enough immediate context to know who the perpetrator was. He nearly shot the wrong man. He almost shot the man who wrested the gun away from the shooter. Moreover, if he had pulled his weapon he could have been confused as a second gunman.[26] The bottom line is, what if there are other non-violent ways to intervene in such cases that are less risky and more effective?

As Preston Sprinkle reminds us, resisting evil with force does not have to be violent. Soon we will hear of an example of *verbal* resistance where a woman confronted a mugger on a train. There is also *sacrificial* resistance such as taking a bullet to protect an innocent person. There's even physical resistance that does not include violence per se, but actions that nevertheless can stop a shooter or attacker—tackling, wresting, kicking, punching, etc.

I love the story that Sprinkle tells that aligns with what we will discover is a third way to confront evil. It's neither passive surrender nor violent resistance toward an aggressor.

There are countless stories about real-life situations where lethal force seemed like the only way to stop the attacker, and yet the victim chose to show radical love. My favorite is the story of a woman who awoke to the sound of a man coming through the window with a knife. As he approached her bed, she yelled out, 'You can kill us, but first let me make you a cup of coffee.' The man accepted the offer, and having slurped down his cup of joe, he decided not to kill.[27]

Nine
THE ROOTS OF PEACE

WE'VE MADE THE CASE that one of the major challenges for change that Jesus posed to his audience was to turn from a violent sacrificial view of God to a non-violent, peaceable view of God. This was based on Jesus' claim that God is not a wrathful, violent judge seeking retribution and punishment for violations of the law, but he is like a loving Father who is merciful to the righteous and unrighteous alike, that he is kind to the ungrateful and wicked, that he does not call for capital punishment of lawbreakers or resistant pagans, or any retribution, for that matter, and that since God actually loves his enemies, that we should too.

Not that Jesus didn't call for a community to hold evil people accountable. He most certainly did. He did with the scribes, Pharisees, and the teachers of the law, calling them whitewashed tombs and a brood of vipers and warning people not to trust in them. He also held them to account by purging the Temple and driving out those taking advantage of the poor and making a profit on the business of divine forgiveness. Yet he did so in a way that did not write wrongdoers off, but in a way that called them to repentance. He told them that prostitutes and tax collectors were entering the kingdom of God before them. The implication was that they would still enter one day in the future. He claimed that all were redeemable, and none were beyond redemption. Paul made this same point when he said, "As in Adam all die, in Christ all will be made alive" (I Corinthians 15:22). What's more, Jesus taught us to do the same, to hold evil people and wrongdoers accountable. But do so humbly without self-righteousness. In other words, Jesus instructed us to check to see if there is a plank in our own eye and take that out before we help take a speck out of others' eyes.

Jesus pointed to examples from the Jewish scriptures of his day that contradicted the violent narratives of Moses, Joshua, Judah, and Phineas—that

God reached out to his enemies with love (the Gentiles in the Elijah and Elisha stories). Jesus also pointed out that any Temple of God, if authentic, would be a house of prayer for all non-Jews (Mark 11:17 and Isaiah 56:7). He taught his disciples that non-Jews were welcome at his table fellowship. He welcomed those who were traditionally enemies: the Roman centurion, the Samaritans, a Gadarene Gentile (Matthew 8:28–34), and a Canaanite woman (Matt 15). In the gospels, it records Jesus going through several towns in the Decapolis, a region where the majority population was "pagan" Greeks and not Jewish.[1] Finally, he argues that many non-Jews would come and sit at God's table feast at the culmination of the ages (Matthew 8:11–12). His statement that many of the subjects of the kingdom would be thrown outside the feast into darkness was typical of his warnings to those who neglected or were unkind to "the least of these." He claimed these people would face the "rehabilitation of the age."

Later, the early disciples of Jesus decided that non-Jews who believed in Jesus did not need to obey the law of Moses to be accepted into the community as "followers" (Acts 15 and Galatians). It's not a conversion to the Jewish religion. It's a conversion to a new way of life based on love for one another, love for enemies, and a peaceable, inclusive, forgiving, restorative community.

THE EQUALITY ETHIC

The first evidence of this is how Jesus treated what he called "the least of these." In Craft Brewed Jesus, using the research of Marcus Borg, I outlined the purity map of first century Judaism.[2] I made the case that Jesus was challenging the purity codes of Judaism that said the purest people were those who most closely obeyed the law of Moses (and the oral tradition if they were Pharisees). Like the Torah stipulates, others had varying levels of purity in God's eyes. The poor, sick, and bleeding were impure, those who consumed the wrong kinds of food were impure, women were, by definition, less pure, the outcasts like prostitutes and tax collectors were impure, and unconverted Gentiles weren't even on the purity map.

Who did Jesus spend most of his time with when he was showing compassion on the masses? The people on the margins of the purity map. Why? Because they were the ones treated the most unequally. Jesus became the "friend of sinners." He was friends with the religious and ceremonially impure or unclean. They needed to be lifted up, and both the religious pure and the rich and powerful needed to be lowered and humbled. The "first will be last and the last will be first" was the equality cry of the reign of God.

When Jesus did engage the "pure" religious folks and the rich and powerful, he called on them to join him to lift up the impoverished and marginalized, to lay up treasure in heaven by giving to the poor and stopping the oppression against them. Zacchaeus, the rich tax collector in Luke (19:1–10), was "saved" when he gave half his possessions to the poor and paid back four times what he had unjustly derived from the poor. He was not saved because he went down the aisle at his local synagogue and "accepted Jesus as his Lord and Savior." Jesus didn't respond to Zacchaeus with, "I'm sorry, sir. Good works won't save you. You are saved by faith, not works...You must accept me, and my future sacrifice on the cross, and be born again in order to be saved." No, Jesus acknowledged that Zacchaeus had proven he has faith by his works—that he had repented from greed and gave restitution to the poor whom he had harmed. Jesus called Zacchaeus—and the rich and religious power elites—to ignore the purity codes of the day, to love their fellow human beings equally regardless of their religious or class standing, and to prove their repentance with their deeds.

As an aside, the phrase "we are saved by faith, not works," (Ephesians 2:8–9) is not referring to the works of doing good to fellow human beings. It's referring to the "works of the law" that Paul said was actually a curse (Galatians). Following religious laws does not save us. What saves us is repenting from religious, political, greedy, harmful, and/or violent power trips. What saves us is starting to trust (have faith) that the peaceable way of equitable, non-violent love for all is the right way. And then acting on that trust by doing good.

INTRODUCING TRUE PEACE

In ancient times, the concept of bringing peace to the world had little to do with making peace with your enemy or establishing democracy. Rather, it was about conquering your enemies and ruling over them with an iron hand. Once your enemy was conquered, peace was maintained by quashing uprisings, keeping order in society (not equality), and punishing the disobedient in a way that put fear in people so they would not try to do the same. It was a peace created through military and political dominance, extraction of resources through taxes, and fear of those in charge. The Romans had this down to a science.

> The Pax Romana (Roman Peace) was a period of relative peace and stability across the Roman Empire which lasted for over 200 years, beginning with the reign of Augustus (27 BCE–14 CE). The aim of Augustus and his successors was to guarantee law, order, and security within the empire, even if this meant separating it from the rest of the world and defending, or even expanding, its borders through military intervention and conquest.[3]

This peace came at a high price. The Roman historian Tacitus quoted a leader of Briton named Calgacus, who commented on the conquest of Britain:

> They [the Romans] are unique in being as violently tempted to attack the poor as the wealthy. Robbery, butchery, rapine [plunder], the liars call Empire; they create desolation and call it peace.[4]

New Testament scholar Hal Taussig explains:

> Romans practiced both random and intentional violence against populations they had conquered, killing tens of thousands by crucifixion. ...By the time crucifixion was a staple of the Roman Empire, its justice system had employed strangling, stoning, burning and even boiling in oil as methods of torture and execution. But crucifixion sent a more lingering message.[5]

Crucifixion became the most famous punishment the Romans carried out. It was used on slaves, pirates, and anyone deemed an enemy of the state. Jesus would have been crucified by the Romans for sedition. The two "thieves" crucified with him were more likely "insurgents," as the Greek word can also mean that.

The main purpose of crucifixion was not to exact justice but to dissuade the public from carrying out similar wrongdoing. With crucifixion, death could take several days, and the victims were sometimes left on crosses after dying to further warn potential criminals. "Crucifixion was usually intended to provide a death that was particularly slow, painful, gruesome, humiliating, and public..."[6] This torture was on display for all to see, as the location of crucifixions were commonly near public thoroughfares. Crucifixion was the ultimate deterrent to crimes of the state, particularly rebellions or other forms of treasonous acts that challenged the authority of Rome.

Through the Roman emperor Augustus (the adopted son of Julius Caesar), Rome conquered new lands and supposedly brought peace to the known world. Augustus was also deemed a keeper of the peace in places like Palestine and Jerusalem, which Rome had conquered over thirty years before his reign. Again, an iron-handed rule with deterrents like crucifixion and stoning were the tools used to keep peace.

"Augustus was hailed as a savior, lord, King of Kings, prince of peace, son of God, the Pontifex Maximus or High Priest of Rome, who brought gospels and glad tidings to the people of Rome."[7] In the Roman mind, the good news was that law and order in the Empire was won and maintained by the use of violence and political weapons.

Then along came Jesus and his first followers who preached a vastly different way of peace. A way that didn't conquer and punish their enemies with violent retribution but rather forgave and loved their enemies with good will. A way that stood up to injustice with calls for equality and kindness for all, regardless of religious, ethnic, moral, or class standing.

To say "Jesus is Lord" or the "Son of God" was not to acclaim some mandatory, theological acceptance of the deity of Christ, but rather to proclaim that the peaceable Way of Jesus was superior to the conquering ways of the world, whether it was from the Roman Empire or Israel's God of Joshua. The road to true peace was not through violent subjection but egalitarian, non-violent love for humankind.

Sometimes people think of the teachings of Jesus as not particularly outstanding compared to our own democratic society's ways of equality, but we forget that in the ancient Roman world conquest context and the Jewish sacrificial religious context—both of which were extremely violent, cruel, and unforgiving—Jesus' teachings were as radical as they were magnanimous.

We also often think that the ways of "the world" that some Bible teachers rail against are mostly things like sexual immorality, hedonistic culture, and lack of religious piety and commitment to the organized church. Although Jesus confronted things like casual divorce[8] and the Jewish definition of adultery, he had nothing to say about sexual taboos, prostitution (except that prostitutes who accepted his good news were more righteous than the religious leaders), or homosexuality. He was considered a glutton and drunkard because he hung out with wine drinkers, welcomed invites from the rich and poor alike, and was the most critical of those entrenched in organized, legalistic religion. He primarily opposed being merciless, unforgiving, retaliatory, retributive, violent, greedy, and using religion or politics to justify power over people.

Jesus was a progressive, universalistic Jew who chose the peaceable narratives of the Bible over the retributive ones. He was not a religious and politically conservative Christian who believed in the inerrancy of the scriptures. He taught a "religion of the heart" (thus women street workers with good hearts can surpass male priests with bad ones) that cares most for the "least of these" in society. He did not teach a religion that one wears on their sleeve in the form of churchgoing, doctrine-believing, religious-code-obeying followers. The "world" that Jesus confronted was an uncaring, brutal, and violent world. The way of the world in that day was violence and unequal treatment of marginalized or broken people by both religious and imperialistic institutions. Opposing this doctrine was about introducing true peace that sought out egalitarian communities of care, love, and restoration, rather than institutions of power, authority, and retribution.

Garreth Higgins says it well: "Jesus comes into a cultural, historical nexus where on the one hand the prevailing empire, Rome, thought domination and conquest through violent retribution and punishment of your enemies is the way, and on the other, the prevailing religion thought that violent rebellion and overthrow of that empire was the way, or least colluding with that violent empire to keep your religious power...so he tells them you're both wrong...of course he was opposed and eventually crucified."[9]

Later on, Jesus' earliest followers actively applied these peaceable teachings for two centuries after his death. They resisted the legalistic, uncaring, inequitable religion of second Temple Judaism by forming communities of compassion that welcomed the marginalized, women, gentiles, and slaves as equals. As Apostle Paul put it, "in Christ, there is no such thing as Jew or Gentile, slave or free, or male and female" (Galatians 3:28). Jesus' followers also practiced benevolence and caring for the poor, even the Roman poor, as the Roman emperor Julian acknowledged in the fourth century. Historian Rodney Stark says they "created a miniature welfare state in an empire which for the most part lacked social services."[10] Historians believe this is the reason for the movement's early growth. It wasn't the promise of a heavenly afterlife over an eternal demise, but rather the attraction of a compassionate and equitable community over the reigning powers of Empire in the here and now, whether it was the empire of second Temple Judaism or the conquering Romans.

The later disciples not only opposed the power of Rome but actively resisted it. They "successfully resisted the Roman Empire. These peoples' [Jesus followers] resistance against Rome often kept violence at bay and gave their people courage and an experience of safety. A key dimension of their resistance to empire was invoking God's compassionate and strange empire, or kingdom, as later translators have it, in contrast to Rome's cruel and dominating one. These various groups made fun of Roman military power and mocked Rome's claim of divine power, even though they themselves had almost no power. The Empire of God challenged the Empire of Rome. Caesar Augustus as Lord conflicted with Jesus Anointed as Lord."[11]

THE EXAMPLE OF JESUS AS THE NON-VIOLENT, FORGIVING VICTIM

In addition to what Jesus taught, there's the example that he demonstrated to the world. When subjected to the authoritarian, violent institutions of second Temple Jewish sacrificial religion and brutal Roman imperialism, he did not respond with violence or call on his followers to take up arms and fight, despite the fact that he was innocent of any crimes. The Jewish leaders convicted him of *blasphemy* based on their warped views of the two-faced Yahweh of the Torah and their fear of him taking away their power over the people. Pontius Pilate convicted him of sedition based on an oligarchic, aggressive, expansionist empire and his own fear of a retributive mob that could make him look bad. Despite Jesus' innocence, he submitted himself to the authorities and took their punishment. He was an innocent victim of grave injustice.

But not only was he an innocent victim, Jesus was a forgiving victim. Not only did he refuse to fight back when he was arrested, tried, and executed, he forgave his perpetrators and enemies. While being tortured with six-inch tapered iron spikes that were driven through his wrists and feet into a wooden beam, he said, "Father, forgive them, for they know not what they do" (Luke 23:34).

The gospel accounts all depict Jesus resurrecting from the dead three days later. Not to take revenge on his enemies who tortured and murdered him. Not to punish his disciples who abandoned or denied him at his time of need. Not to call his allies to take revenge against the Jewish and Roman authorities. But rather to offer terms of peace. "Peace be upon you," he declared when appearing to his disciples and followers, many or most of whom had denied or abandoned him at his time of need. He then told them to spread the good news of the loving God to both Jew and Gentile (in that day, primarily the Romans and Greeks) and for them to keep his teachings to care for the sick and marginalized and love both neighbor and enemy, including those who killed him and those who may kill his followers in the future. Years later, when Stephen was stoned to death by a zealous religious mob, which was seen and approved of by the future apostle Paul, Stephen mirrored Jesus' words right before he died by saying, "Lord, do not hold this sin against them." Jesus was the first, and Stephen was the second forgiving victim. The resurrection of Jesus, whether you literally believe it or not, delivers a message of both peace and vindication. Peace, rather than revenge, is extended to all. Moreover, Jesus' mission and his teachings were vindicated. They did not die with a failed Messiah but have life through a resurrected peace maker and his followers.

WHY MOST CHRISTIANS DON'T SEE THE MESSAGE OF PEACE

Brian Zahnd laments how most Christians today view the teachings of Jesus about engaging society—what Tolstoy called Jesus' *theory of life*—as merely private admonitions rather than what they really are: revolutionary ideas that could change the world:

> Today, there is a tendency to over spiritualize the way Jesus spoke of peace. By making peace primarily a privatized spiritual peace, we are free to carry the banners of war down the road and keep the world as it's always been—just one more war away from peace.[12]

By spiritualizing his teaching on loving our enemies and being true peace makers, we divorce Jesus from his actual ideas. Jesus becomes a means to an end, not a true anointed one to follow.

> Divorcing Jesus from his ideas—especially divorcing Jesus from his political ideas—has been a huge problem that plagued the church from the fourth century onward. The problem is this: when we separate Jesus from his ideas for an alternative social structure, we inevitably succumb to the temptation to harness Jesus to our ideas—thus conferring upon our human political ideas an assumed divine endorsement. With little awareness of what we are doing, we find ourselves in collusion with principalities and powers to keep the world lockstep with the ancient choreography of violence, war, and death. We do this mostly unconsciously, but we do it. I've done it. And the result is that we reduce Jesus to being the Savior who guarantees our reservation in heaven while using him to endorse our own ideas about how to run the world.[13]

When this separation happens, Jesus is drafted into a cultural army for evangelical and fundamentalist Christians to lead a nationalistic agenda. He becomes "a grotesque caricature of Christ." He is no longer a revolutionary, peacemaking teacher on the side of the impoverished and marginalized who calls the political, religious, and wealthy elites to repentance. He becomes a tool for a nationalist and retributive agenda. Mostly the agenda of conservative Christianity, but sometimes the agenda of a more liberal empire. The actual work of non-violent love, forgiveness, and redemption is rejected.

> Certainly, the evangelical view of real-world peacemaking has been something like this: 'Doesn't Jesus have more important work to do?' According to this view, Christianity is mostly about spiritual work of saving souls for an afterlife in heaven, and Jesus' ideas about peace can be put on hold until the age to come. So the argument goes.[14]

Most Christians today—in particular conservative, evangelical, and fundamentalist Christians—don't follow Christ's message of peace. They are not true followers of Jesus. It's hard to say this, but I say it as a former evangelical missionary and church lay leader who also thought I was sincerely following Jesus. But I really wasn't. At best, I was a half-follower, as were many like me. People in the conservative Christian movement follow the Bible, their own evangelical theology, and conservative Christian political and social positions, but they don't really follow Jesus. Following Christ is to follow the way of Christ, which is a peacemaking, restorative way of living life that focuses on what matters most: practicing love toward all of humankind.

At best, evangelicals follow a warped version of Jesus that ascribes to certain commands of Christ—love God with all your heart, love your neighbor as yourself, make disciples by sharing the good news—but reject the full counsel of the good news: love the marginalized, the immigrant, the poor; love your enemies (including political ones), be kind to them, wish/pray them well, forgive them, and challenge them with tact and wisdom, all with the goal of reconciliation. And in extreme circumstances, be willing to nonviolently take up a cross and die, if necessary, in order to help the oppressed and stand up to corruption because that is the example of Jesus. In other words, be a non-passive pacifist.

One reason most Christian conservatives, or even other varieties of Christians, don't follow the way of Jesus is because their churches and leaders have told them that what matters most is having a "saving faith" in Christ. What's of upmost importance is for individuals to accept Jesus as their Lord and Savior (again a phrase that is absent from the Bible) and then believe certain doctrines about Jesus and Christianity. These doctrines include that Jesus is the divine Son of God, he is the second person of the Trinity, and that he took the punishment that we deserved (again, a concept foreign to the earliest Jesus gatherings). They also teach that the Bible is inerrant, the modern "church" is the only way to have community, homosexuality is always sinful (notions that were not taught by Jesus), and that we should evangelize others throughout the whole world so people from every ethnic group come to believe this same way. Moreover, the church is taught that Jesus will return one day to judge the world and will set up his kingdom at the end and in the afterlife. And all of humanity will wind up in heaven or hell.

Finally, that Christians need to promote political goals that have been deemed most important: to criminalize all abortion (even in cases of rape and incest), to overturn Roe vs. Wade at all costs (even if it means electing one of the most un-Christlike Presidents we've ever had in order to do it), to embrace some kind of retributive view of controlling society, and to promote some kind of nebulous form or religious freedom (even if it means disobeying the governing authorities who are trying to save lives during a pandemic). What most Christians fail to see is how Jesus himself defined both salvation and what matters most.

Jesus did not insist that people believe certain doctrines about himself. He insisted that they trust that the ways of the world are evil—its discriminatory, cruel, violent, revengeful, religious, and imperialistic ways—and that the ways of God are good news—its compassion, universal love, forgiveness, and non-violent restoration of relationships in the here and now. In the Parable of the Sheep and the Goats (Matthew 25:31–46), Jesus made it clear that people are judged, not by what they believe or whether they "accept Christ," but by how they treat the most vulnerable and despised members of society. People are not deemed worthy if they promote criminalizing abortion, or if they pray and fast, or if they worship in mega-gatherings, or if they oppose

LGBTQ lifestyles, but rather if they care for the weak and vulnerable: the hungry, thirsty, naked, sick, strangers, immigrants, and prisoners, including criminals. Those who feed them, care for them, help them, and visit them are welcomed into the reign of God even if they don't realize they are doing it for Christ. In other words, even if they aren't Christians. They are rewarded with the "life of the age." Those who don't practice these behaviors are sent to the "rehabilitation of the age" to be refined by spiritual fire and to learn what true righteousness is. This even includes people who claim to "know" him, in other words, people who claim to be Christians. As Jesus warned, "Not everyone who says to me, 'Lord, Lord,' will enter the kingdom of heaven, but only the one who does the will of my Father who is in heaven." (Matthew 7:21) Remember, entering the "kingdom" or "reign" of heaven, or of God, does not mean going to heaven as opposed to hell. It's entering the "realm" of God in the here and now.[15] It's not talking about the afterlife. It means to see or enter into the way of life that Jesus and many of the prophets taught.

As my friend, Chris Kratzer, says, "Some of the best followers of Jesus aren't Christians." What matters most is not what you believe, but how you treat your fellow human beings. Period.

> God doesn't give a rip about what you think about Jesus. Whether He is the son of God or a pre-incarnation of Elvis, born of a virgin or an alien from another planet, or died on the cross for your sins or pulled a David Blaine and never died at all. As one Scripture writer discovered, beliefs only upgrade you to the level of demons. That's the company mere beliefs keep. "You believe that there is one God. Good! Even the demons believe that—and shudder." Instead, Jesus is a way of life, not a way of belief. "Whatever you do for them, you do it unto Me." For Jesus, belief is always connected, not to what you line up in your head, but ultimately to if and how you love. And when you love the way He loves, He counts it as faith, whether you believe or not.[16]

For Jesus, salvation was not about getting a ticket to heaven but about being set free from the violent, retaliatory ways of the world. That includes being set free from the desire to divide the world into "us vs. them" and scapegoat the "thems," so they are blamed for the world's problems (whether it's a conservative or liberal scapegoating) and are worthy of retribution that we are justified in carrying out or doomed to annihilation or eternal conscious torment at the end of it all. The only way to be set free from that is to follow the path of non-violence and enemy love.

This is a very difficult thing to do. It means we must truly believe in a God that is radically different than the ways of world—the world of political control, criminalization, retribution, imprisonment for the sake of punishment (rather than to rehabilitate and redeem), military solutions to the world's conflicts, and the justification of war. We would have to start believing in a God that, as Brian Zahnd says, "would rather die than kill his enemies." We would have to start following such a God (or *theory of life*), and we would have to "rather die than kill our enemies" or harm the oppressed. This is a hard teaching. But soon we will see some examples of how it is done that will help us accept it as a more courageous, honorable, and effective way to live life and make the world a better place.

When we break bad faith, we must reject the caricature of Christ that ignores or minimizes this radical way of life and redefines what matters most, making it into modern evangelical doctrines and political positions. We must expose how Jesus' teachings and revolutionary ideas have been sidelined to irrelevance by cultural warriors and how much we really need those ideas to improve the world. Then we must reclaim the path of peace.

TEN

RECLAIMING THE PATH OF PEACE

LET'S REVIEW WHAT EXACTLY is this peaceable way that Jesus paved and told the world to follow. First, we've made the case that it is an egalitarian way that treats all human beings equitably, regardless of race, gender, or class, with no favoritism toward the rich, powerful, and elite, whether they are the ethnic, religious, economic, or political privileged. It likewise directs no bias against the sick, poor, peasants, oppressed, foreigners, immigrants, and marginalized, but rather raises them up through pursuing social justice. Moreover, it brings down the former through accountability in order to bring the societal playing field into equilibrium. The first will be last and the last will be first, meaning the tables on class and societal norms will be turned.

We just saw how saying "Jesus is Lord" in the mid-to-late first century was not some call to believe in the deity of Christ or the evangelical paradigm. Rather, as David Bentley Hart says, "...it was the claim that all of the orders of power in the world—Empire, Religion, Caste, Class, Wealth, Gods of Nations—had been overpowered and made subject to a peasant called Jesus of Nazareth, whose rule is based on radical charity."[1]

Second, we've made the case that Jesus' way is nonviolent, loving to all including one's adversaries, and redemptive, in that its goal is not punishment of evildoers for punishment's sake. Neither is it revenge, but rather its goal is to restore relationships. We've also established that Jesus and the earliest followers of his way were pacifists.

Moreover, the rationale behind this peaceable way is because it is precisely what humankind needs to survive. "He who lives by the sword, will die by the sword." According to the gospels, Jesus predicted the demise and destruction of the Jewish Temple and city of Jerusalem, because its religious gatekeepers and zealous nationalistic movement would not accept his call for peace with the marginalized masses or with their enemies. Their zeal to punish the "sinful" and hate their enemies would ultimately destroy them.

Rene Girard says this tendency for human self-destruction is born out of mimetic rivalries. The good guys (religious or politically worthy) must conquer the bad guys (the sinful scapegoats) to survive. But that is a fatal mistake.

> Given that Girard believes our desires stem from social rivalry, his warning is: "Choose your enemies carefully because you will become like them." Girard unfashionably denied that there is a significant moral difference between parties to violent conflict: Both are caught up in a demonic logic that will end in mutual destruction.[2]

> Man is creating "more and more violence in a world that is practically without God," if you look at the way nations behave with each other and the way people behave with each other. History, you might say, is a test for mankind. But we know very well that mankind is failing that test...We must face our neighbors and declare unconditional peace. Even if we are provoked, challenged, we must give up violence once and for all.[3]

Give up violence and retaliation approaches to solving social problems. That's a tall order, given our society seems to buy into war and retribution from all sides. The evidence is that Republicans and Democrats alike can be warmongers and generally retributive. George H.W. Bush led us in a Gulf War. George W. Bush got us into the Iraq War, the war in Afghanistan, and the shameful treatment of detainees from the War on Terror. Barak Obama, even though his position was to get us out of the wars in Iraq and Afghanistan, led the effort to kill Osama bin Laden and, along with Hillary Clinton, led us to attack Libya. Obama also ultimately continued the war in Afghanistan. Donald Trump talked a good talk of getting out of foreign wars, but supported Saudi Arabia in their war in Yemen, and he was full of warmongering and hateful rhetoric. Not to mention that he was known for his retributive attitude to relationships, always abandoning and punishing anyone who became disloyal to him. Trump's philosophy of business and life was one of taking revenge on opponents.[4] He also got the federal government back in the execution business. Prior to his presidency, there hadn't been a federal execution of a prisoner since 2003, and there were only three such executions in the last 57 years. In the last six months of Trump's presidency, the federal government executed 13 people.[5]

Republicans and Democrats both called for "tough on crime" legislation that backfired. The Violent Crime Control and Law Enforcement Act of 1994 was hugely bipartisan (a 95 to 4 vote in the Senate), drafted by then-Senator Joe Biden, and signed into law by President Bill Clinton. Despite some good things in the law, such as an Assault Weapons Ban (that expired in 2004) and the Violence Against Women Act, it created 60 new death penalty offenses, eliminated higher education grants for inmates, made membership in gangs a crime, included the three-strikes provision for repeat offenders which created mandatory life sentences under certain circumstances, and accelerated our problem with mass incarceration.

> The legacy of the Violent Crime Control Act and Law Enforcement Act of 1994, better known as the crime bill, has re-emerged in the national debate around criminal justice reform and public safety. Many consider the crime bill to be one of the cornerstone statutes that accelerated mass incarceration. But the law's negative effects did not end there. States and localities were incentivized through a massive infusion of federal funding to build more jails and prisons and to pass so-called truth-in-sentencing laws and other punitive measures that simultaneously increased the number and length of prison sentences while reducing the possibility of early release for those incarcerated. It has been well-documented that these policies were failures.[6]

To reclaim the path of peace, we need to acknowledge, on the negative side, the failure of both war and retributive, or punitive, actions, to both rehabilitate criminals and bring lasting peace to the world. We already addressed this in Chapter 8.

When it comes to war, we must also recognize, on the positive side, that the pursuit of pacifism has a rational basis for it established by social science. Girard has provided some of this for us:

> Whatever the vagaries of his reputation among academics, Girard's most lasting cultural legacy is to provide an intellectual basis for Christian pacifism. Before Girard, pacifists could rely on little more than the sayings of Jesus. Girard's theory of sacred violence provides a comprehensive psychology, anthropology, sociology and theology of peacemaking. If Darwin made atheism intellectually respectable, then Girard has done the same for pacifism.[7]

CHANGE THROUGH LOVE NOT PUNISHMENT

Moreover, in our personal and global conflicts, it is likely the same. You can't change a lost or evil or racist or violent or sexist or homophobic person until they are ready to change—which usually comes after they experience some emotional or mental shock to their lives. And I don't mean punishment from another. The shock typically has to be the variety that pulls them to move toward positive change. Retributive punishment pushes people away and reinforces their tendencies, or just puts fear inside. If it leads to change, it is superficial. If someone changes out of fear, they are only appeasing someone on the outside, not repenting on the inside.

Retribution or punishment does not have any power to change a person. But unconditional love and restoration do. Richard Rohr explains how real change in a person's soul doesn't come from enforcing some tit-for-tat punishment for the crime, but rather from the emotional experience of receiving love. A type of waking up. The apostle Paul put it this way, "God's kindness leads you towards repentance" (Romans 2:4).

This is why love and growth demand discernment, not enforcement. When it comes to actual soul work, most attempts at policing and conforming are largely useless. It took me most of my life as a confessor, counselor, and spiritual director to be honest and truly helpful with people about this. Mere obedience is far too often a detour around actual love. Obedience is usually about cleaning up, love is about waking up.[8]

Our society and most modern Christians have bought into these approaches to address disobedience, criminal behavior, evil deeds, violence, and civil conflicts. Punishment, imprisonment, gun rights, open-carry laws, and war are thought to be answers to these societal and global problems. Yet the peaceable way of Jesus of Nazareth has a profoundly different answer to these problems. "Jesus asks us to consider redemption and posits that only good conquers violence, and that we can covert the violent ones by responding only in love."[9]

Whether one is breaking their own bad and harmful faith paradigm or seeking to find ways of changing our violent, retributive-minded world, the answer is the path of peace. It is not fear of punishment that changes a person, but the experience of being loved, cared for, acknowledged, understood, respected, and corrected with the motivation to restore. Only then can one be challenged to rethink their own harmful, misinformed, and unhistorical worldview. Only then can they change for the good.

JESUS' PATH OF PEACE IN RESPONSE TO VIOLENCE AND HATRED

Shane Claiborne and Michael Martin talk about "the third way of Jesus" in their book, *Beating Guns: Hope for People Who are Weary of Violence*. They cite the two most common responses to violence or the exacting of retribution by victims is to either fight or flee—in other words, the *fight-or-flight* reflex. However, both responses play right into the hands of perpetrators of violence. If you fight back, the perpetrator feels justified in their attack. You have just proven to them you are dangerous and worthy of harm or death. If you flee, the perpetrator feels their attack has proven successful. They were justified in their assault because it worked to drive you away, or it shows you are weak, and they are strong.

The third way is a way that neither fights nor flees. It stands its ground and seeks to disarm the aggressor. Not physically disarm necessarily, although that would be the outcome, but psychologically or spiritually disarm them. It's the way that doesn't overpower and conquer one's enemies, but ultimately changes the enemies to become partners, or even friends.

Jesus gave several examples of disarming one's enemies who were either attacking or abusing. In the Sermon on the Mount, he contradicted the Torah's teaching on resistance and retribution and brought a new ethic of enemy love—one that he said the true Father above practices. And by implication, that the God of Joshua, Judah, Phineas, and other "heroes" of the Jewish scriptures didn't practice.

> You have heard that it was said, "An eye for an eye and a tooth for a tooth." But I say to you, do not resist the one who is evil. But if anyone slaps you on the right cheek, turn to him the other also. And if anyone would sue you and take your tunic, let him have your cloak as well. And if anyone forces you to go one mile, go with him two miles. Give to the one who begs from you, and do not refuse the one who would borrow from you.

> You have heard that it was said, "You shall love your neighbor and hate your enemy." But I say to you, love your enemies and pray for those who persecute you, so that you may be sons of your Father who is in heaven. For he makes his sun rise on the evil and on the good and sends rain on the just and on the unjust. For if you love those who love you, what reward do you have? Do not even the tax collectors do the same? And if you greet only your brothers, what more are you doing than others? Do not even the Gentiles do the same? (Matthew 5:38–47).

> Do to others as you would have them do to you. If you love those who love you, what credit is that to you? For even sinners

love those who love them. If you do good to those who do good to you, what credit is that to you? For even sinners do the same. If you lend to those from whom you hope to receive, what credit is that to you? Even sinners lend to sinners, to receive as much again. But love your enemies, do good, and lend, expecting nothing in return. Your reward will be great, and you will be children of the Most High; for he is kind to the ungrateful and the wicked. Be merciful, just as your Father is merciful (Luke 6:31–36).

The admonitions to turn the other cheek to an aggressor, to give the one suing you for a grievance more than they ask, and to walk a second mile for an occupying soldier, are examples of this disarming technique. All of these ways force the aggressor to recognize the humanity of the victim and force them to see their own unjust violence, greed, or abuse.

But we also know that Jesus didn't merely practice non-resistance to violence and injustice. He also challenged his enemies with uncomfortable truth. The third way is not passive, as the unfortunate term "pacifist" implies. It does not fight with the same armaments that the violent and abusive use, but neither does it flee the scene to save one's skin. It is a heroic way of both disarming and challenging. Of both mercy and truthful confrontation. To his religious enemies, the teachers of the law and Pharisees, Jesus said:

Woe to you, teachers of the law and Pharisees, you hypocrites! You give a tenth of your spices—mint, dill and cumin. But you have neglected the more important matters of the law—justice, mercy and faithfulness. You should have practiced the latter, without neglecting the former. You blind guides! You strain out a gnat but swallow a camel. Woe to you, teachers of the law and Pharisees, you hypocrites! You clean the outside of the cup and dish, but inside they are full of greed and self-indulgence. Blind Pharisee! First clean the inside of the cup and dish, and then the outside also will be clean. Woe to you, teachers of the law and Pharisees, you hypocrites! You are like whitewashed tombs, which look beautiful on the outside but on the inside are full of the bones of the dead and everything unclean. In the same way, on the outside you appear to people as righteous but on the inside you are full of hypocrisy and wickedness (Matthew 23:23–28).

Beware of the teachers of the law. They like to walk around in flowing robes and love to be greeted with respect in the marketplaces and have the most important seats in the synagogues and the places of honor at banquets. They devour widows' houses and for a show make lengthy prayers. These men will be punished most severely (Luke 20:45–47).

The third way is not the way of some wimpy pacifism, but of strong but steady non-violent resistance that challenges and uncovers injustice, hypocrisy, and frauds, (i.e., those who cover up their own inner evil). Some translators of the Greek, like David Bentley Hart's, say a better word for "hypocrites" in these passages is "charlatans."[10] In other words, these enemies of true faith whom Jesus confronted were frauds. Moreover, the words found in the NIV version of the New Testament about these religious enemies being "punished most severely" are misleading. Punishment in Jesus' love ethic is not about retaliation. In his translation, David Bentley Hart translates it as, "they will receive a severer judgment."[11] Greek lexicographer, Ann Nyland translates it as, "These people will be liable to the most severe judgment."[12]

Still, don't be quick to assume the theme of judgment means retribution or going to hell. Jesus said God is kind to the ungrateful and wicked. These same translators, and many more, have stated that the most severe judgment that modern Christians cite from the New Testament (i.e., *hell* and its other term, *eternal punishment*) should be translated as a metaphor for judgment, not hell. As we learned earlier, most of the words translated hell are actually *gehenna*, which is the garbage dump outside Jerusalem.[13] Eternal punishment is not that at all. The accurate translation of the Greek *aionios kolasis* is *"the chastening of that Age"* (Hart) or *"rehabilitation for a set period of time"* (Nyland). In other words, this is an ethic which has an accountability system that restrains, moderates, and rehabilitates evil or unjust people. It does not exact retribution on them for the sake of lawful punishment but intervenes for the sake of change. It's God's Rehab Center, if you will. Jesus loved his enemies, and the New Testament tells us there were several Pharisees, tax collectors, rich people, violence-prone Zealots, and Roman soldiers who were won over. The word mistranslated "punishment," *kolasis*, means corrective chastisement or rehabilitation. Again, as we learned earlier, there's another Greek word for punishment, *timoria*, which was retributive in nature, but that is not the word used in that passage.

In the 20th century, great examples of movements that took this third way are Mahatma Ghandi and his India independence movement in the 1940s, Martin Luther King, Jr., and the non-violent civil rights movement of the 1960s, and Nelson Mandela and the South African Truth and Reconciliation Commission in the 1990s. All of these took an active resistance to injustice, calling out the truth about fraudulent and unjust systems, while not resorting to violence or pursuing retributive justice, but rather reconciliation.

Criminal Justice Reform

In the 21st century, we have the criminal justice reform movement that has recognized the ineffectiveness, injustice, and danger of retributive forms of accountability in our criminal justice system. Bryan Stevenson, attorney, author, and founder of the Equal Justice Initiative (EJI) is a prime example of this call for change. His story and this movement are depicted in the book and movie by the same name, Just Mercy. The EJI "has worked to eliminate excessive and unfair sentencing, exonerate innocent death row prisoners, confront abuse of the incarcerated and the mentally ill, and aid children prosecuted as adults."[14]

The "tough on crime" policies that led to mass incarceration are rooted in the belief that Black and brown people are inherently guilty and dangerous—and that belief still drives excessive sentencing policies today.

More incarceration doesn't reduce violent crime. Using prisons to deal with poverty and mental illness makes these problems worse. People leave overcrowded and violent jails and prisons more traumatized, mentally ill, and physically battered than they went in.[15]

If our goal is to reduce violent crime and wars, we must use means that work. Another example I love to tell of this third way is the story of Daryl Davis.

Convert Racists Rather Than Write Them Off

Let's say the goal is to end racism by fighting white supremacist groups like the Ku Klux Klan. How could it be done? You could take a retaliatory approach, criminalize racist acts, and seek to prosecute and imprison Ku Klux Klan and white supremacist group members. Of course, this might be successful at taking a number of extremists off the streets, but would the fight have been won?

Enter the third way—the way that Daryl Davis follows without calling it that. One day, Davis, a black musician, met a Ku Klux Klansman at a bar where he was performing. The Klansman was impressed with Davis's music and invited him to have a drink with him. Amazingly, the Klansman admitted it was the first time in his life he had sat down one-on-one with a black man. Davis soon discovered the man was in the Klan. That started Davis down a path to meet more Klan members and ask them one critical question: How can you hate me when you don't even know me?

The first step was to learn about their world. "The best thing you do is you study up on the subject as much as you can. I went in armed, not with a weapon, but with knowledge. I knew as much about the Klan, if not more than many of the Klan people that I interviewed. When they see that you know about their organization, their belief system, they respect you."[16]

Davis discovered the major reason cited or implied for hating blacks was that all blacks are inferior. The Klan members sincerely believed that blacks have smaller brains, were incapable of learning higher knowledge, and have a gene that makes them violent. Davis' approach was to befriend Klan members, gain their respect from his knowledge of their organization, and then start challenging these racist views. His goal was not to take revenge or demand retribution on racist people who had harmed individual blacks and society, but rather to seek to understand them and then seek to be understood.

Davis began to turn their internal "logic" on themselves. "I'm not violent. Your theory doesn't hold," he said to one who used the violent gene argument.

"That's because your gene is latent," the man said. Dumbfounded, Davis was speechless. Finally, he thought of reciprocal logic. He claimed everybody knows white people have a gene that makes them serial killers.

"What do you mean?" the man replied.

All serial killers are white, Davis explained. When he asked him to name three black serial killers, the Klan member couldn't, wherein Davis immediately named four very famous white ones. "Son, you are a serial killer," he declared.

"I've never killed anybody," he replied.

"Your gene is latent, it hasn't come out yet," Davis retorted. Ultimately, the man had to concede he had a point, that it's easy to paint someone in a bad light by manipulating facts.

Through befriending Klansmen, doing them favors, visiting their meetings, and calmly challenging their world view, over the years, Davis eventually convinced 200 Klan members to give up their robes. Admittedly, Davis acknowledges some are beyond saving. But his approach works on those who aren't.[17]

> That began to chip away at their ideology because when two enemies are talking, they're not fighting. It's when the talking ceases that the ground becomes fertile for violence. If you spend five minutes with your worst enemy—it doesn't have to be about race, it could be about anything...you will find that you both have something in common. As you build upon those commonalities, you're forming a relationship and as you build about that relationship, you're forming a friendship. That's what would happen. I didn't convert anybody. They saw the light and converted themselves.[18]

A Jewish Couple Changes an Extremist's Mind

In his book, *The Catalyst: How to Change Anyone's Mind*, Jonah Berger tells the story of Michael and Julie Weisser. Michael was a newly appointed Rabbi at the local synagogue in Lincoln, Nebraska. One day they received a call. The caller spoke one sentence and then hung up: "You will be sorry you ever moved to 5810 Randolph Street, Jew boy."

Days later, a package came in the mail with more threats. "The KKK is watching you, scum," a lone note read. The package was full of flyers and brochures with racist and hateful themes that were spouting the inferiority of non-whites and Nazi narratives that were praising the Holocaust. Police believed the man responsible was a notorious KKK leader named Larry Trapp who loved violence and stockpiled automatic weapons.

Scared and intimidated, the Weissers didn't know what to do. Julie ended up doing some research on Trapp and discovered he had serious health problems as a diabetic and both his legs had been amputated.

Later, Michael decided to call Trapp back and try to both reason with him and extend a little kindness. The man never answered the phone, so Michael left the following messages.

"Larry, you better think about all this hatred you're spreading, because one day you're going to have to answer to God for all this hatred, and it's not going to be easy."

He used Daryl Davis' line (not knowing, to my knowledge, who Davis was). "Why do you hate me? You don't even know me, so how can you hate me?" He tried to reason with Trapp about the truth about Nazism. "Larry, do you know the very first laws the Hitler's Nazis passed were against people like yourself who had no legs? ...Do you realize you would have been among the first to die under Hitler? Why do you love Nazis so much?"

"Larry, there's a lot of love out there. You're not getting any of it. Don't you want some?"

Eventually, Larry answered the phone and laid into Michael with some F bombs. "What the fuck do you want? Why the fuck are you harassing me?"

"I'm not trying to harass you, Larry, I just want to talk," Michael said.

"Make it quick."

"Well, I was thinking you might need a hand with something, and I wondered if I could help. I know you're in a wheelchair, and I thought maybe I could take you to the grocery store or something."

That struck a chord. Larry was shocked and at a loss for words. He abruptly ended the call without taking up the offer but seemed to appreciate it. Eventually, things came to a head. One night, Larry called asking for the Rabbi and said, "I want out, but I don't know how." Within a short time, Larry had agreed for Michael and Julie to come over with some food to talk. After they did, Larry ultimately broke down and cried, admitted his problem with hatred, and said he was sorry. Michael and Julie put their arms around him and told him everything would be okay. With time, Larry formally resigned from the KKK and began apologizing to all the people he had hurt.

What blew me away is what happened at the end. Because of Trapp's failing health due to kidney failure, for which the doctors gave him a year to live, and the fact that the Weissers invited him into their home to live so Julie could care for him, Larry Trapp actually converted to Judaism. The restoration of relationships was complete. He had been converted by love, not retribution, punishment, or the threat of hell.[19]

Kindness in a Mosque Stops a Domestic Terrorist in His Tracks

These examples show that the goal in taking the third way is not a conversion to Christianity or any particular religion, but rather a simple conversion to love. An unconditional love that can take many forms and does not need to be communicated through people of faith, nor does it limit what brands of faith are acceptable. Contrary, to what religionists tell you, this is the way of Jesus. It doesn't convert people to another religion, but to a new way of life, or as Tolstoy would say, a new *theory of life*.

Richard "Mac" McKinney, a former Marine, had developed a hatred of Islam from his experience in combat in Iraq and Afghanistan, which taught him to see Muslims as subhuman. He came to believe, through a painfully warped interpretation of Islam, that all of it was a cancer worthy of eradication. When he returned home to Muncie, Indiana, he saw how many Muslim immigrants and converts had since settled in his former community. He was furious. One Friday in 2009, he went to the Islamic Center of Muncie with an overall mission of planting a bomb at the mosque "in hopes of killing or wounding hundreds of Muslims." In this particular scouting visit, something happened that changed the whole trajectory of both his evil philosophy and his life.

Several of the mosque leaders welcomed him. One of them, Bibi Bahrami, called by some "the Mother Teresa of the Muslim community," reached out to Richard and invited him to her home. She prepared a delicious Afghan meal for him. Others in the mosque, including Bibi's husband Moham-mad, spoke to him with kindness, and several literally embraced him. Their philosophy, as Bibi would state, was that "God created all of us to get to know each other and take care of each other—not to despise." In time, a remarkable transformation took place in Richard. He continued to visit the mosque. Within weeks, he formed friendships with Muslims. Astonishingly, he eventually converted to Islam and became one of the mosque's leaders. It was the kindness of the people at the Center that was most decisive in converting him, McKinney shared. His story is told in the documentary, "Stranger at the Gate."[20]

Plotting Peace Not War

The way of Christ is to stop waging war and start plotting peace the way Daryl Davis, Michael Weisser, Julie Weisser, Bibi Bahrami, and Mohammad Bahrami did. In another example that exemplifies this, Claiborne and Martin tell the story of a petite woman who was mugged on a train. At knife point, her assailant told her, "Here's the deal. You're going to give me your bag, get off at the next train station, and not say a word." Her reaction? She looked up at him and introduced herself. She then shared about her loved ones at home and about some photos of her family in the bag. "You want money, I imagine, not these photos," she told him. "In my pocket is $20, which I'm glad to share with you. I will give it to you, and then you get off at the next stop and not say anything." And that's exactly what happened.[21]

Plotting peace is still risky and comes at a cost. The first time Davis met a Klansman privately, he feared for his life. The Weissers had courage to reach back to Larry Trapp, a known, violent leader of the local Klan, and offer to come to his home. When members of the Islamic Center of Muncie first saw an angry-faced McKinney with USMC and skull tattoos, they feared trouble. The petite woman took a chance at not doing exactly what her assailant told her and putting it back on him. Turning the other cheek risks getting hit again. Going another mile with a soldier costs your time and sweat. But showing human kindness while standing up to injustice, without the goal of retribution, bears fruit.

Plotting peace means to use the mistakes, sins, or violence of others in a strategic way, or as Fr. Richard Rohr says, "use them for transformative purposes."[22] Not to punish people, but also not to eliminate the sins as if they were never there. Forgiveness is not forgetting someone's offense altogether. We are acknowledging there is something to forgive, but rather choosing not to punish the person for the offense.

In January 2022, after Bahamian-American actor Sidney Poitier died, I re-watched the classic 1967 movie, *To Sir, With Love*, about an out-of-work engineer (Mark Thackeray played by Poitier) who took on a high school teaching job in inner city London. Exasperated from not getting through to his unruly, obnoxious, out-of-control teenage students through conventional means, he changed his tactics. Rather than being punitive, he began to treat them like adults, to teach them based on their own interests, and to demonstrate unconditional forgiveness and love. For example, an angry boy who opposed Thackeray challenged him to a boxing match in gym class. The student tried to take him down but lost the match. Thackeray did not "finish him off." Afterwards, Thackeray offered to find a job for the student upon graduation, which turned the relationship. The overall result, after a roller coaster of classroom emotions, was the students coming to genuinely love and respect Thackeray and begin taking education and career choices seriously. This is in stark contrast to another teacher with years of experience who had totally given up on helping students and held deep resentments against them.

Another example I like to cite is the critically acclaimed *Ted Lasso* comedy-drama series on Apple TV. Ted is the Christ-figure of the show. As the newly appointed soccer coach from the U.S. for a team in the U.K., no one likes him or treats him well. He also doesn't lead the team to a win the whole first season. Yet, he continually treats others with respect and kindness, while throwing in some friendly humor. Eventually they all come over to his side and become good friends. Kindness and some playful zingers win out. The team actually starts winning a few games. Lasso on scones: "It's like a muffin, except it sucks all the spit out of your mouth." On tea: "I always figured that tea was going to taste like hot brown water. And you know what? I was right. Yeah, it's horrible. No, thank you." After losing a game: "I come bearing sweet treats to numb the sting of defeat."

Finally, two recently published books spell out the path of peace that we want to reclaim. One is *Love Your Enemies: How Decent People Can Save America from the Culture of Contempt* by social scientist, Arthur C. Brooks. Brooks shows how today's American society has developed an "outrage industrial complex" that creates a "culture of contempt" towards people who disagree, typically about politics or religion. Social media has made this much easier to do. Ad hominem attacks against "the other" are common. Rather than a person having a different opinion about something, they are described, or at least perceived, as evil. Those "evil" liberals or "evil" conservatives or "evil" QAnon followers.

The answer? Love people. Love "the other." Not the kind of love that would ignore facts in order to come to some inauthentic middle ground, but a love that acknowledges that while some positions are worthy of contempt, no person is. Treat people kindly, with love and respect, even when you vehemently disagree with their position. This does not mean you never set boundaries in relationships or never stand up to people. It's how you do those things that matter.

The second book is *Saving Grace: Speak Your Truth, Stay Centered, and Learn to Coexist with People Who Drive You Nuts*, by Kirsten Powers. Ah, now that's a great title! Believe me, people like my newly found friend who vehemently insisted JFK, Jr., was alive, or those who are still convinced Biden and the Democrats stole the 2020 election from Trump, or my friends (and family!) who are still evangelicals and staunchly defend hell and the inerrancy of the Bible, they oftentimes drive me crazy. But the thing is, they probably think the same about me.

Powers, a political analyst and columnist, has done us a great service in her book. She tells us how to stand up to people we think take dangerous or deceptive positions and do it with grace. She tells us we don't have to abandon our passionate beliefs and values in order to engage with people with opposing views. Heck, we don't even have to be nice all the time. Jesus wasn't. After all, we just saw how he called the religious priests and "teachers of the law" whitewashed tombs and a brood of vipers. Powers "dismantles the widespread misconception that grace means being nice, letting people get away with harmful behavior, or choosing neutrality in the name of peace. Grace," she argues, "is anything but an act of surrender; instead, it is a kinetic and transformative force."[23]

But it's not only for the person that is driving us nuts, it's for us as well. It frees us from resentments and protects us from personal attacks that foster bitterness inside us.

ELEVEN

MODERN PEACE MOVEMENTS AS OUR GUIDE

MY OWN EPIPHANY ABOUT the horrors of war and violence and the superiority of peace came when I read *All Quiet on the Western Front* when I was in high school. I had heard background noise on the anti-war arguments about the Vietnam War, but it never hit home until I cracked open this small book, considered by many as the greatest war novel of all time. Written from the perspective of a German soldier during World War I, it captures the fear, despair, death, and mindless hatred "that meaninglessly pits young men of the same generation but different uniforms against one another."[1] As a sixteen-year-old, the depictions of gore and violence and the absurd justifications for war haunted me for days after reading it.

A year later, I read Kurt Vonnegut's *Slaughterhouse Five*, a fantasy novel about a man named Billy Pilgrim, based partly on Vonnegut's experience surviving the Allied bombing of the German city of Dresden in 1945. As an American prisoner of war held in the city, Vonnegut lived to tell what it was like in the midst of in a modern-war firestorm that killed up to 35,000 civilians. The Americans and British justified it as a necessary evil to defeat Hitler. The book exposes the hypocrisy of that mindset.

Another, more sophisticated, realization came in my twenties after reading *Vietnam: A History* by Stanley Karnow and hearing of the sad story of war-torn Vietnam, the tragedy of the war, and the many mistakes American presidents made—Johnson and Nixon mostly—that caused the war to escalate and go on for so long. The mind-numbing details of all this came into full focus after reading Robert McNamara's *In Retrospect: The Tragedy and Lessons of Vietnam* years later. Moreover, watching every episode of Ken Burns' documentary, *The Vietnam War: An Intimate History* was like a belt to the side of my head that woke me again to the pointlessness and moral failures of all wars, not just Vietnam. The anti-war peace activists during the Vietnam War got this—often because they were made up of Vietnam veterans like John Kerry and Brian Wilson, members of Vietnam Veterans Against the War, who could attest to the hypocritical and outrageous waging of the war.

Finally, Chris Hedges, who spent 20 years as a global war correspondent, doesn't mince words or real-life war stories told by himself and war veterans, in his latest book, *The Greatest Evil is War*. "The primary lesson in war is that we as distinct individuals do not matter. We become numbers. Fodder. Objects. Life, once precious and sacred, becomes meaningless, sacrificed to the insatiable appetite of Mars [the Roman god of war]." Reading parts of this book reminded me how insensitive and naïve I had become by the time of the Iraq War. I initially supported it based on U.S. Secretary of State Colin Powell's speech at the U.N. where he justified the invasion (later to be discovered his and Bush's rationale was based on lies and speculation). I rationalized Saddam Hussein was so brutally evil the war was a just cause. I forgot, as Hedges reminds us, "there are no good wars." Violence doesn't really solve anything. The testimony of soldiers serving in Iraq and Afghanistan he documents revealed that those wars only created conditions for more hatred and terrorism against us.[2]

EXAMPLES OF NON-VIOLENT MOVEMENTS

Bertha Von Suttner and the Abolition of War Movement

Most of us are well aware of the Vietnam-era peace movements, the non-violent civil rights movement of the 1960s, and the wide opposition to the Iraq War in the 2000s. Yet, we are ignorant of the large-scale peace movements in Europe and America between the Civil War and World War I.

These peace movements got real steam in 1889 when an Austrian noblewoman named Bertha von Suttner wrote a very popular war novel called *Lay Down Your Arms*. Suttner became the founder and chairwoman of the German Peace Society and urged for the establishment of an International Court of Justice, a world organization that would settle disputes between states in accordance with international law. She campaigned for peace all over Europe and regularly met with government officials. Her book "thus contains both the academic arguments in favor of pacifism and an abandonment of conflict as being a way forward for humanity..."[3]

The great Russian novelist and progressive Christian, Leo Tolstoy, was a supporter of Suttner. He wrote *War and Peace* and the faith classic, *The Kingdom of God is Within You*, which extols the virtues of non-violence, peace, and restoration. Tolstoy was the other strong voice to this transatlantic peace movement. He wrote of Suttner, "The abolition of slavery was preceded by the famous book of a woman, Mrs. Beecher Stowe [*Uncle Tom's Cabin*]; God grant that the abolition of war may follow upon yours." Tolstoy hoped Suttner's influential and epic story "would raise consciousness of war's evils so that the old law protecting war would crumble and a new one prohibiting it—God's law of love—would take its place."[4]

Suttner helped inspire the Nobel Peace Prize and later won it in 1905, the first woman to do so. Suttner and Tolstoy shared the same vision of peace and pacifism but had different philosophies on how to achieve it. Suttner favored promoting peace and holding conferences to achieve agreements between states. She supported campaigns that employed the objectives of arbitration treaties, peace unions between nations, and an international body with the strength to maintain law between nations.[5]

Tolstoy's Call for a New Philosophy of Life Based on Non-violence

Tolstoy was suspicious of such methods. He advocated for individual conversions to pacifism. "For the disappearance of war, there is no need of conferences," he said. "As long as every man at the age of twenty or twenty-one abjures his religion [Christian love for enemy and the Jewish call of 'thou shalt not kill'] and promises to kill all those whom his superior orders him to kill...so long war will not cease; and it will grow more and more cruel, as it is already becoming in our day."[6] Contrasted with Suttner, Tolstoy believed that individuals, not states, needed to heed the call to "lay down their arms." Tolstoy supported pacifist communities, such as the Dukhobors of his day, a Christian sect in Russia that was persecuted by the Russian Orthodox Church and the Czar.

Tolstoy arrived at his philosophy of non-violence and pacifism by his understanding of the love ethic of Jesus. He claimed that an objective study of history is the key to religious thought and advocated for an authentic "Christianity not as a mystic religion, but as a new theory of life" in his book *The Kingdom of God is Within You*. This book should be required reading for every person who claims to be a Christian. It advocates for this new theory of life based on restoration rather than retribution in all of life's spheres. It was the book Mahatma Gandhi cited as his chief influence in forming his non-violent methodology to stand up to British colonialism in India.

E. Stanley Jones and the Promotion of a Peaceable Kingdom

E. Stanley Jones also understood Jesus' path of peace. As a Methodist missionary to India starting in the early 1900s, Jones was very popular as a speaker. His practice was to never attack other religions. He separated Jesus from Western culture and was one of the first missionary proponents of "indigenization"—a way to share the good news of Christ through indigenous cultural forms rather than importing Western Christian practices. He did this by founding "Ashrams"—spiritual and monastic communities common among Hindus—rather than planting Western-style churches. Indigenization was updated and renamed "contextualization" in the late 20th century and was one of the strategies I studied and attempted to practice as an evangelical missionary in the 1980s and 90s in Africa (certainly not all evangelical missionaries practiced this). But Jones' indigenization went further than contextualization. He encouraged a universal approach to evangelism, interfaith cooperation, and learning from other faiths.[7] He was not an "us vs. them" conservative Christian.

Jones became close friends with Mahatma Gandhi, the Nehru family (anti-colonial nationalists), and others in the movement for Indian independence. He later wrote a biography of Gandhi. Martin Luther King, Jr., remarked that it was through reading Jones' book that he was spurred to create a strategy of strict non-violent resistance in the civil rights movement.

Jones initiated "round-table" conferences that brought Christians, Hindus, Muslims, agnostics, and atheists together. Rather than arguing for the supremacy of his own Christian faith, he created an environment "in which all voices could speak equally" about their faith experiences and allowed the outcome of the conversation to be left to the Spirit. Rather than watering down the message of Jesus, these meetings brought out a common thirst for faith and meaning in people's lives.[8]

> Mahatma Gandhi...has taught me more about the spirit of Christ than perhaps any other man in East or West. — E. Stanley Jones

Jones was always seeking restoration and peace in relationships and was well known as an effective peacemaker.

> Later in his ministry he traveled around the world speaking about peace and international understanding. He said, "Peace is a by-product of conditions out of which peace naturally comes. If reconciliation is God's chief business, it is ours—between man and God, between man and himself, and between man and man." His efforts of reconciliation in Africa, Asia and between Japan and the United States earned him a nomination for the Nobel Peace Prize. In Japan he was hailed as "The Apostle of Peace."[9]

Resisting Nazism Without Violence

Movements like Gandhi's, Jones', and later Martin Luther King Jr.,'s are peace initiatives done without the use of violence or militarism. Rather than taking up arms and fighting the oppressors with weapons of war, the oppressed people accept the control of the oppressors outwardly but not inwardly. They resist through non-violent means in order to de-escalate the cycle of violence, save lives, protect and stand up for the innocent, and restore economic and social justice.

In Craft Brewed Jesus, I tell the story of how Denmark resisted the Nazis despite not taking up arms to fight them. The story comes from a documentary series called *A Force More Powerful*, which traces six examples of such non-violent resistance in the 20th century (Denmark, India, Poland, Chile, and South Africa) and shows how nonviolent power overcame oppression and authoritarian rule. Here's what I wrote about what was accomplished through non-violent means:

> In 1940, Denmark stood up to Nazi occupation in a most extraordinary way. Rejecting militarism, they first used 're-sistance disguised as collaboration.' In time, through nonco-operation at factories (Nazis had taken them over to build war armaments and ships), acts of sabotage, and governmental stalling, they saved countless lives while opposing the Nazis at every turn. An underground resistance movement supplanted the Danish government that had eventually walked out on Nazi demands. Their indirect tactics and the compassion of the populace protected almost all of Denmark's seven thou-sand Jews from the holocaust.[10]

Peace and Restoration in South Africa

Another example of modern peacemaking is the leadership of Nelson Mandela, Desmond Tutu, and President F.W. De Klerk in apartheid South Africa. In 1990, De Klerk agreed to lift the ban on liberation movements and op-position political parties and release Nelson Mandela from his 27 years in prison. This was an amazing turn of events and a brave decision by De Klerk, who faced severe criticism. It ultimately paved the way for a negotiated peace settlement between the apartheid regime and the anti-apartheid movement. This essentially ended colonialism, the engrained system of racial segregation, and discrimination that had been in place in South Africa for 300 years and led to the country's first democratic elections.

The remarkable part of this historic change was the decision not to pursue the prosecution of people in the apartheid regime for their past crimes. Rather than a retributive approach, the country told the truth about the injustices that occurred, allowed victims to tell their stories, held perpetrators accountable by forcing them to face the truth, granted them amnesty (rather than punishment the way the Nuremberg trials did to Nazi perpetrators), and set a reparations policy. The work of deciding the terms and implementing the project was done by The Truth and Reconciliation Commission, of which Mandela and Tutu were leaders.

The Nonviolent Philosophy of Martin Luther King, Jr.

Martin Luther King, Jr., did not plan to be an icon of the American Civil Rights Movement. He wanted to pastor a church and raise a family. Then he was asked to lead a bus boycott initiative in Montgomery, Alabama. His passion, theology, and oratory skills ultimately propelled him into a leadership role in the wider civil rights movement. He became the founding president of the Southern Christian Leadership Conference, which "advocated confrontation of segregation through civil dissent. This 'direct action' included boycotts, marches, and other forms of nonviolent protest."[11]

As mentioned, King got his ideas and tactics for non-violent resistance from Mahatma Gandhi (E. Stanley Jones' book). Gandhi had gleaned his own philosophy of non-violence from Leo Tolstoy and Tolstoy's book, *The Kingdom of God is Within You*. In the book, Tolstoy spelled out how Christianity has been warped and how we need to understand Jesus' teachings not as a religion but as a new theory of life. He derived his case from Jesus' teaching on turning the other cheek, loving one's enemies, standing up for the oppressed, and challenging people who follow evil ways to change. He asserted that to follow Christ's theory of life is to abolish violence, even the defensive kind, and to stop seeking revenge.

From Tolstoy's assertions, King established his own philosophy of non-violence that many others emulated. For example, black college students in Nashville, Tennessee, organized nonviolent lunch counter sit-ins to fight racial segregation in 1960 as well as marches and boycotts. In his philosophy,

King cited the triple evils of poverty, racism, and militarism as the main targets for nonviolent resistance. We often forget that he was not just fighting for civil rights of non-whites who were oppressed by poverty and racism, but also for the rights of all to live peaceably with equal justice. He said, "A true revolution of values will lay hands on the world order and say of war—'This way of settling differences is not just.' This way of burning human beings with napalm, of filling our nation's homes with orphans and widows, of injecting poisonous drugs of hate into the veins of peoples normally humane, of sending men home from dark and bloody battlefields physically handicapped and psychologically deranged, cannot be reconciled with wisdom, justice and love."[12]

His six principles of nonviolence are an apt lesson for us today:[13]

1. Nonviolence is a Way of Life for Courageous People – It is not for cowards; it is an active form of resistance.

2. Nonviolence Seeks to Win Friendships and Understanding – The end result is redemption and reconciliation.

3. Nonviolence Seeks to Defeat Injustice or Evil, Not People – It recognizes that evildoers are also victims and are not evil people.

4. Nonviolence Holds That Unearned, Voluntary Suffering for a Just Cause Can Educate and Transform People and Societies – It's willing to accept violence if necessary but to never inflict it. It recognizes unjust suffering has tremendous transforming possibilities.

5. Nonviolence Chooses Love Instead of Hate – It resists violence of the spirit as well as the body.

6. Nonviolence Believes That the Universe is on the Side of Justice – It believes that God is a God of justice.

William Barber II and the Poor People's Campaign

The first time I heard Rev. William Barber II speak at the Wild Goose Festival, he reminded me of Martin Luther King, Jr., in TV clips I watched over the years. His low, booming voice and larger-than-life presence had a profound impact on me. Not only was it his impressive nature, but the content of his message. Barber helps lead the nonviolent Poor People's Campaign, a vision that began with Dr. King. They advocate for a moral revival (for equality and social justice) in the spirit of Jesus. Barber reminds us that the good news of Christ is "good news for the poor" (Luke 4:18) and not a religious salvation from a wrathful god. It is glad tidings for the "least of these" in our midst—the poor, immigrants, working-class whites, religious minorities, people of color, and the LGBTQ community—with a call for the affluent and political elites to repent of greed and reckless disregard for the needy. The approach of the movement is not one of gaining justice and equality through retaliation but through love in action. Through "fusion politics," which creates coalitions that often transcend conservative vs. liberal. Their covenant is based on these nonviolent principles: (1) I will act with respect towards all. (2) I will speak truth to power. (3) I will seek to defeat injustice, not people. (4) I will accept the consequences for my actions for justice. (5) I will not resist arrest, use hostile language or insults, carry or use weapons, or make any threats of violence. (6) I will walk in love. (7) I believe the universe is on the side of justice. (8) I am committed to a movement, not a moment.[14] This too is the way of Jesus and the theory of life to which he calls us to embrace. It's not a religious path.

Using Restorative Strategies to Fight Terrorism

In 2013, police in the Danish city of Aarhus had a choice. They could pass tough-on-extremist laws and arrest and jail young Muslims who threatened to go to Syria and fight in the war as Jihadists. Or they could try "The Dutch Approach," a strategy developed in the Netherlands that made friends with one's enemies. They chose the latter, despite detractors that called the move "weak and naïve."

They offered the teenagers tea and someone to mentor them. They mobilized family and friends to reach out and assure them that they were loved. The police strengthened ties with the local mosque. The police chief said it this way:

> What's easy is to pass tough new laws. Harder is to go through a real process with individuals: a panel of experts, counselling, healthcare, assistance getting back into education, with employment, maybe accommodation...We don't do this out of political conviction; we do it because we think it works.[15]

And it did work. In other European cities, the exodus of extremists going to fight in Syria continued at the same high rates. In Aarhus, it dramatically declined to a trickle.[16]

With these historic non-violent peace initiatives as our guide, let's finally turn to the task of how to break bad faith as individuals and as a society. Only then can we recover the path of peace that slowly evolved from the story of Joseph's reconciliation with his family (Genesis) to the prophets telling us to feed our enemies when they are hungry (Proverbs), to Jesus' call to forgive and be kind to the wicked and ungrateful while still standing up to injustice (The Gospels), to our modern non-violent movements to forge civil rights (King), to the heroic tasks to reconcile people within nations (Gandhi and Jones in India and Mandela in South Africa), to the movement to bring equality to the oppressed and least of these (Barber).

Twelve

BREAKING BAD FAITH FOR THE SAKE OF PEACE

HERETICAL, NONSENSICAL, AND HARMFUL BAD FAITH

WE SHOULD WANT TO break the habit of bad faith when we come to recognize that it is heretical. It is actually antithetical to the original message of Jesus. We also should want to break it when we realize that it is nonsensical. Jesus taught his followers to love God with their whole mind (remember, he actually added the word "mind" to the original command in the Torah), and he taught in a way that appealed to common sense. Finally, we should want to break it when we realize that it is harmful. It hurts us, others, and fosters a retributive way of addressing relational problems in the world. These three reasons are precisely why theologies are deemed bad or worth rejecting. They are opposed to sound thinking about history, theology, and love of humanity. Bad faith makes belief in God no different than belief in superstitious paganism.

Michael Hardin makes a concise case how the four major pillars of a bad faith—the punitive-wrathful-God atonement theory, the doctrine of hell, the belief in the inerrancy of the Bible, and the justification of violence practiced by God and our society—are tied together and are in fact all heretical. However, once they are stripped way, broken if you will, we can clearly see the authentic good news (gospel) of peace. Hardin states:

> I remind you that the four pillars of Protestant Orthodoxy, penal satisfaction atonement theory, eternal perdition, the inerrancy view of Scripture and the justification of violence are

all of one piece. Together these constitute what Rene Girard terms "the sacrificial hermeneutic." I am asserting that this way of rendering the biblical message is heresy, for it ultimately violates the integrity of the character of God as revealed in Jesus. This approach to interpreting Scripture can only, in the long run, say that God is no different than all the other gods of human religion only that this God is the true God. If the Living God is no different in character than all the other gods of human religion then what is said about God is idolatry. The logic of the sacrificial hermeneutic leads only to idolatry.

Now this is a bold assertion and I am sure that detractors will say that I am being unkind or unfair. Let it be said, however, that my goal is not simply to deconstruct Protestant Orthodoxy (and its step-children Fundamentalism and Evangelicalism) but to offer a reconstruction that takes quite seriously all the great doctrines of the church. A sacrificial reading of the Bible can only render a Janus-faced god (a god of two faces). In this view God consists of attributes that must "be held in tension." As I said in The Jesus Driven Life, if this is the case, then what we are left with, ultimately, is a god who is just like us, loving and hating, violent and forgiving, merciful and punitive, etc. This is not the God revealed in Jesus. This is a god who needs medication and a shrink.

Here is where my previous assertion that we need to have a "Christ-crucified centered" approach problematizes the sacrificial hermeneutic. If God was in Christ reconciling the world to God's self, and we also assert that the Father was pouring out wrath on the Son, we differentiate the retributive Father from the merciful Son. The work of the Father, to rid God's self of "righteous wrath" and the work of the Son to accept this wrath on our behalf as a merciful substitute creates a schism in the Trinity and overlooks the critical element in atonement. How is God reconciling the world to God's self? "By not counting sins against us" (2 Cor 5:16-20). This is exactly the same work as the Son who cried repeatedly from the cross, "Father, forgive them" (Luke 23:32). And God did. Forgiveness freely given, without consideration of repentance or even faith. In other words, the attitude and posture of the loving divine Trinity towards us begins with forgiveness apart from some sort of transaction between the Father and the Son. The fact is that nowhere in the New Testament can the Protestant Orthodox believer find a single verse that says the Father was pouring out wrath on the Son. This is a conclusion that can only be derived from a number of faulty premises, but it is never asserted as a datum in the apostolic writings.

If one believes in the penal satisfaction theory of the atonement, one is bound then to assert equivalence between the sacrificial system of the Old Testament and the death of Jesus. This is precisely the opposite direction of the apostolic tradition and of Jesus' message and ministry which is anti-sacrificial in character. In order to assert this equivalence the Protestant must then assert the equivalence of the two Testaments thus forming the basis for both the [inerrancy] logic and a corresponding hermeneutic.

This false atonement theory and the view of the Bible as "the Word of God" are of a single piece. To deconstruct one is to deconstruct the other. Once this is done then the concept of eternal perdition and the justification of violence follow and are also deconstructed. When that occurs what we are left with is the "evangel," truly good news![1]

Hardin's statement describes the bad faith that our society and religious establishments have bought into. We desperately need to break it, and by so doing, rediscover good news.

THE CHALLENGES AND REWARDS
OF BREAKING BAD FAITH

In my experience, whether it's religious, cultural, or personal, people don't change unless something very painful or very emotional happens in their life. People become drug addicts or alcoholics largely because they are masking some underlying pain, or, in the case of opioid addiction, they are desperate to alleviate physical pain. Often people finally overcome addictions because they hit rock bottom and start to admit they have a problem and need help. Oftentimes, a person who experiences great loss, trauma, depression, or other emotional pain, begins to rethink other areas of their life that they may need to change.

Likewise, with some exceptions, I believe people don't come into the evangelical church unless they have grown up in it or have had some crisis in their life—usually during their formative years—that drives them to seek answers. Droves of young people came into the church in the late 60s and then the 70s and 80s due to disillusionment with their generation's social and drug-fueled revolution. "The Jesus Revolution," as Time Magazine called it, ensued. I didn't seriously come into the evangelical church until I had a nervous breakdown in college. Notwithstanding a positive spiritual experience that I had shortly thereafter, my coming into the church was driven by a pressing personal need for love, acceptance, and community.

Moreover, I never directly addressed my own harmful evangelical theology, except on the edges, until I fell into clinical depression in the mid-to-late 1990s and began to question it more seriously. There is countless documentation of people leaving the evangelical church mostly due to suffering spiritual abuse caused by church leaders and harmful religious systems.

It is the same for someone who realizes they need to break a bad-faith habit. Usually, unless something very difficult or emotional happens in their life, they are not ready to deconstruct their faith. But once a door is opened, that is, something has happened to open their eyes to alternative ways of thinking, a faith shift can begin to occur. More often than not, it happens slowly, like peeling layers of an onion, as one addresses their harmful paradigms on God and theology and then discovers more historical and restorative views. In the end, it is a beautiful transformation that sets people free from destructive religious thought patterns. And in the case where people find more historic, theistic views, it helps people reconstruct a beautiful, non-religious "faith" based on the restorative and subversive way of Jesus.

We need to break bad faith in our society in two ways. One, for individuals who have embraced both violent sacrificial religion and various frauds and myths in Western Christianity (whether inadvertently or not), they need to deconstruct these paradigms as they are able and willing. This is the individual, one-by-one spiritual evolution that is going on today where so many evangelicals and fundamentalists are leaving the conservative-minded church. Or, in some cases, they are trying to radically reform it (whether it's worth trying to reform is another debate).

And it's not just conservatives who need this change. Many in the progressive Christian movement—liberals, if you will—may have more historically-grounded ideas about Christianity. However, they may still have retributive notions of how to right the ideological ship to fight racism, homophobia, white supremacy, injustice, and the like. Some of them, like those who resorted to violence during the Black Lives Matter protests, have not fully embraced nor practice the enemy-love and forgiving-victim ethic of Jesus. These folks still want to impose changes on others, from mandating politically correct language and history to calling for punishments and monetary reparations. It's not that requiring good historical studies or agreeing to reparations is bad. They can be very good. Rather, it's often about the goal behind this approach. For some, their goal is not necessarily extending forgiveness and seeking reconciliation of relationships. It's more about punishing people for punishment's sake. It's more about retribution. This individual reformation is not an easy task, nor will it happen overnight. Patience is called for.

The second thing that needs to happen is within our society as a whole. The world is still obsessed with retributive tools and war as instruments of change. Just-war theory is not even followed, but even if it was, it appears to be a pipedream. Claiming that war is a necessary evil appears to be a myth. Violence only begets more violence and prolongs war. Making war more humane has backfired, putting us into circumstances where war becomes inevitable and ongoing. For both combatant and non-combatant survivors, the effects of war ruin lives through PTSD or physical and economic destruction.

Public opinion needs to shift on this. It already has, to some degree, when it comes to criminal justice reform. People have recognized our method of holding people accountable for crimes, when only focused on punishment and retribution, is counterproductive, resulting in high recidivism rates for prisoners. Although sometimes supporting such measures for different reasons, some Republicans have joined Democrats supporting legislation to reform our criminal justice system. President Trump did at least one good thing when he was in office. He signed the bipartisan First Step Act, formally known as the Formerly Incarcerated Reenter Society Transformed Safely Transitioning Every Person Act (Trump was initially skeptical of the legislation and was persuaded to sign by his son-in-law Jared Kushner). But there is still a long way to go, and the ideas around spreading Restorative Justice Centers need to be taken seriously.

But in regard to war, we have an even longer way to go. There needs to be a groundswell of public opinion that it's time to try worldwide peace movements again. It's time for another movement to abolish war, or at the very least, a commitment to pursue every non-violent means of solving domestic and international conflicts before a physical war is even considered, let alone pursued.

Now let's take a closer look at these two ways of breaking bad faith.

Individual Religious Deconstruction and Reclamation

How does an individual break bad faith associated with violent sacrificial religion and the various frauds and myths in Western Christianity? Once they are open to the possibility that at least some aspects of their faith are bad or unhistorical or misguided, it's a matter of going on an historical journey. Bad theology is based on a bad study of history. Good theology can only be derived from a sound study of history—one that starts with the foundation, not the observation tower. So, one must rediscover a good study of the original Jesus Movement, learn how it differs from most (not all) versions of modern faith, and how much of later Christian history warped the original "good news of the reign of God" that Jesus taught. It's important to make the journey one's own so individuals think for themselves, are open-minded to look under a lot of rocks, and come to their own conclusions. Thinking for oneself is discouraged among evangelicals or fundamentalists but is paramount in any deconstruction and reconstruction process. We will not all land in the exact same place, and that's fine. The goal is to follow the historical evidence where it leads as we see it but to be open to all ways of looking at things.

This historical journey can be a private research project where one does their own work at uncovering more accurate historical narratives. Or it can be centered on participating in one of the emerging "faith deconstruction workshops" available, such as former Baptist and Vineyard pastor Keith Giles' "Square One" workshops, which take people back to the beginning to rethink their faith.[2] I also offer a workshop that helps people both deconstruct evangelicalism and reconstruct a more historical faith path or philosophy of life. In my experience, there are five areas that are absolutely key. I cover all of these in my freedom workshops, the first being an on-demand *Religious Deconstruction Workshop* available on the website, The Spiritual Brewpub:[3]

1. Uncover and Overcome Fear-based Religion: Most people in evangelicalism/fundamentalism have a fear-based faith. They have a fear of falling away, losing one's salvation, going to hell, not being "biblical," not remaining orthodox, being influenced by demons, being gay, losing their Christian friends, becoming a heretic, not having a church covering, losing their Christian job, ruining their religious career, or any manner of other fears. "Perfect love casts out fear" and "Anyone who fears has not been perfected in love," says the New Testament book of I John. People with a fear-based religion have not experienced true, unconditional love. The love they "know" is conditioned on measuring up to please a transactional and two-faced god who demands something in return and is unprincipled in meting out love and forgiveness. People need to break out of this cycle of fear.

2. Identify One's Own Cognitive / Emotional Dissonance: People have both cognitive and emotional disconnects that they need to identify and address. In the cognitive area, it could be the intellectual inconsistencies in their faith (e.g., the disconnect between the violent, retributive god found in some parts of the Old Testament and the non-violent, forgiving Father described by Jesus of Nazareth). Or other contradictions they find in the Bible. Or the inconsistencies found in the history of Christianity. On the emotional side, it could be the disconnect between one having a sincere, emotional love for certain individuals who are not considered part of the family of God—the LGBTQ community, ex-evangelicals, atheists, agnostics, people of other religions—and having to reconcile that with the belief that those said individuals will supposedly go to hell if all things remain the same.

3. Learn How the Bible was Compiled and How the First Followers Viewed the Bible: Embarking on an honest study of how the modern Bible was compiled and viewed over the centuries, starting with the Jewish people and later the followers of Jesus, is probably the most important thing one can do to break bad faith. For example, believing in the biblical doctrine of inerrancy and practicing a "flat reading" of the Bible can really screw with one's head. Earlier, we highlighted how the Jewish scriptures were viewed and how they weren't canonized by Jews—establishing the definitive list of inspired books—until the second century. This was after the Jesus movement had already begun. Likewise, the New Testament wasn't finalized into a definitive list until the fourth century after hundreds of years of relying on oral tradition, mixed agreements on a variety of writings and what was worthy of scripture, and disputes about certain works, such as the books of Revelation, Hebrews, some of Paul's epistles, 2 Peter, and Jude. Not to mention the variety of scriptures deemed worthy by many orthodox believers that didn't make it into the New Testament. The Bible is a product of human decisions made in history. We need to know that history and how the Jews, Jesus, and his earliest followers viewed and used the Bible before we can decide how we should.

4. Learn How the Early "Church" Didn't Go to Church but Did Build Compassionate Communities: Adding to what we covered in this book, one can learn a lot more about what the earliest Jesus gatherings were like in the first and second century and get an understanding of what the original "ekklesia" was like. This includes its valuation of women as equals, its practices of equitable table fellowship, its outreach to the poor and marginalized. The creeds and fights over "Christology" (precisely how to view Christ's deity) came much later. Then one can compare that history to the modern church and do a fit-gap analysis on what the differences are, as well as learn where most of our modern church practices came from—many derived from pagan practices that were part of Roman and Greek religious cults and subsequently evolved through the centuries. When this is fully understood, one can clearly see that modern church is optional for a sincere believer and is actually problematic when we are honest about the failures of so many church movements in our time. These failures include the Catholic Church sexual abuse scandal and Protestant churches, denominations, and parachurches financially or spiritually abusing people (or covering up sexual abuse). These include the scandals of Jim and Tammy Baker, Jimmy Swaggert, Bill Gothard's Institute of Basic Life Principles, Sovereign Grace Ministries (formerly People of Destiny and the denomination I was in for five years), Mars Hill Church (Mark Driscoll), Calvary Chapel, the Southern Baptist denomination, and Hillsong, to name the most famous ones. For every one of these there are myriad more, both large and small churches or ministries that you have never heard of.[4]

5. Learn How the Very First Generation of Followers Viewed Salvation and Rejected All Violence: Another key is learning the historical facts around what modern Christians believe and call the "penal substitutionary atonement" (PSA)—that on the cross, Jesus was a substitute for all sinners who took the punishment that all humanity deserves (being tortured and murdered by Roman crucifixion) in order to appease God who will then offer forgiveness. The forgiveness only comes IF, and only IF, an individual accepts Jesus as their Lord and Savior (acknowledging PSA). As discussed, history teaches us PSA was foreign to the earliest church and wasn't even developed until the 13th century and not fully articulated until the 16th century. Another area to be addressed is where the concept of eternal damnation and hell came from and how it was never taught by Jesus or his earliest followers. In fact, Universalism—the belief that all of humanity will ultimately be reconciled to God—was the prevailing view of the Jesus movement for the first 500 years. Moreover, it is learning how the overwhelming majority, if not all, of earliest Jesus followers were pacifists who swore off violence and militarism of any kind. All this opens one's mind and heart to consider a new paradigm on what salvation really is for humanity.

6. Learn How to Deprogram Oneself from Bad Faith Habits and Overcome the Trauma of Abusive Religion: My experience is that secular, cognitive behavioral therapy saved me from clinical depression, which stemmed from abuse inflicted by evangelical churches and leaders (wittingly or unwittingly). Cognitive therapy is just retraining your brain to think differently. In religious deconstruction, it's about aligning with the ideas of a compassionate and rational God rather than the abusive, manipulative, cultic, fear-based beliefs that conservative Christianity teaches. I recognized cognitive therapy as coming from a God of love who used it to set me free from abusive religion. Another technique I learned was from Dr. David Smith, a philosophy and religious studies instructor for the Osher Lifelong Learning Institute at the University of Washington. It's call "If-Then Logic." You ask yourself over periods of time questions like "If God is perfectly good, would he or she punish me for sincerely using God-given reason and historical studies to change my mind about certain religious beliefs?" and "If God is truly good, unchanging, and principled, would he or she be two-faced and order genocide of whole peoples in one age of time and offer unconditional forgiveness to humankind in another age?"

My online, on-demand Religious Deconstruction Workshop[5] takes people through these six steps and helps them be set free from the cloud of guilt, fear, and depression that usually accompanies deconstructing evangelical or some other form of conservative Christianity. It also points people toward ways to reconstruct a vital faith on the path of Jesus' love ethic or a new restorative theory of life based on what one learned in their deconstruction process. Finally, it introduces people to a new community of like-minded folks who have similar experiences with whom they can build relationships, which is also critical to healthy spiritual deconstruction and reconstruction.

Society Deconstructing Retribution and Reconstructing Peace

In late December 1914, during World War I, a great example of "deconstructing retribution" occurred in the battlefield trenches of Europe. Masses of Allied and Central Powers soldiers spontaneously decided to stop fighting, instituted a truce, and began peacefully fraternizing with each other. Unfortunately, it did not grow beyond field soldiers/officers and influence public military opinion, let alone the military high command. It also didn't last long enough to have a lasting impact on the war. But, for a brief time, soldiers deconstructed killing one's enemy in wartime and extended peace to one another. On both sides, they left behind the patriotic aggression usually required in any war. I described it in my book *Craft Brewed Jesus:*

> As I write this, it is exactly one hundred years to the day from the start of the infamous Christmas truce of 1914 between mostly British and German, and some French and Belgian soldiers on the western front during World War I. [Story told in the 2005 movie, *Joyeux Noelle*] Locked in static trench warfare five months into the war, the practice of occasional cease-fires and fraternization among enemy soldiers in "No Man's Land" had already developed due to the close proximity of enemy lines. For short periods of time, soldiers would engage in conversation, barter for cigarettes, or recover wounded and dead comrades. On December 7, 1914, Pope Benedict XV suggested an official cessation of warfare during Christmas. Political and military leaders refused to initiate a formal cease-fire. Nevertheless, reports say up to one hundred thousand troops took part in an unofficial Christmas truce that lasted at the very least through Christmas Eve and Day and in some cases up until New Year's Day. The scale of this truce went way beyond earlier ones.
>
> In some cases, troops made a formal agreement for a truce for a specified period of time. In other locations, it was more infor-mal. For many, it started on Christmas Eve when German sol-diers began singing Christmas Carols and songs and lit candles on top of the trenches. German tradition celebrated more on the eve of Christmas, rather than the day itself. Soon, British troops, and apparently some French and Belgian troops, en-tered into a time of fraternization with the Germans. Each side sang their favorite Christmas songs, both secular and religious oriented. They allowed each other to bury their dead in No Man's Land and said prayers over them. They met together

and exchanged things like cigarettes, cigars, bottles of wine, food, and souvenirs. They swapped jokes and information about the war. Some accounts say some of them even played one or more football (soccer) matches.

Unfortunately, this widespread cessation of war for Christmas over several days was never repeated in the following years during the war, although it was attempted. Afterward, all holiday ceasefires in World War I were quashed by threats of disciplinary action.

In the midst of the horrors of trench warfare, thousands of troops spontaneously followed their hearts. They discovered a light within that led them to submit to Christ's command to love their enemies. That light won out over the military command to fight.[6]

This is the kind of mindset one needs to break society's trust in militarism to solve the world's problems. Military solutions only cause more death and suffering. As we have learned, historians argue that World War I, the supposed "war to end all wars," and the post-war, ill-conceived Treaty of Versailles (that economists deemed counter-productive, too harsh on Germany, and eventually crippled the German economy) led to World War II. The treaty was retributive in nature and caused German resentment that Hitler later took advantage of to manipulate the masses to support his Nazi party. In contrast, the Marshall Plan after World War II, heralded as the greatest diplomatic effort in history, gave aid to our enemies to rebuild cities and infrastructure. Although part of its motivation was to deter communism, the affect was restoring relationships of previous enemies to the point that Germany and Japan soon became economic power houses as well as allies and friends to the United States. Some say the Marshall Plan helped avert World War III.

A World Without Traditional Prisons?

If we took the notion that restorative justice works better than retribution and punishment, how would we handle hatred, crime, and violence in our society? Is holding people accountable for wrongdoing, whether non-violent or violent, only done by punishing them with prison sentences? Aren't our prisons supposed to be institutions of "correction," not merely a means of meting out a penalty?

Why does the United States have the highest incarceration rate in the world (664 per 100,000)? Even compared to countries with similar and higher crime rates? Why is it five times more than the United Kingdom, six or seven times more than Canada and France, and nine or ten times more than Denmark, Netherlands, and Norway?[7] Why are black Americans incarcerated at nearly five times the rate as White Americans?[8]

Why is our recidivism rate—the percent of incarcerated who relapse into criminal behavior—at 70% after five years compared to countries like Norway that are only at 20% after five years?[9] Could it be that other countries have discovered a better way to handle crime that fits the ethic of restoration over retribution that Jesus of Nazareth and other prophets taught? Could it be that we still haven't overcome our racist past to apply justice in an equitable way? Could it be that we need a whole new paradigm on how to treat people as human beings and restore peace after someone commits a non-violent or violent crime? Here's what one woman has discovered that introduces a new mindset:

> Deanna Van Buren designs restorative justice centers that, instead of taking the punitive approach used by a system focused on mass incarceration, treat crime as a breach of relationships and justice as a process where all stakeholders come together to repair that breach. With help and ideas from incarcerated men and women, Van Buren is creating dynamic spaces that provide safe venues for dialogue and reconciliation; employment and job training; and social services to help keep people from entering the justice system in the first place.[10]

In this TED Talk from 2017, Architect Van Buren laid out her vision that has culminated in designing Restorative Justice Centers with the capacity to replace prisons. Van Buren began designing these Centers and promoting their expansion across the country.

In these spaces, the focus is on first addressing the needs of those who have been harmed by a crime. And then to hold those who have committed the offense accountable, but not through punishment, but through meeting their obligation to make amends. The goal is to find a way to repair the breach in the relationship.

Research has shown this approach builds empathy, reduces violent re-offending by up to 75%, and lessens post-traumatic stress that victims of severe violence experience. Because there is a track record of these advantages, judges and prosecutors have started to divert cases from going to court and rather send them to these Centers to minimize the numbers entering the criminal justice system to start.

The big idea is to address the root causes of crime not merely the outcomes of crime. That is, to repair broken relationships and pursue education, job training, and workforce development instead of imprisonment.

How About Rethinking What Prisons Should Be?

Earlier, we discovered that Norway's recidivism rate for prisoners is much, much lower than the United States. In fact, they boast the lowest recidivism rate in the world, while America's prison system is among the highest in the world. Why? Because Norway has a completely different paradigm on the purpose of imprisonment. Prison isn't so much about punitive consequences for past behaviors to balance the scales of justice but rather preventing criminals from having bad intentions towards others in the future. In other words, to change hearts.

Norwegian prison guards have to complete a two-year training program where they're taught that it's better to make friends with inmates than to mistreat or punish them. It's called "dynamic security." It is a system that restores human beings rather than trap them in barred cells surrounded by fences with barbed wire. "We talk to the guys. That's our weapon," said a guard. Guards don't mirror the prisoners' behavior. They turn the other cheek. Even their maximum-security prisons have this approach. Inmates have private rooms, TVs, kitchens where they can cook, a library, a climbing wall, and a fully equipped music recording studio, where they can record their own music. In minimum security facilities, it's sometimes hard to tell the inmates from the guards. In those spaces, inmates are significantly free to move around but have responsibilities to keep gardens, harvest food, cook, chop wood, and do their own carpentry.

The results? Norwegian prisons have no major problem with bullying, inmates get along fine, and they are prepared to go back into the society without harmful intentions toward others. As a warden explains, "Treat people like dirt, and they'll be dirt. Treat them like human beings, and they'll act like human beings. I tell people, we're releasing neighbors every year. Do you want to release them as ticking time bombs?"

Admittedly the cost of these prisons is almost twice as much as in the U.S. But when you factor in that ex-convicts commit fewer crimes, which saves money in law enforcement, and most of them find employment and pay taxes and don't need government handouts, the overall cost is low. At the end of the day, "the Norwegian prison system pays for itself more than two times over. Norway's approach isn't some naïve, socialist aberration. It's a system that's better, more humane and less expensive."[11]

There is also a movement in the United States to reform prisons and reduce recidivism through the establishment of "Rehabilitation Programs" within prisons. These programs include efforts to build a school district within the prison system for educational programs, develop marketable job skills for inmates, target an inmate's "criminogenic needs" with courses on and services for cognitive behavioral therapy, getting inmates more active in productive activities, provide treatment for mental health and substance abuse, strengthen their family ties, reduce use of solitary confinement, phase out use of private prisons, and strengthen federal halfway houses.[12] As citizens, we should be supporting such programs and voting for representatives that can change the existing penal system through legislation and cultural change.

MODERN PACIFISTS IN OUR TIME

There aren't many true pacifists and restorationists around these days and for the ones that are, most of the media, including the liberal left, don't pay much attention to them. Pacifism, especially in the face of defending against acts of war and violence, seems naïve and ineffective. Yet, we know from history that Jesus taught and emulated pacifism and that for the first few centuries of the Jesus movement, his followers were overwhelmingly pacifists. And they weren't passive pacifists. On the contrary, they resisted evil with nonviolent tools, just as we've seen in many examples described in this book. We also know that many people in modern history took Jesus' teaching seriously and successfully forged pacifist and nonviolent restorationist movements that changed the world for the better.

We have talked about Bertha von Suttner and Leo Tolstoy in the anti-war movement at the turn of the 20th century, Mahatma Gandhi and E. Stanley Jones and the Indian non-violent fight for independence and peace, Martin Luther King, Jr., and the Civil Rights Movement, Nelson Mandela and Desmond Tutu and South Africa's Truth and Reconciliation Project, and William Barber II's efforts with the Poor People's Campaign. There is also a variety of Danish activists—modern ones and those who non-violently resisted Nazism during World War II—as well as people like defense attorney Bryan Stevenson, author of *Just Mercy*, and "progressive prosecutors" who fight for criminal justice reform that challenges racial injustice, helping to end mass incarceration and excessive punishment and establishes rehabilitation programs in and outside of prison.

We also know that pacifism and restorative justice is based on a new paradigm of how to treat one's enemies that can be found in certain ancient Jewish historical accounts (not the entire Old Testament but certain passages from the Old Testament and prophets) and later eloquently articulated by Jesus of Nazareth. We also know that you don't have to be a sworn pacifist dead set against all war to start treating your enemies and society's criminals with love and reason, rather than revenge. We saw this in the stories of people like Daryl Davis, Michael and Julie Weisser, Deanna Van Buren, Bibi and Mohammad Bahrami, and the guards and wardens of Norway's prisons.

With the Russian attack on Ukraine in February 2022, pacifism seems even more unattainable in our modern day. How can you expect a sovereign nation like Ukraine to refrain from defending itself against Russian aggression? I have to admit that it's realistic to think such a war as the one in Ukraine is truly a "just war." At the very least, we must accept the suffering of Ukrainians at the hands of Russian attacks as worthy of military defense that can save lives of innocent people. And we should naturally praise the courage of Ukrainian defensive efforts and the heroism of its people and its president, Volodymyr Zelensky.

However, we also have to keep in mind several things about the nature of wars and how they are prevented, how they start, and how they end. First, we must resist the temptation to demonize the enemy as pure evil. In wars, leaders start them, and soldiers have to be motivated (and sometimes coerced) to fight them, by propaganda, promises, fear of punishment, shame of letting down fellow soldiers, and anger towards an aggressor. In Ukraine, Chris Hedges argues that Russia started the war at least partly because the U.S. and NATO broke a series of agreements over many years—not to extend NATO beyond a certain line, not to deploy NATO troops in certain regions, and the refusal to implement a prior peace agreement.[13] Of course, this does not justify or condone Russian aggression, especially some of the atrocities they have committed once the war began. But it does help us understand the motivation of the enemy. And that the motivation for war is rarely black and white, one side being altogether good and honest and the other side being altogether evil and dishonest. Hedges believes the war could have been averted if those agreements had been honored.

We know that defensive wars will usually have better battle morale because they are easier to motivate people to fight. They are easier to promote as a just cause. But Ukrainians and anyone who supports their cause, especially if they believe in redemptive strategies rather than retributive ones to fight evil, must ask themselves, what of the enemy Russian soldiers? Are they not fellow human beings? What about their children, wives, parents, and families who also suffer when their loved ones are fighting a war? Are many if not most of the Russian soldiers persuaded (brainwashed by propaganda), at least initially, into thinking they are fighting a worthy cause? In addition to knowledge of broken NATO promises, aren't most Russians told lies by the Kremlin that Russia is liberating Ukraine from neo-Nazis and fascists? Should Ukrainians kill Russian soldiers for being misled by their own government? If Ukrainians found a way to oppose Russia nonviolently, would they still be worthy of international support? If so, wouldn't Russia still be deserving of resistance via strategic (not vengeful) sanctions?

Second, pacifism is not a strategy only to be executed after violent aggression begins. Michael McKoy makes this point:

Pacifists are often asked to justify their beliefs after the bullets have started flying, but pacifism does not begin 'in the breach' when the situation is dire and violent retaliation is the best bad option. Rather, it begins before the breach when multiple options are possible that may preclude destructive violence. Pacifism warns that when leaders prioritize violence as a policy option, they more often disregard 'modest stillness and humility' and risk escalation to war.[14]

This reveals how the work of pacifism is chiefly preventing war through honest diplomacy, honoring prior agreements, and pursuing peacemaking negotiations prior to armed conflict. In fact, studies show one can find ways to stop war through strategic settlements that would have more long-term benefits for all, given what happens during and after war—death, destruction, suffering, PTSD, etc. "Policial science research on war finds that there always exists a pre-war settlement that is more materially advantageous to all sides than any outcome following war."[15]

For example, prior to the war, Ukrainians strongly opposed Ukrainian neutrality as a political position, something that Russia proposed months before the invasion. As of April 2022, Ukrainian leadership admitted Ukrainian neutrality is a requirement to reach a peace settlement with Russia, and it is a centerpiece of peace negotiations. McKoy argues that the refusal by NATO and Ukraine to consider Russia's neutrality proposal "only served to further militarize the conflict, provoke Russian pride, and give Ukraine false hope. More 'stillness and humility' were needed to make difficult compromises and avoid the devastations of war."[16]

Third, it is pacifist foreign policy strategies during this war that offer the best hope to end the conflict. Experts have prioritized de-escalation and are always looking for peaceful "off ramps" to offer Vladimir Putin that will allow him to withdraw from Ukraine while enabling him to save face. International opposition to the war has primarily used the nonviolent strategy of unified economic sanctions by at least a dozen countries. These have been successful in weakening Russia both economically and militarily.

Although most Russians still support the war and blame the West, it appears they do so because they believe a few small truths and several big lies told them by Kremlin propaganda. Indications are that while only 20 percent of Russian citizens oppose the war, that number is growing. Moreover, even some of the supporters are ambivalent and express anxiety about it. "Nearly half of Russians who support the war also want peace talks." These public opinions can lead to more widespread discontent.[17] Another nonviolent strategy, although it's unclear how much it has been pursued, is to fight the pro-war propaganda within Russia with the dissemination of news stories that tell the truth. In other words, using internet-sourced news strategically to combat the narratives heard on the official Russian state television. The twenty percent of Russians who oppose the war are already getting their news from the internet. A propaganda war can help change minds among the populace and turn people against the lies of the war. Yet this would probably have to entail the West also being honest about any broken agreements with Russia.

What's more, we should listen to experts in nuclear politics who tell us of the real possibility of Putin using nuclear weapons should he become desperate. "Despite how untrustworthy or repugnant Putin may be, refusing to negotiate with him is worse policy."[18]

At the end of the day, the most promising nonviolent route to end the war may be through a Russian internal regime collapse due to rising dissent between the public and the military and stress on Russia's overcentralized system. Their political machine is not conducive to handling the accumulating crises of the war, battlefield losses, conscription protests, economic failure, falling revenues, and continuing labor unrest.[19] A former Russian soldier-turned-commander in a Russian mercenary organization deserted and defected over the brutality (forcing prisoners to fight and shooting them if they refused) and incompetence he saw on the frontline. "Sooner or later," he said, "the propaganda in Russia will stop working, the people will rise up and all our leaders ...will be up for grabs and a new leader will emerge."[20]

CHOOSING RESTORATION
OVER RETRIBUTION

Whatever our opinions about the war in Ukraine, the lessons of the past about war should still haunt us. The price we paid for our American wars, the absurdity of World War I, the arguable inevitability of World War II due to an ill-conceived treaty, the outrageous civilian deaths in that war, the tragedy of Vietnam, the mistakes of Iraq, and the embarrassing torture of detainees by Americans at Abu Gharib. These tragic events beg these questions: Is there a better way to respond to violence and aggression? Can we limit deaths by a pacifist, nonviolent resistance to evil? Can we achieve more long-lasting peace by not actually going to war but pursuing nonviolent strategies? Can we solve our problems with rising crime and violence through more drastic, rational, criminal justice reform that has the goal of restoring hearts and not merely exacting punitive measures? Can we start believing in a God who genuinely loves all of humanity and goes out searching for lost, evil people to restore and redeem them in love, not punish them with violent acts or eternal damnation? Can we start doing that ourselves and imitate people like Daryl Davis, Michael and Julie Weisser, Bibi and Mohammad Bahrami, and Deanna Van Buren?

Millions of people believe the answers to the questions above are Yes. And modern Christian pacifists, although an almost-silent voice among us, are making the case that war is not necessary to achieve equilibrium in the world. Certainly, Christian author and ethicist Stanley Hauerwas has in his book, *The Peaceable Kingdom: A Primer in Christian Ethics*. As has Jesuit priest, Daniel Berrigan, who founded the Plowshares anti-nuclear weapons and pacifist movement. And pastor Brian Zahnd in his book, *A Farewell to Mars: An Evangelical Pastor's Journey Toward the Biblical Gospel of Peace*, as well as theologian Michael Hardin in *The Jesus Driven Life: Reconnecting Humanity with Jesus*. I was recently reminded of the work of Walter Wink and his book, *Jesus and Nonviolence: A Third Way*. We have also mentioned Preston Sprinkle's vision in *Fight: A Christian Case for Non-Violence*. What's more, there's the Community Peacemaker Teams (formerly Christian Peacemaker Teams), which supports peace work in areas of conflict all over the world. Moreover, Jesuit Priest, John Dear, once nominated for the Nobel Peace Prize by Desmond Tutu, has spent decades working in the modern peace movement fighting injustice, war, capital punishment, and poverty. His take on following Jesus: "Jesus was totally nonviolent and calls us to practice and teach Gospel nonviolence and welcome God's reign of peace and nonviolence, which means from now on, we work for the abolition of war, poverty, racism, gun violence, the death penalty, nuclear weapons, environmental destruction, and all violence."[21] Finally, there's people like

Logan Mehl-Laituri, who wrote *Reborn on the Fourth of July: The Challenge of Faith, Patriotism, and Conscience*. An army veteran who served in the Iraq War, Mehl-Laituri was a fire-support specialist before applying to become a noncombatant conscientious objector. Not to mention the fact that these writers, activists, and movements are standing on the shoulders of the Quakers, Tolstoy, King, Rene Girard, and many more unnamed peacemakers.

Not only are there Christian or Christ-influenced pacifists, but secular ones are also sounding a call for change. In their book, *Why Civil Resistance Works: The Strategic Logic of Nonviolent Conflict*, Erica Chenoweth and Maria J. Stephan say the long-term effects of war are so detrimental as to not justify its waging. They conclude "that successful nonviolent resistance ushers in more durable and internally peaceful democracies, which are less likely to regress into civil war. Presenting a rich, evidentiary argument, they originally and systematically compare violent and nonviolent outcomes in different historical periods and geographical contexts, debunking the myth that violence occurs because of structural and environmental factors and that it is necessary to achieve certain political goals. Instead, the authors discover, violent insurgency is rarely justifiable on strategic grounds."[22]

Moreover, historians are rediscovering the wisdom of Jesus' teaching on nonviolence and love. Turning the other cheek is not just for saints. Rutger Bregman admits:

> Only recently did I realize Jesus was advocating a quite rational principle. Modern psychologists call it non-complementary behavior. Most of the time...we humans mimic each other. Someone gives you a compliment, you're quick to return the favor. Somebody says something unpleasant, and you feel the urge to make a snide comeback. When you're treated with kindness, it's easy to do the right thing. Easy, but not enough. To quote Jesus again, "If you love those who love you, what reward do you have? Do not even the tax collectors do the same? And if you greet only brothers and sisters, what more are you doing than others?" The question is, can we take things a step further? What if we assume the best not only about our children, our co-workers, and our neighbors, but also about our enemies? ...Are you and I capable of turning the other

cheek? And can we make it work on a large scale—say, in prisons and police stations, after terrorist attacks or in times of war?[23]

What's more, Christopher Blattman, in his work, *Why We Fight: The Roots of War and the Paths of Peace*, takes his expertise in economics, political science, and history to argue that violence is actually not the norm when conflicts arise. Societies already "are surprisingly good at interrupting and ending violence when they want to."[24] The book inspires us to stop concluding that war is inevitable and unfolds a vision to "give peace a chance."

Moreover, we are reminded how Samuel Moyn, in his book *Humane: How the United States Abandoned Peace and Reinvented War*, exposed the dark side of trying to wage war more humanely and how it has only perpetuated war and made us abandon consistent peace strategies.

Whatever the answer is to the questions above, we who have been victims of a bad faith system need, at the very least, to choose the goal of restoration and redemption over retribution as the answer to how we deal with evil, lost souls based on what a God of love would truly be like. When confronted with historical facts about the original essence of the first-through-third-century Jesus movement, we must find a way to deconstruct unhistorical and harmful theologies. We must reconstruct a faith that better fits the facts and experience of a God of love or a philosophy of life that better fits the facts of social and political science. We must break bad faith for the sake of peace; we must do this to bring harmony to our lives, our families, our communities, and the world. The question for the reader is this: what do you need to do to break bad faith and start pursuing a path of peace? This is not about conversion to a reformed Christianity. It's about changing one's mind about what is the wisest way to live life in the face of human conflicts and injustice. What brings true restoration and redemption? What suppresses evil behavior? Physical force or genuine love for humanity? Waging war or plotting peace? We all must decide.

Bless those who persecute you; bless and do not curse...Do not repay anyone evil for evil...If your enemy is hungry, feed him...Do not be overcome by evil, but overcome evil with good. — The Apostle Paul (Romans 12:19–20)

END NOTES

INTRODUCTION: EXPOSING BAD FAITH

1 Ellul, *The Subversion of Christianity*, 3.

2 Tolstoy, *The Kingdom God is Within You*, 32.

3 *Exegesis* is defined as examining biblical passages in literary, historical, and cultural context to determine original meaning. *Hermeneutics* is determining the best way to interpret a passage and apply it today.

1: UNCOVERING VIOLENT SACRIFICIAL RELIGION

1 "Billy Graham in Twilight: His New Thinking on Politics, the Bible, and the Prospect of Death," Newsweek, August 14, 2006.

2 Ramelli, *The Christian Doctrine of Apokatastasis*.

2: HOW RELIGIOUS MYTHS AND FRAUDS WORK

1 Buhler, "3 Poll Workers."

2 Claimed to be a hidden organization within the government seeking to manipulate the system.

3 Horton, "After Truth."

4 Hertenstein, *Selling Satan*.

5 Ibid.

6 "We Used Her," CBC Radio, May 21, 2020, https://www.cbc.ca/radio/asithappens/as-it-happens-wednesday-edition-1.5576923/we-used-her-minister-regrets-paying-roe-vs-wade-plaintiff-to-speak-out-against-abortion-1.5576924.

7 Rob Schenck, "A Movie That Bares the Soul," May 18, 2020, https://www.revrobschenck.com/blog/2020/5/18/a-movie-that-bares-the-soul-behind-roe-v-wade-along-with-my-own-.

8 Ibid.

9 "Final Report: Select Committee to Investigate January 6th Attack on the U.S. Capital."

10 "Most White Evangelicals Still Believe the 2020 Election was Stolen," Relevant Magazine, November 8, 2021, https://relevantmagazine.com/faith/church/most-white-evangelicals-still-believe-the-2020-election-was-stolen/.

11 Jack Dawes, Jr., "Most White Evangelicals Embrace 'The Big Lie,'" Good Faith Media, May 14, 2021, https://goodfaithmedia.org/most-white-evangelicals-embrace-the-big-lie/.

12 "In more than 60 cases," Politifact, January 8, 2021, https://www.politifact.com/factchecks/2021/jan/08/joe-biden/joe-biden-right-more-60-trumps-election-lawsuits-l/.

13 Zachary B. Wolf, "The 5 key elements of Trump's Big Lie," CNN, May 19, 2021, https://www.cnn.com/2021/05/19/politics/donald-trump-big-lie-explainer/index.html.

14 "Donald Trump Speech," Rev, January 6, 2021, https://www.rev.com/blog/transcripts/donald-trump-speech-save-america-rally-transcript-january-6.

15 Claire Lampen, "The MyPillow Guy Has Been Banned From Twitter," The Cut, January 26, 2021, https://www.thecut.com/2021/01/mike-lindell-pro-trump-my-pillow-ceo-banned-from-twitter.html.

16 "Mike Lindell: Absolute Proof 2021," https://www.bitchute.com/video/gNplqDH0ttlo/.

17 "MyPillow CEO's election fraud 'proof' implodes in front of live audience," Bit Chute, February 8, 2021, https://www.cnn.com/videos/business/2021/08/13/mike-lindell-symposium-osullivan-pkg-ac360-vpx.cnn.

18 "Mike Lindell," Wikipedia, accessed February 6, 2023, https://en.wikipedia.org/wiki/Mike_Lindell.

19 "Dinesh D'Souza Pleads Guilty," FBI, May 20, 2014, https://www.fbi.gov/contact-us/field-offices/newyork/news/press-releases/dinesh-dsouza-pleads-guilty-in-manhattan-federal-court-to-campaign-finance-fraud.

20 "Barr Laughs Off Election Fraud," YouTube, accessed February 6, 2023, https://www.youtube.com/watch?v=Nz6smxo-MkE

21 Ali Swenson, "Gaping Holes," AP, May 3, 2022, https://apnews.com/article/2022-midterm-elections-covid-technology-health-arizona-e1b49d2311bf900f44fa5c6dac406762.

22 Ja'han Jones, "Right Wing Group behind '2000 Mules' could face federal scrutiny," MSNBC, October 17, 2022, https://www.msnbc.com/the-reidout/reidout-blog/arizona-fraud-investigation-2000-mules-rcna52549.

23 "Fact Check – Does '2000 Mules' provide evidence?" Reuters, May 27, 2022, https://www.reuters.com/article/factcheck-usa-mules/fact-check-does-2000-mules-provide-evidence-of-voter-fraud-in-the-2020-u-s-presidential-election-idUSL2N2XJ0OQ.

24 Chris Ingalls, "Skagit County Republicans," King 5 News, November 3, 2022, https://www.king5.com/article/news/investigations/investigation-truth-voter-fraud-skagit-county.

25 Brian Naylor, "Read Trump's Jan. 6 Speech," NPR, February 10, 2021, https://www.npr.org/2021/02/10/966396848/read-trumps-jan-6-speech-a-key-part-of-impeachment-trial.

26 "Trump, Republicans incite crowd," YouTube, accessed February 6, 2023, https://www.youtube.com/watch?v=mh3cbd7niTQ.

27 "Mel Brooks gives FIERY speech," YouTube, accessed February 6, 2023, https://www.youtube.com/watch?v=ZKHwV6sdrMk&t=250s.

28 Garrison, "The Door Interview: Mark Yaconelli."

29 Ehrman, *Did Jesus Exist?*

30 Koine Greek was the common supra-regional form of Greek spoken and written during the time of Jesus and in which the New Testament was written.

3: THE MAJOR MYTHS VERSUS REALITY

1 Vearncombe, *After Jesus Before Christianity*, 3.

2 Ibid., 4.

3 Shanks, *Partings: How Judaism and Christianity Became Two*, 3.

4 Isaiah 1:11–23, Psalm 51:16–17, Micah 6:6–8, Hosea 6:6.

5 Shisley, "Biblical Views: From Supper to Sacrament."

6 Camp, *Craft Brewed Jesus*, 127–128.

7 In 2012, James Dobson blamed the Sandy Hook school shooting on God's judgment due to America not being Christian enough. See https://relevantmagazine.com/faith/james-dobson-calls-sandy-hook-shootings-judgment/.

8 Shanks, *Christianity and Rabbinic Judaism*, 63.

9 "Spotlight," IMDb, accessed February 6, 2023, https://www.imdb.com/title/tt1895587/.

10 Stanley, "The Sex-Abuse Scandal That Devastated a Suburban Megachurch."

11 "Our Investigations," The Roys Report, accessed February 6, 2023, https://julieroys.com/investigations.

12 Vearncombe, *After Jesus Before Christianity*, 6.

13 Camp, *Craft Brewed Jesus*, 72–96.

14 See Bernstein, *Which Came First: The Church or the New Testament?*, Enns, *The Bible Tells Me So* and *How The Bible Actually Works*, Flood, *Disarming Scripture*, Smith, *The Bible Made Impossible*, and Wills, *What Paul Meant*.

15 Smith, *The Bible Made Impossible*.

16 David Platt, "Behold His Wrath," November 6, 2017,

https://radical.net/podcasts/radical-podcast/behold-his-wrath/.

17 "Francis Chan's Warning to the church!" accessed February 6, 2023,

https://www.facebook.com/watch/?v=393291054724027.

18 Matthew Cortina, "Mark Driscoll Sermons: Tells Congregation 'God Hates Some of You,'"

Christian Post, November 10, 2011, https://www.christianpost.com/news/mark-driscoll-

sermons-tells-mars-hill-congregation-

god-hates-some-of-you-video.html.

19 Ibid.

20 Janus is the Roman mythological god who literally had two faces and represented duality.

21 "The Origin of Heaven and Hell," *Biblical Archaeology Society*, October 31, 2018.

22 Nyland, *The Source New Testament*, 63.

23 Hart, *The New Testament*, 543–548.

24 "Hellbound?" accessed February 6, 2023,

https://www.amazon.com/Hellbound-William-Paul-Young/dp/B00CHI51DO.

25 In addition to the two books cited above, there is: Baker, *Razing Hell*, Jersak, *Her Gates Will Never Be Shut*, MacDonald, *The Evangelical Universalist*, Talbot, *The Inescapable Love of God*, Hart, *That All Shall be Saved*, Ferwerda, *Raising Hell*, Artman, *Grace Saves All*, Stenson, *Christian Universalism: God's Good News for All People*, Hanson, *Universalism: The Prevailing Doctrine of the Christian Church During Its First Five Hundred Years*, and Giles, *Jesus Undefeated: Condemning the False Doctrine of Eternal Torment*.

26 Camp, *Craft Brewed Jesus*, 57-59.

27 Hanson, *Universalism: The Prevailing Doctrine of the Christian Church During Its First Five Hundred Years*.

28 Nyland, *The Source New Testament*, 63.

29 Josephus, *The Jewish War*, Book 6.

30 Aristotle, *Rhetoric Book 1*, Chapter 10.

31 Nyland, *The Source New Testament*, 63.

32 Arnold, *Orthodoxy Revisited*, 112.

33 See Bregman, *Humankind* and Schaeffer, *Fall in Love*.

34 Heim, *Saved from Sacrifice*.

35 Shanks, *Partings: How Judaism and Christianity Became Two*, 21.

36 Wright, *Jesus and the Victory of God*, 360–365.

37 DeMar, *Last Days Madness*, Sproul, *The Last Days According to Jesus,* and Giles, *Jesus Unexpected.*

38 Once, James Dobson blamed the Sandy Hook shooting on America's recent change on gay marriage. See "James Dobson Calls Sandy Hook Shootings 'Judgment,'" Relevant,

December 8, 2012, https://relevantmagazine.com/faith/james-dobson-calls-sandy-hook-shootings-judgment/.

39 Nyland, *The Source New Testament*, 304.

40 Robin Gallaher Branch, "Who Was Phoebe?" BAS, March 3, 2022, https://www.biblicalarchaeology.org/daily/who-was-phoebe/.

41 Fee, "First Epistle to Corinthians" and Ehrman, *Misquoting Jesus*.

42 Nyland, *The Source New Testament*, 330.

43 Wills, *What Paul Meant*.

44 Ibid.

45 Ellul, *The Subversion of Christianity*, 69.

46 Ibid., 70.

47 Ibid., 71.

48 Martin, *Unclobber*, 115.

49 Dr. Roland Chia, "The Dangerous Distortions of Dominion Theology," Ethos Institute, September 21, 2020, https://ethosinstitute.sg/distortions-of-dominion-theology/.

50 "The Call," accessed February 6, 2023, https://louengle.com/the-call/.

51 "The Story," accessed February 6, 2023, https://thesend.org/story/.

52 Meyers, *The Underground Church*, Chapter 4.

53 Hardin, *The Jesus Driven Life*, 126.

54 Ibid., 127.

55 Ibid., 129.

56 Nyland, *The Source*, 52. Also see Instone-Brewer, *Divorce and Remarriage in the Church*.

4: THE TWO-FACED GOD OF POPULAR THEOLOGY

1 Flood, *Disarming Scripture*, 13.

2 Enns, "John Piper on Why It's Right to Slaughter Women and Children."

3 Ibid.

4 Ibid.

5 Girard, *I See Satan Falling*, Foreword.

6 Sprinkle, *Fight*.

7 Nyland, *The Source New Testament*, 25.

8 Ibid., 84.

9 *Porneia* denotes idolatry, adultery, and ritually unclean sexual acts—incest, sex with in-laws, sex with animals, sex during menstruation, and sex with temple prostitutes (homosexual or heterosexual). See Nyland, *The Source New Testament*, 45.

10 The Torah defines adultery for a man differently than for a woman. A woman commits adultery when having relations with *any* man other than her husband while a man commits adultery only when he has relations with another man's wife.

11 Hardin, *The Jesus Driven Life*, 67.

12 Shanks, *Christianity and Rabbinic Judaism*, 59.

13 Under Roman law the Sanhedrin could not execute someone themselves. If they wanted to kill Jesus, they would have to either make it look like an accident (fall off a cliff), do it under cover, or convince the Romans to do it.

5: THE ERRONEOUS WAY PEOPLE VIEW THE BIBLE

1 Camp, *Confessions*, 79.

2 Ibid., 84.

3 Lim, *The Formation of the Jewish Canon*.

4 Bernstein, *Which Came First?*

5 Wills, *What Paul Meant.*

6 Camp, *Craft Brewed Jesus*, 72-96 and Bernstein, *Which Came First?* 5–11.

7 Bernstein, *Which Came First*, 11.

8 "The Bible Critiques Itself," Trinity College Dublin, accessed February 6, 2023, https://www.youtube.com/watch?v=_BLP0V4bFEY.

9 Some translations like the NIV, New Century Version, and the Berean Standard Bible, add words like "just", "only, and "merely" to the text, so it states, 'I did not *only* give them commands about... sacrifices.' But none of those words are in the original Hebrew! All other translations do not have one of those qualifying words. They read, "I did not give them commands about burnt offerings and sacrifices." See: https://biblehub.com/jeremiah/7-22.htm.

10 Flood, *Disarming Scripture*, 33.

11 Tverberg, *Walking in the Dust of Rabbi Jesus*, 60.

12 "Accurate 2 Timothy 3:16 translation," Biblical Criticism History and Archives, March 8, 2004, https://bcharchive.org/2/thearchives/showthread25cf.html?t=79637.

13 See examples in Flood, *Disarming Scripture*, 81–82.

14 Enns, *How Bible Actually Works*, 218.

15 Ibid., 174.

16 Chuck McKnight, "My Long Fight to Defend Inerrancy," Patheos, April 2, 2016, https://www.patheos.com/blogs/hippieheretic/2016/04/my-long-fight-to-defend-inerrancy-why-i.html.

17 Hart, *The New Testament*, 313.

18 Flood, *Disarming Scripture*. 53.

19 Julie Roys, "John MacArthur Shamed, Excommunicated Mother for Refusing to take Back Child Abuser," March 8, 2022, https://julieroys.com/macarthur-shamed-excommunicated-mother-take-back-child-abuser/.

6: THE PROBLEM WITH A TRANSACTIONAL GOD

1 Rohr, *Universal Christ*, 71.

2 James Bernard Murphy, "Does Religion Give Rise to Violence—or the Other Way Around?" Religion News, November 15, 2025, https://religionnews.com/2015/11/15/religion-violence-islam-christianity-atheism-isis-terrorism-paris-rene-girard/.

3 Kevin Miller, "J.E.S.U.S.A.," March 27, 2020, https://vimeo.com/ondemand/jesusa.

4 Rohr, *The Universal Christ*, 72.

5 Jersak, *A More Christlike God*, 257.

6 Ibid., 260.

7 Kevin Miller, "J.E.S.U.S.A.," March 27, 2020, https://vimeo.com/ondemand/jesusa.

8 Now called Beyond at beyond.org.

9 Translation of Matthew 28:19 in Nyland, *The Source New Testament*, 70.

10 If the evangelical interpretation is correct, at most only two of the 12 disciples actually obeyed Jesus' command. Tradition says Mark went to Egypt to preach and plant communities and Thomas went to India to do the same. None of the others went into "the nations" and even Mark and Thomas did not target specific ethno-linguistic groups.

7: VIOLENCE IN POPULAR THEOLOGY AND AMERICAN CULTURE

1 Howard Zinn, "Holy Wars," Democracy Now, January 8, 2010, https://www.democracynow.org/2010/1/8/howard_zinn_three_holy_wars. Also see, Keith Giles, " American Impatience: How We Could Have Avoided 3 Holy Wars," Patheos, June 12, 2020, https://www.patheos.com/blogs/keithgiles/2020/06/american-impatience-how-we-could-have-avoided-3-holy-wars/.

2 Howard Zinn, "Holy Wars," Democracy Now, January 8, 2010, https://www.democracynow.org/2010/1/8/howard_zinn_three_holy_wars.

3 Ibid.

4 Rossiter, *The Abolition of Slavery*, 45–55.

5 Howard Zinn, "Holy Wars," Democracy Now, January 8, 2010, https://www.democracynow.org/2010/1/8/howard_zinn_three_holy_wars.

6 "Bombing of Tokyo (10 March 1945)," Wikipedia, accessed February 6, 2023, https://en.wikipedia.org/wiki/Bombing_of_Tokyo_(10_March_1945).

7 "The United States Bombing Surveys," 107.

8 "Fact Sheet: US Nuclear Weapons in Europe," Center for Arms Control, August 18, 2021, https://armscontrolcenter.org/fact-sheet-u-s-nuclear-weapons-in-europe/.

9 Howard Zinn, "Holy Wars," Democracy Now, January 8, 2010, https://www.democracynow.org/2010/1/8/howard_zinn_three_holy_wars.

10 Victoria Barnett, "Dietrich Bonhoeffer: Resistance and Execution," The US Holocaust Memorial Museum, accessed February 6, 2023, https://www.ushmm.org/information/exhibitions/online-exhibitions/special-focus/dietrich-bonhoeffer/resistance-and-execution.

11 Ibid.

12 Kevin Miller, "J.E.S.U.S.A.," March 27, 2020, https://vimeo.com/ondemand/jesusa.

13 Zahnd, A Farewell to Mars, Chapter 1.

14 "Getting Away with Torture," Human Rights Watch, accessed February 6, 2023, https://www.hrw.org/report/2011/07/12/getting-away-torture/bush-administration-and-mistreatment-detainees.

15 Kevin Miller, "J.E.S.U.S.A.," March 27, 2020, https://vimeo.com/ondemand/jesusa.

16 Ibid.

17 Anthony B. Robinson, "The anti-Mark Driscoll: Resisting cage-fighter Jesus," Crosscut, February 24, 2010, https://crosscut.com/2010/02/the-antimark-driscoll-resisting-cagefighter-jesus.

18 Hedges, The Greatest Evil is War, 73.

19 Eliza Griswold, "God, Guns, and Country: The Evangelical Fight Over Firearms," The New Yorker, April 19, 2019, https://www.newyorker.com/news/on-religion/god-guns-and-country-the-evangelical-fight-over-firearms.

20 Kevin Miller, "J.E.S.U.S.A.," March 27, 2020, https://vimeo.com/ondemand/jesusa.

21 Laurie Goodstein and Richard Fausset, "Welcoming Worshipers With Open Arms and Concealed Ones, Too," The New York Times, November 10, 2017, https://www.nytimes.com/2017/11/10/us/church-shooting-security.html.

22 Tom Dunkel, "Locked and Loaded for the Lord," The Washington Post, https://www.washingtonpost.com/news/style/wp/2018/05/21/feature/two-sons-of-rev-moon-have-split-from-his-church-and-their-followers-are-armed/.

23 Ibid.

24 Jon Schwarz, "By Far the Worst Thing Trump Did Was Flirt With Nuclear War With North Korea," The Intercept, January 20, 2021, https://theintercept.com/2021/01/20/

biden-inauguration-trump-north-korea/.

25 Kevin Miller, "J.E.S.U.S.A.," March 27, 2020, https://vimeo.com/ondemand/jesusa.

26 Sprinkle, *Fight*, Chapter 1.

27 Ibid.

28 "Q&A: Guantanamo Bay, US Detentions, and the Trump Administration," Human Rights Watch, June 27, 2018, https://www.hrw.org/news/2018/06/27/qa-guantanamo-bay-us-detentions-and-trump-administration#q7.

29 "Getting Away with Torture," Human Rights Watch, accessed February 6, 2023, https://www.hrw.org/report/2011/07/12/getting-away-torture/bush-administration-and-mistreatment-detainees.

30 A. L. Smeulers, "Abu Ghraib and the War Against Terror," VU Amsterdam, November 18, 2008, https://research.vu.nl/ws/files/2403096/215948.pdf.

31 "Thousands of Trump supporters hold 'Jericho March,'" WRAL News, December 12, 2020, https://www.wral.com/thousands-of-trump-supporters-hold-jericho-march-ahead-of-electoral-college-vote-6-arrested/19426443/.

32 Richard Weikart, "Metaxas's Counterfeit Bonhoeffer," CSU Stanislaus, accessed February 6, 2023, https://www.csustan.edu/history/metaxass-counterfeit-bonhoeffer.

33 Aaron Rupar, Twitter, accessed February 6, 2023, https://twitter.com/atrupar/status/1337848438239662085?s=20.

34 David French, "The Dangerous Idolatry of Christian Trumpism," The Dispatch, December 13, 2020, https://thedispatch.com/newsletter/frenchpress/the-dangerous-idolatry-of-christian/.

35 Tom Dreisbach and Tim Mak, "Yes, Capital insurrectionists were armed," Witf, March 19, 2021, https://www.witf.org/2021/03/19/yes-capitol-insurrectionists-were-armed-here-are-the-weapons-prosecutors-say-they-used/.

36 Sharp, "Hijacked Christianity: How An Aberrant Eschatology Enables a Grievance Culture That Supplants Christian Grace For an Extremist Meritocracy," 145.

37 Ibid., 205.

38 Ibid., 171.

39 Jill Filipovic, "Death sentence for abortion?" The Guardian, April 11, 2019, https://www.theguardian.com/commentisfree/2019/apr/11/death-sentence-abortion-hypocrisy-pro-life.

40 Sarah Frostenson, "40 years of attacks on abortion clinics," Vox, December 1, 2015, https://www.vox.com/2015/12/1/9827886/abortion-clinic--mapped and "Anti-abortion violence," https://en.wikipedia.org/wiki/Anti-abortion_violence.

41 Gerald R. Thompson, "A Pro-Life Attorney Explains Why Abortion is Not Murder,"

Lonang Institute, accessed February 6, 2023, https://lonang.com/commentaries/
foundation/family/why-abortion-is-not-murder-theology-of-the-unborn/.

42 Although I would support well-crafted laws that restrict late term abortions, there is still the need
for exceptions to protect the life of the mother and serious fetal anomalies, which are the reasons later
abortions are pursued. Later abortions (after 21 weeks) are extremely rare representing only 1% of total
abortions. Anti-abortion advocates like Ahn often claim anyone pro-choice is okay with an abortion
right up until the moment of birth. This is just not true.

43 Jeff Diamant and Besheer Mohamed, "What the data says about abortion in the U.S.,"
Pew Research Center, January 11, 2023, https://www.pewresearch.org/fact-tank/
2023/01/11/what-the-data-says-about-abortion-in-the-u-s-2/.

44 Gabrielle Stanley Blair, "Ejaculate Responsibly," Amazon Summary, accessed
February 6, 2023, https://www.amazon.com/Ejaculate-Responsibly-Whole-Think-
Abortion-ebook/dp/B0B5HWBKNC/.

45 Camille, Caldera, "Fact check: Democrats have condemned violence linked to BLM,"
USA Today, August 13, 2020, https://www.usatoday.com/story/news/factcheck/2020/08/
13/fact-check-democrats-have-condemned-violence-linked-protests/3317862001/.

46 "Rob Schenck Exposes Disturbing Gun Culture," The Spiritual Brewpub, accessed
February 6, 2023, https://www.youtube.com/watch?v=S1k1KUD6T5Q.

47 "CCW Gun Cases," Garrison Grip, accessed February 6, 2023,
https://garrisongrip.com/ccw-gun-cases/.

48 "The Armor of Light," accessed February 6, 2023, https://www.armoroflightfilm.com/.

49 Zach Despart, "Systemic failures in Uvalde shooting went far beyond local police,"
The Texas Tribune, July 17, 2022, https://www.texastribune.org/2022/07/17/law-
enforcement-failure-uvalde-shooting-investigation/.

50 "What is Grooming?" ADL, September 16, 2022, https://www.adl.org/resources
/blog/what-grooming-truth-behind-dangerous-bigoted-lie-targeting-lgbtq-community.

51 Amanda Musa and Christina Maxouris, "A Texas man was arrested and charged," CNN,
December 3, 2022, https://www.cnn.com/2022/12/03/us/texas-man-threats-boston-
doctor-transgender-care/index.html.

52 "Supporting the LBGTQ+ Community Amidst Escalating Violence," Sahan Journal,
December 12, 2022, https://sahanjournal.com/sponsored/supporting-the-lgbtq-
community-amidst-escalating-violence-blue-cross-blue-shield-of-minnesota/.

53 "Man Accused in Paul Pelosi Attack," PBS, December 28, 2022, https://www.pbs.org/
newshour/politics/man-accused-in-paul-pelosi-attack-pleads-not-guilty-to-six-charges.

54 Em Steck and Andrew Kaczynski, "Marjorie Taylor Greene Indicated Support for Executing
Prominent Democrats," CNN, January 26, 2021, https://www.cnn.com/2021/01/26/politics/

marjorie-taylor-greene-democrats-violence/index.html.

55 Gillian Morley, "Nicholas Roske, accused of trying to kill Brett Kavanaugh, pleads not guilty," CBS News, June 22, 2022, https://www.cbsnews.com/news/nicholas-roske-brett-kavanaugh-attempted-assassination/.

56 Wehner, "The Evangelical Church is Breaking Apart."

57 Ibid.

58 Ibid.

8: THE MYTH OF REDEMPTIVE VIOLENCE

1 Kevin Miller, "J.E.S.U.S.A.," March 27, 2020, https://vimeo.com/ondemand/jesusa.

2 "Incarceration," accessed February 6, 2023, https://www.healthypeople.gov/2020/topics-objectives/topic/social-determinants-health/interventions-resources/incarceration.

3 Shanley, *Many Sides of Peace*, 57.

4 Gilligan, *Violence*, 84.

5 Ibid., 113.

6 Bregman, *Humankind*, xiv-xv.

7 Ibid, xvi-xvii.

8 Claiborne, *Beating Guns*, 223.

9 Anthony H. Cordesman, "America's Failed Strategy in the Middle East," CSIS, January 2, 2020, https://www.csis.org/analysis/americas-failed-strategy-middle-east-losing-iraq-and-gulf.

10 "How Common is PTSD in Veterans?" U.S. Department of Veteran Affairs, accessed February 6, 2023, https://www.ptsd.va.gov/understand/common/common_veterans.asp.

11 Kevin Miller, "J.E.S.U.S.A.," March 27, 2020, https://vimeo.com/ondemand/jesusa.

12 Bregman, *Humankind*, 81.

13 Ibid, 82–83.

14 Kevin Miller, "J.E.S.U.S.A.," March 27, 2020, https://vimeo.com/ondemand/jesusa.

15 Hedges, *The Greatest Evil is War*.

16 Armstrong, *Fields of Blood*, Introduction.

17 Bregman, *Humankind*, 220.

18 Ibid., 219–220.

19 Ibid., 220.

20 Kevin Miller, "J.E.S.U.S.A.," March 27, 2020, https://vimeo.com/ondemand/jesusa.

21 Moyn, *Humane*, 135.

22 Ibid., 134.

23 Ibid., 135.

24 Ibid., 134.

25 Ibid., 136.

26 William Saletan, "Armed Giffords hero nearly shot wrong man," NBC News, January 11, 2011, https://www.nbcnews.com/id/wbna41018893.

27 Sprinkle, *Fight*, Chapter 11.

9: THE ROOTS OF PEACE

1 "Significance of Decapolis," Got Questions, accessed February 6, 2023, https://www.gotquestions.org/Decapolis-in-the-Bible.html.

2 Camp, *Craft Brewed Jesus*, 23–36.

3 Donald L. Wasson, "Pax Romana," World History, December 8, 2015, https://www.ancient.eu/Pax_Romana/.

4 Ibid.

5 "How Romans Used Crucifixion—Including Jesus's—as a Political Weapon," Newsweek, April 4, 2015, https://www.newsweek.com/how-romans-used-crucifixion-including-jesus-political-weapon-318934.

6 "Crucifixion," Wikipedia, accessed February 6, 2023, https://en.wikipedia.org/wiki/Crucifixion.

7 Sprinkle, *Fight*, Chapter 13.

8 Nyland, *The Source New Testament*, 51–52.

9 Kevin Miller, "J.E.S.U.S.A.," March 27, 2020, https://vimeo.com/ondemand/jesusa.

10 See Camp, *Craft Brewed Jesus*, Chapter 7.

11 Vearncombe, *After Jesus Before Christianity*, 6.

12 Zahnd, *Farewell to Mars*, Chapter 1.

13 Ibid.

14 Ibid.

15 The gospels of Luke and Mark tend to prefer the term "kingdom of God." Matthew's use of the "kingdom of heaven" is often seen as a reflection of the sensibilities of the Jewish audience this gospel was directed to, and thus tried to avoid the word "God." Most scholars feel the two phrases are theologically identical. https://en.wikipedia.org/wiki/Kingdom_of_heaven_(Gospel_of_Matthew) Some translators also use the terms "reign" or "realm" for "kingdom."

16 Chris Kratzer, "Some of the Best Followers of Jesus Aren't Christian," November 15, 2022, https://chriskratzer.com/some-of-the-best-followers-of-jesus-arent-christian/.

10: RECLAIMING THE PATH OF PEACE

1 Kevin Miller, "J.E.S.U.S.A.," March 27, 2020, https://vimeo.com/ondemand/jesusa.

2 Murphy, "Does religion give rise to violence – or the other way around?"

3 Haven, "History is a Test: Mankind is Failing It."

4 Once at a National Day of Prayer Breakfast event, Trump heard Arthur Brooks speak on *Love Your Enemies: How Decent People Can Save America from the Culture of Contempt*. Remarking immediately afterward, Trump said he didn't believe "love your enemies" was good advice.

5 Lee Kovarsky, "The Trump Executions," University of Texas School of Law, December 14, 2021, https://papers.ssrn.com/sol3/papers.cfm?abstract_id=3891784.

6 "The 1994 Crime Bill Continues to Undercut Justice Reform," CAP, March 26, 2019, https://www.americanprogress.org/article/1994-crime-bill-continues-undercut-justice-reform-heres-stop/.

7 Murphy, "Does religion give rise to violence – or the other way around?"

8 Rohr, *The Universal Christ*, 73.

9 Shanley, *Many Sides of Peace*, 58.

10 Hart, *The New Testament: A Translation*, 555.

11 Hart, *The New Testament. A Translation.*

12 Nyland, *The Source New Testament.*

13 Besides *gehenna*, two other words, *hades* (*sheol* in Hebrew) and *tartarus* are also translated *hell*. *Hades* is the place of the dead for both the righteous and unrighteous. *Tartarus* is a term from Greek mythology for a dark realm of hades. It is only used once in 2 Peter, a book whose authorship is the most disputed of all NT books.

14 "Equal Justice Initiative," Wikipedia, accessed February 6, 2023, https://en.wikipedia.org/wiki/Equal_Justice_Initiative.

15 "Criminal Justice Reform," EJI, accessed February 6, 2023, https://eji.org/criminal-justice-reform/.

16 "How One Man Convinced 200 Ku Klux Klan Members to Give Up Their Robes," NPR, August 20, 2017, https://www.npr.org/2017/08/20/544861933/how-one-man-convinced-200-ku-klux-klan-members-to-give-up-their-robes.

17 Ibid.

18 "Accidental Courtesy," PBS, February 13, 2027, https://www.pbs.org/independentlens/films/accidental-courtesy/.

19 Berger, *The Catalyst*, 51–60.

20 John Blake, "A Marine who hated Muslims went to a mosque..." CNN, October 8, 2022, https://www.cnn.com/2022/10/08/us/marine-mosque-islam-blake-cec.

21 Claiborne, *Beating Guns*, 220.

22 Rohr, *The Universal Christ*, 72.

23 Kirsten Powers, "Saving Grace," Amazon Summary, accessed February 6, 2023, https://www.amazon.com/Saving-Grace-Centered-Coexist-People-ebook/dp/B08V4XDPZQ/.

11: MODERN PEACE MOVEMENTS AS OUR GUIDE

1 "All Quiet on the Western Front," https://www.amazon.com/All-Quiet-Western-Front-Novel/dp/0449213943/.

2 Hedges, *The Greatest Evil is War*.

3 Bertha von Suttner, "Lay Down Your Arms: The Autobiography of Martha von Tilling – Anti-war Activist and Crusader for Peace," January 1, 1914, https://www.amazon.com/Lay-Down-Your-Arms-Autobiography/dp/1789871468/.

4 Moyn, *Humane*, 48.

5 "Bertha von Suttner. Nobel Lecture." The Nobel Prize, accessed February 6, 2023, https://www.nobelprize.org/prizes/peace/1905/suttner/lecture/.

6 Moyn, *Humane*, 49.

7 "E. Stanley Jones," Read the Spirit, accessed February 6, 2023, https://readthespirit.com/interfaith-peacemakers/e-stanley-jones/.

8 "Finding Christ at the Round Table," Christian History Institute, accessed February 6, 2023, https://christianhistoryinstitute.org/magazine/article/finding-christ-at-the-round-table.

9 "E. Stanley Jones," Read the Spirit, accessed February 6, 2023, https://readthespirit.com/interfaith-peacemakers/e-stanley-jones/.

10 Camp, *Craft Brewed Jesus*, 170.

11 "Southern Christian Leadership Conference," National Park Service, accessed February 6, 2023, https://www.nps.gov/subjects/civilrights/sclc.htm.

12 "Dr. Martin Luther King in 1967," Democracy Now, January 21, 2013, https://www.democracynow.org/2013/1/21/dr_martin_luther_king_in_1967.

13 "Six Principles of Nonviolence," King Institute Stanford, accessed February 6, 2023, https://kinginstitute.stanford.edu/sites/mlk/files/lesson-activities/six_principles_of_nonviolence.pdf.

14 "Poor People's Campaign Covenant of Nonviolence," accessed February 6, 2023, https://www.poorpeoplescampaign.org/covenant-of-nonviolence/.

15 Bregman, *Humankind*, 343.

16 Ibid., 343.

12: BREAKING BAD FAITH FOR THE SAKE OF PEACE

1 Hardin, *What the Facebook?* 51-52.

2 "Keith Giles Brings You Back to Square One," ReKnew, September 29, 2019, https://reknew.org/2019/09/keith-giles-brings-you-back-to-square-one-podcast/.

3 "Religious Deconstruction Workshop," The Spiritual Brewpub, accessed February 6, 2023, https://www.spiritualbrewpub.com/spiritual-freedom-deconstruction-workshops.

4 "Our Investigations," The Roys Report, accessed February 6, 2023, https://julieroys.com/investigations.

5 "Religious Deconstruction Workshop," The Spiritual Brewpub, accessed February 6, 2023, https://www.spiritualbrewpub.com/spiritual-freedom-deconstruction-workshops.

6 Camp, *Craft Brewed Jesus*, 153–154.

7 Emily Widra and Tiana Herring, "States of Incarceration," Prison Policy Initiative, September 2021, https://www.prisonpolicy.org/global/2021.html.

8 Ashley Nellis, Ph.D., "The Color of Justice," The Sentencing Project, October 13, 2021, https://www.sentencingproject.org/publications/color-of-justice-racial-and-ethnic-disparity-in-state-prisons/.

9 "U.S. Prison Population vs. the World," accessed February 6, 2023, https://backgroundchecks.org/us-prison-population-vs-the-world.html.

10 Deanna Van Buren, "What a world without prisons could look like," TEDWomen, accessed February 6, 2023, https://www.ted.com/talks/deanna_van_buren_what_a_world_without_prisons_could_look_like.

11 Bregman, *Humankind*, 326–330.

12 "Prison Reform: Reducing Recidivism," US Department of Justice, accessed February 6, 2023, https://www.justice.gov/archives/prison-reform.

13 Hedges, *The Greatest Evil is War*, 1.

14 Michael McKoy, "What Does Pacifism Have to Say about Ukraine?" Providence, April 12, 2022, https://providencemag.com/2022/04/what-does-pacifism-say-ukraine/.

15 Ibid.

16 Ibid.

17 Robyn Dixon, "Russians back war in Ukraine, but report finds notable opposition," The Washington Post, September 7, 2022, https://www.washingtonpost.com/world/2022/09/07/russia-war-ukraine-public-opinion/.

18 Michael McKoy, "What Does Pacifism Have to Say about Ukraine?" Providence, April 12, 2022, https://providencemag.com/2022/04/what-does-pacifism-say-ukraine/.

19 Daniel, Treisman, "What Could Bring Putin Down?" Foreign Affairs, November 2, 2022, https://www.foreignaffairs.com/ukraine/what-could-bring-putin-down.

20 Muhammad Darwish, Katharina Krebs and Tara John, "Former Wagner commander describes brutality and incompetence," CNN, January 31, 2023, https://www.cnn.com/2023/01/30/europe/wagner-norway-andrei-medvedev-ukraine-intl/index.html.

21 John Dear, "Biography," accessed February 6, 2023, https://johndear.org/biography/.

22 Erica Chenoweth and Maria Stephan, "Why Civil Resistance Works," Amazon Summary, accessed February 6, 2023, https://www.amazon.com/Why-Civil-Resistance-Works-Nonviolent/dp/0231156839.

23 Bregman, *Humankind*, 323.

24 Blattman, *Why We Fight*, Amazon Summary, accessed February 6, 2023, https://www.amazon.com/Why-We-Fight-Roots-Paths-ebook/dp/B099VV73ZH/.

BIBLIOGRAPHY

Armstrong, Karen. Fields of Blood: Religion and the History of Violence. New York: Anchor, 2015.

Arnold, Robert Lloyd, *Orthodoxy Revisited: Contrasting the Faith and Practice of the Eastern Orthodox Church with Evangelical Doctrine.* Salisbury, MA: Regina Orthodox, 2005.

Artman, David. *Grace Saves All: The Necessity of Christian Universalism.* Eugene, OR: Wipf & Stock, 2020.

Baker, Sharon L. *Razing Hell: Rethinking Everything You've Been Taught About God's Wrath and Judgment.* Louisville: Westminster John Knox Press, 2010.

Bregman, Rutger. *Humankind: A Hopeful History.* New York: Back Bay Books, 2019.

Buhler, Rich. "3 Poll Workers Arrested in Alabama for Voter Fraud – Fiction!" Truth or Fiction, December 18, 2017. https://www.truthorfiction.com/3-poll-workers-arrested-alabama-voter-fraud/.

Bernstein, James. *Which Came First: The Church or the New Testament?* Ben Lomond, CA: Conciliar, 1994.

Berger, Jonah. *The Catalyst: How to Change Anyone's Mind.* New York: Simon & Schuster, Eugene, OR: Resource Publications, 2016. 2020.

Blattman, Christopher. *Why We Fight: The Roots of War and the Paths of Peace.* New York: Viking, 2022.

Brooks, Arthur C. *Love Your Enemies: How Decent People Can Save America from the Culture of Contempt.* New York: Broadside Books, 2019.

Camp, Michael. *Confessions of a Bible Thumper: My Homebrewed Quest for a Reasoned Faith.* Seattle: Engage Faith, 2012.

_____, *Craft Brewed Jesus: How History We Never Knew Taps a Spirituality We Really Need.* Eugene: OR, Resource Publications (Wipf & Stock), 2016.

Claiborne, Shane and Michael Martin. *Beating Guns: Hope for People Who are Weary of Violence.* Grand Rapids, MI: Brazos Press, 2019.

"WWI's Christmas Truce." History. Accessed February 7, 2023. http://www.history.com/topics/world-war-i/christmas-truce-of-1914.

Cox, Harvey. *The Future of Faith.* New York: HarperCollins, 2009.

Dean, Jonathan Geoffrey. *Salt & Light: The Complete Jesus.* Jonathan Dean, 2022.

DeMar, Gary. *Last Days Madness: Obsession of the Modern Church.* Atlanta: American Vision, 1999.

Ehrman, Bart D. *Did Jesus Exist? The Historical Argument for Jesus of Nazareth*. New York: HarperOne, 2013.

_____, *Misquoting Jesus: The Story Behind Who Changed the Bible and Why*. New York: HarperOne, 2005.

Ellul, Jacques and Geoffrey Bromiley. *The Subversion of Christianity*, Eugene, OR: Wipf & Stock, 1986.

Enns, Peter. *The Bible Tells Me So: Why Defending Scripture Has Made Us Unable to Read It*. New York: HarperOne, 2014.

_____. *How the Bible Actually Works: In Which I Explain How an Ancient, Ambiguous, and Diverse Book Leads Us to Wisdom Rather Than Answers—and Why That's Great News*. San Francisco: HarperOne, 2019.

_____. "John Piper on Why 'It's Right for God to Slaughter Women and Children Anytime He Pleases and Why I Have Some Major Problems with That." Patheos. July 2012.https://www.patheos.com/blogs/peterenns/2012/07/john-piper-on-why-its-right-for-god-to-slaughter-women-and-children-anytime-he-pleases-and-why-i-have-some-major-problems-with-that.

Ferwerda, Julie. *Raising Hell: Christianity's Most Controversial Doctrine Put Under Fire*. Rathdrum, ID: Vagabond Group, 2014.

"Final Report: Select Committee to Investigate January 6th Attack on the U.S. Capital." December 22, 2022, 117th Congress Second Session, House Report 117-663.

Flood, Derek. *Disarming Scripture: Cherry-Picking Liberals, Violence-Loving Conservatives, and Why We All Need to Learn to Read the Bible Like Jesus Did.* San Francisco: Metanoia, 2014.

French, David. "The Dangerous Idolatry of Christian Trumpism," The Dispatch, December 13, 2020, https://thedispatch.com/newsletter/frenchpress/the-dangerous-idolatry-of-christian/.

Garrison, Becky. "The Door Interview: Mark Yaconelli," *The Wittenburg Door*, December 21, 2022. https://wittenburgdoor.substack.com/p/the-door-interview-mark-yaconelli.

Girard, Rene. *I See Satan Fall Like Lighting.* New York: Orbis Books, 2001.

Giles, Keith. *Jesus Unexpected: Ending the End Times to Become the Second Coming.* Oak Glen, CA: Quoir, 2020.

_____, *Jesus Undefeated: Condemning the False Doctrine of Eternal Torment.* Orange, CA: Quoir, 2019.

Hanson, J. W. *Universalism: The Prevailing Doctrine of the Christian Church During Its First 500 Years.* Boston: Universalist, 1899.

Hardin, Michael, and Hardin, Lorri.. *The Jesus Driven Life: Reconnecting Humanity with Jesus.* Lancaster, Pa: JDL Press, 2013.

_____, *What the Facebook? Posts from the Edge of Christendom.* Lancaster, PA: JDL Press, 2014.

Hart, David Bentley. *That All Shall be Saved: Heaven, Hell, and Universal Salvation.* New Haven: Yale University Press, 2019.

Haven, Cynthia. "History is a Test. Mankind is Failing It." Stanford Magazine, July/August 2009.

Heim, Mark S. *Saved from Sacrifice: A Theology of the Cross*. Grand Rapids, MI: William B. Eerdmans Publishing, 2006.

Hedges, Chris. *War is the Greatest Evil*. New York: Seven Stories Press, 2022.

Horton, Adrian. "After Truth: how ordinary people are 'radicalized' by fake news." The Guardian, March 19, 2020. https://www.theguardian.com/tv-and-radio/2020/mar/19/after-truth-hbo-fake-news-pizzagate-documentary.

Hertenstein, Mike and Jon Trott. *Selling Satan: The Evangelical Media and the Mike Warnke Scandal*. Chicago: Cornerstone Press, 1993.

Instone-Brewer, David. *Divorce and Remarriage in the Church: Biblical Solutions for Pastoral Realities*. Downers Grove: InterVarsity, 2003.

Jenkins, Phillip. *Lost History of Christianity: The Thousand-Year Golden Age of the Church in the Middle East, Africa, and Asia—and How It Died*. New York: HarperOne, 2009.

Jersak, Bradley. *A More Christlike God: A More Beautiful Gospel*. Pasadena, CA: Plain Truth, 2015.

_____, *Her Gates Will Never Be Shut: Hope, Hell, and the New Jerusalem*. Eugene, OR: Wipf & Stock, 2009.

Josephus, Flavius. *The Jewish War*. Rev. ed. Translated by G. A. Williamson. New York: Penguin, 1970.

Lim, Timothy H. *The Formation of the Jewish Canon*. New Haven: Yale University Press, 2013.

Macdonald, Gregory. *The Evangelical Universalist*. Eugene, OR: Cascade, 2006.

Martin, Colby. *Unclobber: Rethinking Our Misuse of the Bible on Homosexuality*. Louisville: Westminster John Knox Press, 2022.

Mehl-Laituri, Logan. *Reborn on the Fourth of July: The Challenge of Faith, Patriotism, & Conscience*. Downers Grove, IL: IVP Books, 2012.

Meredith, Edward, *The Rhetoric of Aristotle, Volume 1*, Palala Press, 2016.

McKnight, Chuck. "My Long Fight to Defend Inerrancy and Why I Finally Accepted the Bible We Have," https://www.patheos.com/blogs/hippieheretic/2016/04/my-long-fight-to-defend-inerrancy-why-i.html.

McNamara, Robert. *In Retrospect: The Tragedy and Lessons of Vietnam*. New York: Vintage Books, 1996.

Moyn, Samuel. *Humane: How the United States Abandoned Peace and Reinvented War*. New York: Farrar, Straus and Giroux, 2021.

Meyers, Robin. *The Underground Church: Reclaiming the Subversive Way of Jesus*. San Francisco: Jossey-Bass, 2012.

Murphy, James Bernard. "Does religion give rise to violence – or the o ther way around?" Religion News Service, 2015. https://religionnews.com/2015/11/15/religion-violence-islam-christianity-atheism-isis-terrorism-paris-rene-girard/.

Nyland, Ann. *The Source New Testament: With Extensive Notes on Greek Word Meaning*. Australia: Smith & Stirling, 2004.

Powers, Kirsten. *Saving Grace: Speak Your Truth, Stay Centered, and Learn to Coexist with People Who Drive You Nuts*. New York: Convergent Books, 2021.

Rohr, Richard. *The Universal Christ: How a Forgotten Reality Can Change Everything We See, Hope For, and Believe*. New York: Convergent, 2021.

Rossiter, Edward. "The Abolition of Slavery in the Western Hemisphere: Its Consequences for Africa." OAH Magazine of History, Volume 7, Issue 4, Summer 1993.

Schaeffer, Frank. *Fall in Love, Have Children, Stay Put, Save the Planet*. Boca Raton, FL: HCI Books, 2021.

Shanks, Hershel (Editor). *Partings: How Judaism and Christianity Became Two*. Washington, DC: Biblical Archaeology Society, 2013.

_____. *Christianity and Rabbinic Judaism: A Parallel History of Their Origins and Early Development*. Washington, DC: Biblical Archaeology Society, 1992.

Shanley, Brayton. *The Many Sides of Peace: Christian Nonviolence, the Contemplative Life, and Sustainable Living*. Eugene, OR: Resource Publications, 2013.

Sharp, David. "Hijacked Christianity: How an Aberrant Eschatology Enables a Grievance Culture That Supplants Christian Grace for an

Extremist Meritocracy." Georgia State University, 2022.
https://scholarworks.gsu.edu/cgi/viewcontent.cgi?article=1133&
context=communication_theses.

Shisley, Steven. "Biblical Views: From Supper to Sacrament: How the
Last Supper Evolved." BAS Library. March/April 2017.
https://www.baslibrary.org/biblical-archaeology-review/43/2/8.

Smith, Christian. *The Bible Made Impossible: Why Biblicism is Not a
Truly Evangelical Reading of Scripture*. Grand Rapids: Brazos, 2012.

Sprinkle, Preston. *Fight: A Christian Case for Non-Violence*. Colorado
Springs: David C. Cook, 2013.

Sproul, R. C. *The Last Days According to Jesus: When Did Jesus Say
He Would Return?* Grand Rapids: Baker, 1998.

Stanley, Tiffany. "The Abuse Scandal That Devastated a Suburban
Megachurch." Washingtonian. February 14, 2016. https://www.
washingtonian.com/2016/02/14/the-sex-abuse-scandal-that-
devastated-a-suburban-megachurch-sovereign-grace-ministries/.

Stenson, Eric. *Christian Universalism: God's Good News for All People*.
Mobile, AL: Sparkling Bay Books, 2008.

Talbott, Thomas B. *The Inescapable Love of God*. Eugene, OR: Cascade,
2014.

The United States Bombing Surveys, Maxwell Airforce Base, AL:
Air University Press, September 30, 1945. https://www.airuniversity.
af.edu/Portals/10/AUPress/Books/B_0020_SPANGRUD_
STRATEGIC_BOMBING_SURVEYS.pdf.

Thompson, Gerald R. "A Pro-Life Attorney Explains Why Abortion Is Not Murder: (So Please Stop Saying It Is)," https://lonang.com/commentaries/foundation/family/why-abortion-is-not-murder-theology-of-the-unborn/.

Tolstoy, Leo. *The Kingdom of God is Within You*. Kshetra Books, 2016. First edition, 1894.

Tverberg, Lois. *Walking in the Dust of Rabbi Jesus: How the Jewish Words of Jesus Can Change Your Life*. Grand Rapids: Zondervan, 2012.

Vearncombe, Erin and Brandon Scott and Hal Taussig. *After Jesus Before Christianity: A Historical Exploration of the First Two Centuries of Jesus Movements*. New York: HarperOne, 2021.

Wills, Garry. *What Jesus Meant*. New York: Penguin, 2006.

_____. *What Paul Meant*. New York: Penguin, 2007.

_____. *What the Gospels Meant*. New York: Penguin, 2009.

Wright, N. T. *Jesus and the Victory of God*. Minneapolis: Fortress, 1996.

Wehner, Peter. "The Evangelical Church is Breaking Apart." *The Atlantic*, October 2021.

Zahnd, Brian. *A Farewell to Mars: An Evangelical Pastor's Journey Toward the Biblical Gospel of Peace*. Colorado Springs: David C. Cook, 2014.

For more information about Michael Camp,
or to contact him for speaking engagements,
please visit www.spiritualbrewpub.com.

Many Voices. One Message.

www.quoir.com

Printed in Great Britain
by Amazon

30176085R00143